PRAISE FOR
ON PURPOSE

'To define a purpose that will galvanize the entire organization is a leap of faith and requires strong leadership, but it also requires the clear and compelling process outlined in this book if you are to embark on this incredible journey.'
Patrick Dempsey OBE, Managing Director, Whitbread Hotels and Restaurants

'Shaun and Andy have created another great book in *On Purpose*, describing simply how great businesses use purpose and focus to fulfil customer needs and create value.'
Vernon W Hill II, Founder and Chairman, Metro Bank

'Every now and then a truly cutting-edge book comes along which changes everything we know about the secrets of organizational greatness. *On Purpose* is a profound and practical book no leader should miss reading. Full of powerful examples and pragmatic practices, it reveals the mysteries of long-term enterprise success.'
Chip R Bell, author of *The 9½ Principles of Innovative Service*

'Shaun Smith and Andy Milligan have added another strong chapter to their purpose. This is a must-read for any leader who is looking at differentiating their business by asking the important "why?" and "why us?" questions. It will provide excellent guidance in how to create your own journey and, most importantly, how to stick to it once your purpose has been found.'
Frans-Willem de Kloet, Managing Director and CEO, UPC Czech Republic

'Since the publication of *Uncommon Practice* in 2002, Shaun Smith and Andy Milligan have published a series of books rigorously examining the DNA of brands that deliver outstanding customer experiences.
In *On Purpose*, they delve even further into the fabric of customer-focused companies, exploring the very purpose of these brands, and making a convincing correlation between customer advocacy and a strong sense of company purpose. Often books on the topic of customer experience are fairly passive affairs, celebrating the achievements of successful brands. But *On Purpose* isn't just thought-provoking – it is also action-provoking. It will surely generate an urgent

sense of soul-searching amongst those whose brands are built as money-making machines. But it will also encourage those brands built on more purposeful foundations to revisit their philosophies and ensure that these are being clearly communicated both to employees and customers.

The key message of this terrific book is that brands need to be engaging and inspiring to stand out from the crowd. And without a clear sense of purpose – within the company, its leaders, its staff and its communications – brands will struggle to be distinctive.'
Neil Davey, Editor, MyCustomer.com, Group Editor, SIFT MEDIA

'No successful business leader of the future can feel exempt from reading this remarkable book. It is by two global experts, extremely readable and compelling in its key message to place customer experience at the very core of every business.'
Roger Harrop, The CEO Expert, author and international speaker

'Great book – highly recommended!'
Joe Pine, co-author of *The Experience Economy*

ON PURPOSE

Delivering a branded
customer experience
people love

Shaun Smith
Andy Milligan

KoganPage

LONDON PHILADELPHIA NEW DELHI

First published in Great Britain and the United States in 2015 by Kogan Page Limited

2nd Floor, 45 Gee Street
London EC1V 3RS
United Kingdom
www.koganpage.com

1518 Walnut Street, Suite 1100
Philadelphia PA 19102
USA

4737/23 Ansari Road
Daryaganj
New Delhi 110002
India

© Shaun Smith and Andy Milligan, 2015

The right of Shaun Smith and Andy Milligan to be identified as the authors of this work has been asserted by them in accordance with the Copyright, Designs and Patents Act 1988.

ISBN   978 0 7494 7191 0
E-ISBN   978 0 7494 7192 7

British Library Cataloguing-in-Publication Data

A CIP record for this book is available from the British Library.

Library of Congress Cataloging-in-Publication Data

Smith, Shaun, author.
   On purpose : delivering a branded customer experience people love / Shaun Smith, Andy Milligan.
      pages cm
   ISBN 978-0-7494-7191-0 (paperback) – ISBN 978-0-7494-7192-7 (ebk)   1. Customer relations.
2. Relationship marketing.   3. Branding (Marketing)   I. Milligan, Andy, author.   II. Title.
      HF5415.5S595 2015
      658.8'12–dc23
                                                            2015031282

Typeset by Graphicraft Limited, Hong Kong
Print production managed by Jellyfish
Printed and bound by CPI Group (UK) Ltd, Croydon, CR0 4YY

Contents

For online resources to accompany this book go to:
www.koganpage.com/onpurpose or to:
www.smithcoconsultancy.com/cem-toolkit

Introduction

'**E**very business must serve a social purpose.' These are not the words of a social campaigner or a politician; they are the words of a banker, Ashok Vaswani, the chief executive officer (CEO) of Retail and Business Banking at Barclays, one of the world's largest banks. Barclays has been involved in at least one major trading scandal and holds the dubious honour of the most fined bank in Britain. There will be some people who will treat his words with understandable cynicism but that would be to miss the point. The point is not that the words are sincere or not – it is that they should have been said at all. Banks are concerned with the control of money – why should they concern themselves with any purpose beyond that? The reason is that society is demanding they do. When banks first started they fulfilled a social need in the community, to enable ordinary people to fund their ambitions. Over the years banks forgot that purpose and focused most of their efforts on funding their own ambitions through obscene profits, often at the consumer's expense. The bubble burst in spectacular fashion with the downfall of Lehman Brothers in the United States and RBS in the UK. The rot seemed widespread across the sector. HSBC, one of the world's largest banks, became involved in a range of banking scandals, including foreign exchange manipulation and rigging of international interest rate benchmarks. Stuart Gulliver, group chief executive for HSBC, said it had caused 'damage to trust and confidence' in the company.[1] So much so that HSBC are considering bringing back their old brand, 'Midland', because the HSBC name is so tarnished.

But it isn't just the banks that have lost their way; it is now critical for any business to demonstrate it has a purpose before, and beyond, profit; that it seeks to improve the lives of its customers as a primary goal. Failure to have such a purpose, to be clear about it and to ensure it directs everything you do, will lose customers, employees and ultimately business value. Purpose drives profits.

The power of purpose to answer the question 'Why?' has also become a powerful concept in its own right. Simon Sinek's TedX talk 'Start with why' has become one of the most viewed online videos ever, with its central message of 'People don't buy what you do; they buy why you do it'. It has inspired millions of people, including Sir Richard Branson who wrote a blog called 'Why all businesses should ask themselves why'. However, neither Sinek's video and book nor Branson's blog tell you 'how'. That is why we have written this book.

The purpose of *On Purpose*

Since the publication of our book *Uncommon Practice* in 2002 we have been championing those businesses that have made delivery of outstanding customer experiences their focus. We have shared the stories of companies around the world who have been bold, who have sought to differentiate dramatically what they offered to customers. We believe that the most effective marketing and the best business development are achieved through customer advocacy, and you only get advocacy from people who love what you do, not what you *say* you'll do.

More and more companies have taken seriously the customer experience and as a result have become better at delivering what customers want. Customer experience was once seen as only one of a number of important things that CEOs wanted to address. However, by 2011, Forrester's report into the state of customer experience showed it had become their top priority and, in 2014, a lack of strategy for customer experience was cited as the number one reason for preventing profitable business performance.

Overall, customers' experience of businesses has reflected this shift in corporate priorities. According to the National Customer Satisfaction Index in the United States, satisfaction with companies across all sectors has risen from a low index score in 1998 of 70 to a high of almost 77 by 2013.

Take the banking sector, for example. At the turn of the 21st century, First Direct in the UK and Umpqua in the United States were rare examples of entirely customer-focused brands. Now, in an attempt to mend the relationship with consumers, almost all the high street or retail banks have published customer charters and many are measuring the net promoter score (NPS) as an indication of customer satisfaction or otherwise.

But though more companies have become better at what they do, few have articulated well 'why' they do it and translated that meaningfully into 'how' they do it. So the second use of our title *On Purpose* is to explore the intentionality of customer experience. How can brands be much more deliberate and focused in serving their customer and go beyond the vague (and usually uneconomic) desire to 'delight' customers? Following the publication of our book *Bold: How to be brave in business and win* (2011) many executives and organizations asked us to give speeches or advice on 'how' they might apply the principles. We came to realize that the book was inspiring because it talked a great deal about what these great brands did to transform their markets, but less about the 'why' and the 'how'. This book aims to address both of these needs and we shall share examples of companies that have done so.

As we have worked and talked over the years with all kinds of different companies and their customers, consumers and employees, it has become clear to us that the 'why' and the 'how' have become the most important sources of meaningful differentiation for businesses – 'meaningful' in terms of our ability, as consumers, to understand what the business is offering and its relevance and appeal to us.

Why purpose is important

Quite simply, showing you have an authentic and credible sense of purpose – a reason 'why' you exist beyond the desire to make profit – drives commercial value in an increasingly competitive world.

Purpose matters to consumers

The attitudes and motivations of people in many countries towards what they buy and why they buy it – whether it is a consumer product, a business service or even a political party – has changed.

The phrases 'conscious consumption' and even 'conscientious consumption' have entered the language of economists. People are looking not simply for a product that fulfils their practical need combined with an image that reflects their personal identity. They want to buy brands that have an authentic sense of purpose, run by people who are passionate about or at the very least genuinely interested in what they are selling. And they want those brands to be contributing in some way to solving, or at least addressing, the wider societal challenges we all face.

Michael Porter, widely regarded as one of the world's leading authorities on business strategy, identified this change in consumer or customer motivation. It led him to establish the 'Shared Value Initiative'. He argues that the businesses that will succeed will be characterized by a common sense of identity and motivation between owners, employees and customers. This goes beyond 'we're people who make the chocolate bars you like' to a more fundamental sense of what you 'believe in', your 'values' and ultimately to a recognition of the social impact that businesses have. 'The purpose of the corporation,' he writes, 'must be redefined as creating shared value, not just profit per se. This will drive the next wave of innovation and productivity growth in the global economy.'[2]

In one sense, we are going back to the future. The businesses of the early 19th century were often founded on strong principles, often social or religious beliefs. WK Kellogg, Joseph Rowntree and John Stuart of Quaker Oats, for example, founded commercial organizations inspired by a strong sense of a higher purpose. The difference now is that this sense of purpose is so shared that customers feel they have an affinity, a sense of loyalty and a sense of identity wrapped up in that business.

The global public relations business Edelman conducts an annual survey called the Global Trust Barometer. They look at the importance that people say they ascribe to factors such as 'trust' and 'the values of an organization'. From 2011 onwards they have recorded a rise in the importance of those factors among consumers. The 2015 Global Trust Barometer found that four in five respondents wanted to see companies pursue a higher purpose, not just profit.[3] However, only 24 per cent of the consumers surveyed globally believed that business was driven by the desire to make the world a better place.

People are looking to buy from and work for organizations that share their values and stay true to them. They will reward with their loyalty, or punish with their defection, businesses that do or don't put their customer at the heart of how they operate. A recent example of this in the UK is the retail giant Tesco.

When we wrote about Tesco in our book *Uncommon Practice* in 2002, it was riding high. Its CEO, Sir Terry Leahy, was adamant that its success was due to its clarity of purpose: 'to earn our customers' lifetime loyalty'. The words 'earn' and 'loyalty' are key – indicating a direct link between the focus of effort towards customers and the reward from their behaviour. Few people doubt that Tesco's strength was due to its unrelenting focus on its customers' needs and wants, even if some people felt that this strength was strong-arming suppliers and local authority planners into giving Tesco what they wanted. Tesco grew from a business that turned over £16 billion in 1998 to £65 billion by 2012 when Sir Terry Leahy stepped away.

However, between 2012 and 2014, Tesco's results and reputation tumbled, culminating in a false accounting scandal. Regardless of the alleged actions of a few individual executives, the consensus from analysts was that Tesco's poorer performance has been due to its failure to focus on its core customer. Business observers generally agreed with Sir Terry Leahy's own assessment that Tesco 'focused too much on what it isn't, rather than remembering what it is'. How could a company with a core purpose 'to earn our customers' lifetime loyalty' end up selling those customers horsemeat labelled as beef? Failure to control the supply chain suggested to some that profit, not purpose, had become Tesco's primary concern.

Authentic concern for delivering to customers is key to business success because it drives customer, employee and ultimately all stakeholder satisfaction. People are increasingly testing how 'authentic' organizations are, judging them by the actions and words of the average customer and the average customer-facing employee, not the CEO's shareholder-directed statements. Customers are judging, to put it simply, on what they hear from the people to whom they can most easily relate – 'ordinary' people just like them. Edelman revealed in its 2013 Global Trust Barometer that two sources of credibility for a company had seen dramatic rises: 'other customers' and 'ordinary employees'. These had risen by 22 per cent and 16 per cent respectively to 65 per cent and 50 per cent, compared with only 38 per cent for the CEO, a drop of 12 per cent.

Purpose matters to employees

Employees are, similarly, looking to work for companies with whom they can share a common sense of purpose and derive dignity from their daily work, not just a pay cheque. Southwest Airlines, the largest low-cost carrier and the most consistently profitable airline in the world (42 years and counting!), placed the recruitment of people who shared its culture at the heart of its business philosophy. As Herb Kelleher, its CEO and chairman for most of those 42 years, memorably said: 'the business of business is people'. True differentiation, he argued, could only come from culture, from behaviour, because everything else was replicable; as he pointed out in a speech in 2008, 'All airlines have planes.' The management guru Peter Drucker agrees, saying: *'Culture eats strategy for lunch.'*

Many companies have followed the Southwest Airlines route to success. Umpqua Bank and First Direct deliberately hired people who had no previous banking experience so that they would only focus on what customers wanted, not what banks could do. Zappos, the online retailer snapped up by Amazon for $1 billion in 2009, offers newly recruited employees $4,000 to leave after one week of training. Why? Because they only want the people who really want to stay.

The business benefits of engaged employees were highlighted in a study by the Temkin Group in 2011. Looking across a number of different industries in the United States, they discovered that employees who were 'engaged' (people who understood and shared a sense of common purpose with the business, and felt empowered to deliver that purpose) were more productive, more loyal and delivered greater customer satisfaction than those who were not.[4] A staggering 99 per cent of employees who worked for businesses that the Temkin study had identified as delivering excellent customer experiences agreed that they were 'committed to helping their company succeed'. Whereas, of the employees who worked for companies that delivered poor customer experiences, only 17 per cent agreed with the statement. Doing the right thing for the customer is a universal motivator.

Why purpose became important

What has caused the importance of purpose to rise among so many people in so many countries?

The evidence is that there are three reasons:

1 A shift in consumer values caused by both generational change and especially by the financial crisis of 2008.

2 The rise of new technologies that empower people.

3 The shift in the value base of many developed economies.

1 *A shift in values*

It seems that as baby boomers have been succeeded by generation Xers, who in turn have been succeeded by generations Y, Z and millennials, attitudes to and expectations from life have been changing. This is true about why people buy what they buy. The baby boomers have now entered their 60s and even generation X have begun to turn 50. These were people who were brought up with some deeply held beliefs about empowerment, about freedom and about 'living life to the full'. They have little desire to retire gracefully, thus earning themselves the 'Ageing Ravers' tag – and they have money to spend. They are at once interested in enjoying themselves and doing what is right for their succeeding generations. Consumption for them is less about 'having' and more about 'doing' and doing good while they do it. Extreme examples of this are entrepreneurs such as Bill and Melinda Gates and Sir Richard Branson. It is not exclusive to baby boomers, of course. According to *Forbes* magazine, Warren Buffet's entire holding in Berkshire Hathaway, ome $58 billion, will be donated to charity before or upon his death.

ere have always been philanthropists but why is it that baby boomers eration X seem to be applying this on a commercial scale? For the need to go all the way back to 1943. It was then that Abraham ed his groundbreaking paper 'A theory of human motivation'. bed his 'hierarchy of needs', which has become one of the sychology models in business. He suggested that our f-actualization', which means, essentially, achieving ch less well known is that shortly before his death called 'Critique of self-actualization theory' model and proposed another dimension as notivation. He called it 'self-transcendence' and concluded the self only finds its actualization in giving itself to some higher goal outside itself, in altruism and spirituality. It seems that the increasing wealth of the older generations is allowing them to turn their attention from 'me' to 'we'.

So there seems to be a psychological need for purpose, but the shift towards values is probably also a product of our times. The global financial crisis (GFC) of 2007–08 has, of course, accelerated some of our underlying beliefs: that you 'can't trust the man', that life is too short, that we owe a responsibility to those who come after us. Certainly, the breakdown in trust in institutions – financial, political and religious – seems to have been fuelled by the collapse in confidence that the GFC fostered if not created.

The GFC has also focused people on 'meaningful' or true value. People expect their hard-earned euro, pound or dollar to give them much more. And the 'reassuringly expensive' pitch of many brands convinces fewer people. Primark, the European retail phenomenon, is a great example of the shift in value perception. Instead of regarding cheap clothes as unfashionable, millions of consumers recognize that Primark offers good quality, fast fashion that costs little and can be easily given away. Teenagers can enjoy a form of retail therapy for a few pounds – it is no longer the preserve of the well-to-do.

The savvy consumer that has been created by this combination of changing generation and financial environment is at once keen to get good value and to espouse good values. Primark has, for example, worked hard to reassure its customers that the inexpensive prices of its clothes are not the direct result of the exploitation of low-cost labour.

The importance to customers of putting 'purpose' before profit can be seen in the success of organizations such as Fairtrade and the World Wildlife Fund (WWF). Major branded-good companies have realized that it is a commercial advantage to them to source from fair trade-approved suppliers and so carry the fair trade logo on their products. This includes multinational powerhouses such as Nestlé, whose Nescafé coffee brand has been so dominant in Europe for so long that you would think it had little need of external endorsemen from a not-for-profit brand. But consumers are putting their money into tho brands that they perceive as doing 'the right thing'. And Nestlé, like any g brand should, is responding to its customers. In 2012, there were €4.8 b of fair trade-endorsed products sold in Europe.

So the search for a higher purpose is becoming a vital factor in t sumer's choice of products and it is becoming of vital commercial im for brands themselves. This is clearly shown by Havas Media's ann into 'Meaningful Brands'. Paul Frampton, the CEO, introduced the

Key
— Meaningful Brand Index
— STOXX 1800 × 120%
— FTSE4 Good Index × 175%

Figure 0.1 Havas Meaningful Brands Index 2013

by saying, 'In our survey of 134,000 consumers across 23 countries we found real people crying out for brands to have a purpose, and live that purpose in what they do.' Their 2013 report also found that the meaningful brands outperformed the market by 120 per cent and this increased significantly in their 2015 study, so focusing on purpose makes you more profitable (see ~ure 0.1).

~re is a danger, of course, in reporting compelling statistics such as these.

~w with the rush to corporate social responsibility (CSR) some years

~rt-sighted CEO motivated by the potential to generate positive

~l conclude 'We need a purpose statement' and delegate some

~ate one or, perhaps even worse, ask their ad agency to craft

~ do so misses the point entirely. It is about the 'doing',

nologies and breakdown of

aspect of our lives. Our ability to render

~n can then be translated into anything

~D printing to mobile money, has simplified,

speeded up and more often than not improved our experience. We shop online, pay our bills online, and even undertake mass political protest online. If we have a digital device connected to the internet, we have access to a world of information. And, as always, with information comes knowledge and with knowledge comes power. So pervasive and relentless is this process that experts now refer to the 'internet of things', a world where all devices – from a fridge to a phone – are connected and can communicate intelligently with each other. Soon your fridge will identify that it doesn't have enough milk and will automatically order extra pints from your online supermarket, which will deliver it either to your house or to a location of your convenience somewhere on your journey home from work.

We can find out how to write business plans, how to rent our spare rooms, how to raise money through crowdfunded investment, how to fix a computer, cook a meal for a multitude, even buy weapons, all by accessing applications on the internet. There is a thriving digital currency independent of the currencies controlled by the central banks of countries and economic unions. Bitcoin is just one of these currencies and it is fuelling the growth of entirely new businesses. Around $250 million was estimated to be in bitcoin businesses during 2014, an increase of 150 per cent on 2013.

All of the above is making it easier for everyone to start businesses that disrupt the normal way of doing things – businesses that are nimble, agile, highly responsive to customer needs and, most importantly, launched with an avowed purpose of making a difference rather than simply making a buck.

Accompanying the Digital Revolution has been a rapid deregulation, which has made it easier for companies to cross borders, enter new markets and reduce costs dramatically. Let's take two examples: Airbnb and Uber. Both of these brands are disrupting their respective sectors (guest accommodation and vehicle hire) by helping to redefine and reshape expectations. Airbnb allows anyone (as long as they pass some essential security checks) to rent out any part or whole of their house to anyone else at rates far more appealing than many hotels or traditional guesthouses. It can only do this because of the ubiquity of digital technology, our increasing comfort with online payment systems and a regulatory environment that is less stringent about what you can or cannot do with the subletting of your home. Uber is the same. It relies on our familiarity with and the ubiquity of hand-held digital devices, fast connectivity and a regulatory environment that allows them to trade as vehicles for hire, not taxis. Of course, disruption of this kind is often met with resistance from traditional channels, as Uber found in France.

Other sectors are constantly subject to regulatory change aimed at bringing in greater competition, greater customer or consumer choice, greater efficiency and effectiveness, including health care, education and finance. This is creating a fertile environment for extreme competitiveness. The power of technology and the breakdown of traditional forms of business are allowing business to operate in unprecedented ways. However, power – without the moderating hand of purpose – can be a dangerous force. Google's purpose is to 'organize the world's information and make it universally accessible and useful' but perhaps, recognizing the danger inherent in the sheer sweep of their purpose, their mantra is 'Don't be evil'. Even so, Google has come in for its fair share of criticism over the years.

Interestingly, Google recently partnered with agencies TNS and Ogilvy to research how digital platforms and social media have changed the relationship between advertisers and consumers. They concluded that with the limitless options open to consumers they 'are choosing to engage only with content that is personally relevant to them, their purpose and their passions'. They summed up their research by saying 'their (the consumers') path to purchase is actually their path to purpose'.

3 *A shift in the source of value*

The source of value for business and for an economy has always come from access to or control of a key resource that people need or want. For centuries, that was land and natural resources, then it became access to financial and human capital required for the development of the manufacturing base of the industrial age. Somewhere in the 20th century we entered the 'Information Age', where access to data became a key source of advantage as services and communications began to dominate developed economies.

Now a new shift in value is occurring. In 1999, Joseph Pine and James Gilmore wrote the book *The Experience Economy*, predicting that consumers would increasingly demand and pay premiums for an 'experience' beyond the mere consumption of any branded product or service. Starbucks coffee houses were the most conspicuous example of this. People visited them as much to 'hang out' or catch up on some work as to drink coffee. Howard Schultz, its CEO, described Starbucks as 'the third place' between home and work where because of its ambience, and the time you could linger, people would pay up to $4 for a coffee.

This desire for an experience beyond the product or service has grown. It requires the mingling or merging together of marketing, operations and human resources because, for the consumer or the customer, the people, the messaging and the product or service provision become integral parts of a bigger whole and, in some cases, indistinguishable from each other. People who buy Innocent drinks rather than other smoothies are buying its quirky sense of fun as much as the healthy product.

Above all, the experience economy requires constant innovation or invention as a key source of value. Customers want predictability of outcome but they don't want sameness of experience. They want to know they will get something of value that is consistent with their perceptions of the brand but which is updated, upgraded or has the capacity to surprise them in a relevant way. In order to invent and innovate regularly and relevantly, companies need to achieve unprecedented levels of intimacy with their customers. They need as much as possible real-time information about what their customers like or don't like, what they want or desire. This goes far beyond gathering the opinions of customers in a way that is remote from the experience, such as through focus groups or gathering their reactions through high street or online surveys. It means being in a continual conversation with customers, who will give you as much information as they want in the expectation that you will use it to improve their experience. In fact, it goes beyond a conversation into the co-creation of the experience itself.

In an effort to refresh constantly the relationship with customers, companies are investing in experiences that are 'immersive', by which we mean that customers or consumers are actively engaged in or participants in them. This is a trend best exemplified in the entertainment business. Punchdrunk, for example, an innovative theatre company, puts on shows in unusual, 'non-theatrical' venues and then involves the audience in the performance in unique ways where the audience 'controls' the experience. Its award-wining production of *Sleep no More*, a version of *Macbeth*, at the time of writing has run in New York for more than three years. It takes place in 100 rooms over six floors of an old warehouse building and each member of the audience can walk through the warehouse and the story at his or her own pace, choosing which part of the story they want to follow.

This personalization, co-creation and 'participation' in the experience is increasingly what other commercial sectors are aspiring to. It might be as simple as having your favourite picture on your bank credit card or your name on a Coca-Cola can, or more useful such as Amazon's profiling, or more immersive such as Google Cultural Institute or Burberry's Bespoke tab on its website.

For this to work, the participation has to be relevant to the brand and its consumer, of course, and it also has to be relevant to its purpose. Just because organizations *can*, doesn't mean that they *should*. Technology allows us to engage with customers whenever we choose, but the question is 'Should we – does it add value for the consumer?' You only need to think of the irritating customer relationship management (CRM)-driven cold calls that interrupt our Saturday evenings, or the spam that clogs up our e-mail on a daily basis. We often joke in speeches that CRM, rather than standing for 'customer relationship management', actually stands for 'constantly receiving mailshots' from the customer perspective. The filter of an effective purpose places a check on how, and when, we engage with customers over these channels to ensure that we are doing so in a way that creates value for the consumer and the business. O2, the telecom operator and one of the most successful purpose-driven brands, has a proposition called 'Priority Moments' where it texts customers with invitations to concerts at the O2 Arena or sporting events. Its purpose is '*Helping our customers connect to the people and things that matter to them*' and this provides the lens through which the brand makes those decisions about what to communicate to whom.

Since Shaun and Joe Wheeler wrote their book *Managing the Customer Experience* in 2002, customer experience has gone mainstream, but it has been made hugely more important and complex by the addition of the 'omni-channel' approach. Omni-channel includes not only traditional media channels but also every touchpoint through which the customer experiences the brand. The product, the packaging, the place in which it is sold and the people who represent or sell the brand across every channel – including physical, social and digital – have to deliver a consistent experience of the brand. They are all 'channels' for establishing a conversation with the customer and creating a perception of the brand. If any of them operates in a way that is inconsistent or at odds with the sense of purpose of the brand, it will dilute or, at worst, destroy value for the business.

We said that our title *On Purpose* has a double meaning – the notion of purpose beyond profit and also the sense of being intentional about delivering the customer experience. This becomes all the more important when delivering an experience across multiple channels because the variables increase exponentially and therefore the opportunity for inconsistency is massive. All the more reason, then, to take a joined-up approach. As Ronan Dunne, CEO of Telefonica UK, the owner of O2, says, 'it only works when it all works'.

How to be on purpose

Organizations that are 'on purpose' do three main things:

> They *Stand up* for something that they believe will deliver true value or otherwise improve the lives of their customers or consumers.

> They *Stand out* from competitors by intentionally and consistently delivering a distinctive customer experience across all channels that is consistent with their promise.

They *Stand firm* by creating the appropriate culture to ensure sustainable and authentic delivery over the long term.

This book therefore explores and explains these three dimensions in some detail. It also explains how these businesses 'never stand still', responding and anticipating continuously to the changing needs of customers and society.

How to use *On Purpose*

We received many compliments about our previous books, *Uncommon Practice*; *See, Feel, Think, Do*; and *Bold: How to be brave in business and win*. The stories they contain and their underlying customer-centric philosophy has inspired many people. However, some readers wanted more help and tools in order to apply the thinking to their own organizations, especially long-established corporations or business-to-business organizations.

We also learnt from our last book, *Bold: How to be brave in business and win*, the importance of having supplementary material to the printed book that could be accessible online – and, of course, embedded into digital versions of the book.

We have structured this book in such a way that you first read about each of the three dimensions of being *on purpose* (stand up, stand out, stand firm) and the numerous examples to illustrate them. We also provide the story of a brand to illustrate each of the three main parts of the book. We offer an implementation process that distils our years of experience working with leading brands to apply this thinking and two major case studies of organizations – Liberty Global and Premier Inn – that have done so where the executives concerned tell you what they did, why they did it, how they did it and what they learned 'warts and all'.

Finally, at the end of the book, we provide links to a comprehensive online 'toolkit', which contains many of the tools we use and supports the implementation process we describe. You can, of course, skip straight to the toolkit, but that would be to miss out on some insightful case studies and, in particular, would prevent you from thinking constantly throughout the reading of this book about the most important question: 'What purpose does my business serve?'

We hope you enjoy the book and find it relevant and useful for your own business, whatever its type or size. If you do, then we will have achieved *our* purpose.

Notes

1 http://www.bbc.co.uk/news/business-31627068.

2 www.sharedvalue.org.

3 http://www.edelman.com/insights/intellectual-property/2015-edelman-trust-barometer/.

4 Temkin Group Q4 2011 Consumer Benchmark Survey; base 2,435 employees of for-profit organizations in the United States.

Part One
Stand up

Chapter One
Purpose driven

The wrong kind of purpose

A few years ago, we were working for a Japanese consumer electronics company whose major competitors included Fuji. At a workshop with the leadership team we asked what their purpose was – the reply was 'F..k Fuji'.

Destroying or displacing your competitor is certainly one kind of purpose. Some managers can find it easier to motivate their people by making an enemy of the competition and giving people the objective to defeat them. It is a mindset that sees business as a war game and uses other military terms and strategies to achieve victory.

Kevin O'Leary, the Canadian businessman behind Shark Tank, said, 'Business is war. I go out there, I want to kill the competitors. I want to make their lives miserable. I want to steal their market share. I want them to fear me.' There are numerous books on the theme of business as war, including adaptations of *The Art of War* by the ancient Chinese military strategist, Sun Tzu.

This approach works when it is easy to see who the enemy is: Pepsi versus Coca-Cola in the 'rock and roller Cola wars'; IBM versus Apple in the 1980s; Sainsbury versus Tesco, or Nike versus Reebok. But in a world where competitors are coming from anywhere, where digital has transformed the ability of brands to nimbly and quickly forge new relationships with customers, where new categories and subcategories are being created and consumers are deciding on a daily basis, it seems that what they perceive as competing alternatives – this 'battle of the brands' approach – is less relevant.

Moreover, it can seem absurd. The satirist PJ O'Rourke, in a brilliant article for *Forbes*, mocks the inherent nonsense of comparing war with business: 'They have as much in common as a sucking chest wound and a lunch expense account.' He went on to write, 'Good business produces what the best war can't, mutual satisfaction – pleased customers, investors, employees or bosses. At the end of a war, they are in a grave. At the end of a business day, usually not.' The machismo surrounding the 'business as war' analogy is also, we suspect, unappealing to at least half of the world's population.

Of course, the 'military style' objective does not need to be couched in such overtly aggressive language. Many organizations motivate their people with a target or goal that is about 'hitting market share', 'reaching a profit level', and 'maximizing sales'. People like these targets because they are SMART (specific, measurable, actionable, realistic and time-critical).

But the problem at the heart of the 'kill your competitor' or 'hit your objective' 'become number one' types of purpose is that they are self-serving and ultimately self-limiting. What happens when you *are* number one? Who do you go and kill then? How inspiring is it for your minimum-wage employees to know that you are the most profitable organization in your industry? And how motivating is it to your customers to know that your purpose is to destroy your competitors – or, worse still, that your objective is to 'sell them stuff'? Because in this day and age, when customers are peering behind the veil of secrecy that companies have maintained in the past, when the 'truth is out there', they will find out. In 2014, the UK retailer Sainsbury ran into a media storm when an internal campaign instructing store staff to sell an extra 50p worth of product to every customer, became public knowledge. Unfortunately, one of Sainsbury's store staff had accidentally pinned up the poster carrying the instructions at the front of the store where consumers could see it.

As we mentioned in our introduction, Barclays Bank is one of a number of financial service businesses undergoing transformative change around its sense of purpose. Matt Hammerstein, its head of customer experience for retail banking, explains the challenge of changing people's motivation from a 'business target' to a 'higher purpose':

'A lot of people talk about change fatigue, they complain that there's too much change. But we cannot slow the pace of change. So, I don't think it's change fatigue; I think it's "lack of purpose" fatigue. I think people are struggling to answer the question, "Why the hell am I doing this?" Let me give you an example. I was with someone who leads a very big global business here and I said, "What's your biggest challenge?" He said, "Communications. To get the troops fired up, five years ago I used to go out and say we're number three on the league table, we want to be number one, numbers one and two are ___, go beat the pants off them. It used to be so simple." I said, "Well, it's not about life being more complex or more simple; the fact was the purpose was absolutely clear. The purpose was to become number one. And you don't know what your purpose is right now. That's not a communication problem, that's a fundamental challenge because you don't know what to tell people about why they come to work and work hard. You've got to figure out in your own mind what the purpose is, and then the communication is pretty simple. Because once you've figured it out and you're clear in your own head, people will jump off a cliff for it, like they used to. You've just got to figure out what your purpose is now – and that's hard."'

There is one other problem with the 'beat your competitor' approach to purpose: it requires little 'insight'. There is little you need to discover or be inspired by, if all you want to do is kill the guy who is standing in your way, or find ways to extract more profit from customers.

Of course, we strongly believe that companies must make profits. Profits are a good thing: you can invest them in improving your customer experience, in funding research and development, in paying your employees better wages, and in making returns to your investors. Businesses don't exist unless they make money (or are heavily subsidized by someone who has lots of it). And no customer is going to thank you for delivering an experience that costs you more than they can afford to pay. They won't be happy if you go out of business in order to give them a great service. But profits should come from providing value.

There are organizations who put their social purpose first and foremost and money is less important. These are not-for-profit organizations. They have a very strong sense of purpose, which is altruistic. They need to 'raise' money rather than make it. Profits are not an outcome for them as they are for businesses. The outcome and the purpose are one and the same for many not-for-profit organizations. In fact there are some organizations whose purpose is to make themselves disappear. Oxfam wants to rid the world of poverty. If it does, it makes itself immediately redundant.

These organizations are purpose driven but they are not businesses and we are exclusively concerned in this book with businesses. Of course, businesses can learn enormously from not-for-profit organizations about purpose and how it drives behaviour – just as not-for-profits can learn about customer experience from great businesses.

There are three types of purpose, therefore, which we have identified: commercial purpose, which is primarily about your financial goal; brand purpose, which is about your customer ambition; and social purpose, which is about your societal vision. These three purposes have to be reconciled (Figure 1.1). Even not-for-profits have a financial goal, otherwise they lack the funds to effect any change, and commercial organizations need to concern themselves with the society within which they exist otherwise they may not be around for very long. The question is: which of these is your primary purpose?

Robert Stephens is the founder of the Geek Squad. He grew a business that went from essentially one man (himself) to a phenomenon that became the number one provider of domestic computer repairs in the United States. Robert built his business with a refreshing approach that turned what most people saw as a boring but necessary activity conducted by geeks into a fun business that has 20,000 'special agents' servicing customers – and millions of fans.

He did so through insight. He saw that when someone's PC stopped working at home that person would become emotionally distressed, bereft of the kind of IT support that he or she would get at their workplace, and often with highly emotional content on their personal computers that they risked

Figure 1.1 The three purpose drivers

losing. He saw there was a business opportunity in taking away the stress, making customers smile and in helping them to get the most out of their computers in a really engaging way.

Robert is probably the leader that has been most often quoted from our previous books. He has a knack of reducing things to their fundamental truths. He explains in his uniquely entertaining and straightforwardly honest way how companies balance the three types of purpose we identify – commercial, brand and social:

> 'I think purpose is part of a major trend, and that trend is related to global commerce. As we learn about how connected things are, whether it's the environment or the global supply chain or the gigantic debris field of plastic in the ocean that gathers there because of the currents, we're learning that everything has its price. Even Apple with its wonderful vision has to be vigilant on behalf of factory workers. Apple could not do what they do without lower-cost Chinese labour, and Zara and others couldn't produce what they do.
>
> 'The consumer could ignore that before, and may not have even been aware but, because of global communications, once you see the relationship you can't unsee it. Companies can ignore it if they want but at some point I believe that lack of authentic purpose will be a tax not just on your growth and revenues, but on your talent acquisition.
>
> 'So as long as an organization is honest with itself, it can have a totally capitalist world view. How does this apply to business? We have to

support the AIDS crisis, we have to help starving children in Africa, because they are our future customers; we must save them so they can buy from us one day. I take care of my employees and I provide them with benefits because I don't want them worrying about s..t like that – so they can be super-productive. With this super-cynical but super-honest world view, you can be a capitalist pig, you can love Wall Street and Gordon Gekko, but you can still take care of the environment for capitalist reasons – as long as you're doing the right thing.

'You know, personally, I'm not really interested in the environment; I don't really think the world can be saved and, politically, I don't believe in climate change. So purpose doesn't have to be altruistic in my view. It doesn't have to be all about hugging trees. And that's where you can be authentic. You can be authentically "greedy", because, if I'm truly a true greedy person, I would not steal from somebody because at some point it will come back to hurt me. It ruins the virtuous cycle. Businesses need to behave ethically because in the long run, if they don't it short-changes them anyway. So this is a more refreshing, more honest way that people can think about this notion of purpose.'

The right kind of purpose

So what is the right kind of purpose for businesses? It is one that is *primarily* customer driven. The social purpose is attendant on it because customers live in society, and financial goals are consequent to it because if you delight customers you should make money. That might sound cynical to some but, as Robert Stephens says: '*A cynic is just a romantic with higher standards.*'

Because businesses' primary purpose must be customer driven, it is vital that they gain insight into what customers need or want, now or in the future. Barclays Bank's purpose is 'Helping people achieve their ambition – in the right way'. Matt Hammerstein explains the insight that led Barclays to that purpose:

'The financial crisis and the subsequent recession revealed there were organizations that had figured out how to make money and that was their principal purpose. That was not unique to banking. It was the 1980s spirit of shareholder returns: the only thing that you needed to do as a company was to make sure that you were producing good shareholder returns. That became problematic because an attitude developed that "anything goes"; as long as it contributes to a shareholder return then we can justify it.

*'We have to reconnect the question "What are we in business for?"
with a higher order of magnitude than just to make money. As a bank,
we are at the heart of what our customers need in order for them to be
as successful as they want to be. And ultimately the things that they are
trying to do are about being good citizens, contributing to their own and
society's wealth and happiness. So it becomes fundamentally incumbent
on us, if we aspire to try and serve those needs, to be clear about what
our social purpose is. There are lots of stakeholders who affect our
licence to operate, specifically regulators and legislators. If they don't
understand that what we are doing for our customers also benefits them
as custodians of society, they can take that licence away.'*

So the best businesses will have a purpose that is driven by insight, first and
foremost, into its customers' needs but also considers the demands of the
society in which they will operate. And there is increasing evidence that
customers will reward businesses that do this.

Since 2010 Havas Media Group have invested in a regular study into people's
attitudes to brands – called 'Meaningful Brands'. Essentially, this looks at how
relevant to people any brand is – not merely in delivering a specific functional
or aspirational image benefit, but within the context of what they are concerned about in their world as well as their values or beliefs about what is
important. Essentially, how does that brand help them to improve their quality
of life and wellbeing? The 2015 analysis covered 34 countries, involving
300,000 consumers, revealing that the majority of people could not care
whether 74 per cent of brands they bought existed or not. However, it also
found that the brands that people found most 'meaningful' to them – and
there were not many – were regarded as essential to their lives. Moreover,
those brands were also the ones that were growing or performing strongly in
terms of traditional business measures, outperforming the others by 133 per
cent stock market value. Analysis of the survey also revealed that a brand's
'Share of Wallet' – a metric used to measure the percentage spent with a
brand versus the total annual expenditure within its category – is on average
46 per cent higher for meaningful brands and can be up to as much as
seven times larger.

Furthermore, the performance of marketing key performance indicators
(KPIs) set by top meaningful brands can grow at twice the rate of those set by
lower-scoring meaningful brands. For example, for every 10 per cent increase
in meaningfulness, a brand can increase its purchase and repurchase intent
by 6 per cent and price premiums by 10.4 per cent. The results have led Havas
to conclude that brands that contribute significantly to our quality of life are

rewarded with stronger business results – they earn a 'return on meaning': ie business benefits gained by a brand when it is seen to improve our wellbeing.

Dominique Delport, the global managing director of Havas Media Group, summarized the impact of 'meaning' on marketing: 'Great marketing has a cumulative effect as it's shared. We will only share ideas if brands do stuff that matters to us. We now look to brands for meaningful connections – big or small.'

There is plenty of other evidence that customer-centric businesses with strong brands (ie ones to which customers feel a high level of affinity) out-perform their markets. For example, in 2003, a joint study by the University of Carolina and Harvard Business School reviewed the business performance of the Top 100 brands in the Interbrand Global Brand Value survey. They con-cluded that the businesses that owned these brands not only delivered higher returns to shareholders than other stocks, they also did so at a lower risk rate. In February 2015, Apple's market capitalization was $765 billion, which is twice as much as the second most valuable company on the planet, Exxon Mobile.[1] Paradoxically, Steve Jobs was famously known to be disinterested in making money. Rather, his purpose was, 'We're here to put a dent in the universe.'

Insight helps to keep purpose relevant

The digital world and the 'internet of things' have transformed how we experi-ence the promises that brands make. They have also transformed our ability to shape and co-create those experiences and to tell millions of other people about our experiences, good or bad. But brand owners have had to face trans-formative challenges before. In the early 20th century, transformations occurred in the mass production, storage and transportation of goods and, later, in mass media, especially radio and television.

Such transforming factors have, though, never changed the fundamentals of brand building: gain continuous insight into what your customers want, know how the purpose of your brand helps them, be clear about your pro-mises and deliver them brilliantly. Brand owners as diverse as Coca-Cola, Kellogg's, Guinness, Procter & Gamble (P&G), Disney, Ritz-Carlton and IBM have prospered over centuries because they have understood those simple fundamentals. They have also understood that the trust that the brand earns endures, while what the brand actually sells can change dramatically. IBM does not sell computers any more but its purpose is still driven by the same insight that Thomas R Watson had in 1915 – that 'information technologies would benefit mankind'. Today, IBM speaks publicly through its advertising of a purpose to create a 'smarter planet'. The best brands have adapted to the changing needs of society, not just to the individual needs of consumers in that society. In fact, they have anticipated those needs and develop their advanced planning and research and development process to provide the goods and services that will be needed in the future.

Returning to Barclays Bank, if Matt Hammerstein is right and it is incumbent on banks to serve a social purpose, then it becomes essential to them to understand what is happening in society and provide services that help people to cope with its changes, not just to put their money somewhere safe.

Hammerstein explains how Barclays Bank has been looking at those changes:

> 'Right now, we're somewhere in the midst of what I call the third
> industrial revolution. In the first, there was mechanization in the 18th
> and 19th centuries; so in the United States, the cotton gin came and
> it completely disrupted labour economics. In the second, you had
> motorization in the early part of the 20th century, with the same impact;
> it completely transformed the way in which the economy worked. Now
> you've got digitization and it's having exactly the same impact on society.
>
> 'As a bank, we could just sit back, observe that and say "Well, that's
> fine, we're aware of that, we can sympathize with it; it's going to have a
> big impact on our business because we're going to digitize certain things,
> and there'll be certain people who won't be able to do what they do
> today." Or we can recognize that actually all of our customers, clients and
> our colleagues are going through that one way or another and we can
> orient what we are doing in our business around helping them.
>
> 'In the midst of industrial revolutions, lots of people prosper and lots
> of people get left behind. So we said that our mission must be to leave
> no one behind. Now, we're not literally going to be able to help all
> 65 million people in the UK, but if we have the ambition of doing
> whatever we possibly can, it's going to stretch our imaginations to do
> things we probably wouldn't have otherwise done.'

This has led Barclays to launch a programme called 'Digital Eagles' (named after the famous logo of the bank). The Digital Eagles are specially trained members of staff on hand in all Barclays branches to provide technology advice to both customers and non-customers. It is a free service, an opportunity for people to build confidence in digital skills. Steven Roberts, director of strategic trans-formation at Barclays, explains:

'We firmly believe that Barclays has a commercial and social responsibility to ensure that no one is left behind on the digital journey, so we are on a mission to help and enable people to understand and embrace coding and the new Digital Revolution – whether they are seven or 107.

'As we transform Barclays into a truly digital business we now have more than 25,000 Digital Eagles worldwide, with over 12,000 in the UK. We've even created our own accreditation, called the Digital Driving Licence. Accredited by City & Guilds, it started out for colleagues and is now available and accessible to everyone, free to download as an app. We've already got registered users from more than 20 countries around the world and we're aiming for a million downloads. We've already seen the benefit that the Barclays Digital Driving Licence can bring as an accessible and non-intimidating introduction to the digital world.'

Barclays Bank has a long way to go – as do most of the other traditional banks – to persuade people, including its own customers, that it is putting its customer-driven purpose at the heart of all its activities. In 2014, its chairman Sir Anthony Jenkins stated that he thought it would take 10 years for the banks to gain people's trust. But as the Chinese proverb puts it, the journey of 1,000 miles starts with a single step. It seems that the other Board members were not prepared to make that journey with him, because he was asked to step down in 2015.

Banks, as we have said, are not the only targets of customer and social criticism. Another industry sector at the heart of the 'digital storm', which has also attracted much scrutiny from society, is media. Media brands such as newspapers, TV channels and film studios have had their entire operational

Image 1.1 Barclays digital eagles

and regulatory business models disrupted. Print media have particularly suffered. Print media once effectively controlled the news agenda, even in flourishing democracies. Newspapers told us what to think, or at least what to think about. They were the main way in which the institutions that sought to control people's behaviour (political parties, businesses, religious organizations) influenced us. With only limited competition, newspapers often appeared to act in a form of cartel – setting rules for themselves under the privilege of freedom of speech not granted to other forms of media, such as television. Their relationship with their consumers was what, in psychology, a transactional analyst would have called 'parent–child'. They claimed to be the 'voice of the people' and, in order to prove their point, could use the selective editing of letters from readers and 'campaigns' supported by their readers.

They operated behind 'closed doors' where they could engage in practices that their readers, had they known about them, would probably have deserted in droves, which is in fact what happened as soon as the digital revolution hit them. Suddenly, readers could consume their news, gossip or entertainment any time they liked in any way they liked at any pace they liked. Consumers showed an enthusiasm to 'get behind the story', to lift the veil of secrecy to understand 'what was really going on' and to which newspapers could not respond. Such a world exposed what was the primary purpose of these print brands, and when readers did not share that purpose, they would quickly turn against it.

Let's compare two print brands, both established in the same year, 1843. The first is the *News of the World* in the UK, established in October 1843 by John Browne Bell and heralded as 'The Novelty of Nations and the Wonder of the World'. Its founder said: 'Our motto is the truth, our practice is fearless advocacy of the truth.' Bell's insight was that as the political franchise was extended to more and more people, and as standards of education and levels of prosperity increased, more people would want to read more about and be entertained by what was going on in the world. The purpose of the *News of the World* was 'to give the poorer classes of society a paper that would suit their means, and to the middle as well as the richer a journal which, by its immense circulation, should command their attention'.

For many years, the newspaper certainly fulfilled part of its purpose: it did command attention. However, by the early 2000s it was embroiled in what appeared to be a war not to bring the truth to its readers but to win more market share and thus greater advertising revenue. The pressure to get more and more exclusives of more salacious detail resulted in journalistic practices that were illegal, offensive and even betrayed their own readers. It culminated in the phone-hacking scandals, which led to its parent company, News

International, concluding that the brand was so contaminated that the newspaper had to be closed down and the brand withdrawn from the market.

Compare that brand with an entirely different publication: *The Economist*. Established in September 1843 by businessman James Wilson with the following purpose: 'to take part in a severe contest between intelligence, which presses forward, and an unworthy, timid ignorance obstructing our progress'. Wilson had a similar insight to Bell about the need for engaging more people with knowledge, but its difference was that he saw the need to *drive* the world's progress, not simply report it.

The brand has flourished by consistently staying true to that purpose and finding new and relevant ways to deliver on it. Its owner, Pearson International, with its core product, *The Economist* weekly magazine as its engine, has found new ways to engage new audiences intelligently through *The Economist* brand. The Economist Intelligence Unit publishes books, organizes conferences and has a thriving online offer, which attracts an upscale, educated and usually affluent audience, which in turn attracts advertisers with good money to spend. So institutionalized is *The Economist* culture – its style guide is one of the best books we have read on how to write – that it is impossible to think of it betraying its purpose and editorial principles. Rest assured, should it be tempted to do so, its readers would soon let it know.

How purpose informs building your brand and your business

Robert Stephens explains how building business is driven by the relationship between 'purpose' (what you stand for) and 'brand' (what customers experience of you):

'I think purpose is part of brand and brand really is the wrapper that represents the complete package in the customer's head. Everybody has a need for labels. The human mind has a need for organization, so when we are comparing more than just price, purpose and brand are the thing that people really look at. Can I trust you? Especially if it's a complex service; it's not just about the price.

'Customers look for subtle signs. When you get a bid from somebody, is there handwriting somewhere on it or are they simply using a computer to generate it; do they use a barcode, how fast do they get the bid to you? All of those things tell you a lot about how the supplier is going to behave if you choose to do business with them.

'The more commoditized something gets, the less we value it, just like the less we have to work for something, the less meaning it has for us. I think you can run a fine company with no higher purpose but, when you have one, it can serve as the glue that holds people together during tough times. It can lower the cost of operating. Purpose acts like an invisible manager to make the organization operate more efficiently and to help people do the right things.

'Go back a few years and if you had some great people and you had an interesting brand, you could probably deliver an experience that was distinctive and different and appealing to customers, but I think it's just so much more difficult now, because yes, you can have a brand, and yes, you can have maybe a little bit of a distinctive experience, but unless you're able to convey that, to communicate it, to deliver it intentionally across all of these different channels, be that the web or social media or retail or whatever, then, you know, it's suboptimal.'

Purpose drives and informs all aspects of brand building. If you can't answer the simple question, 'If our brand didn't exist, would we need to create it?' with a resounding 'Yes, because...' and articulate your purpose, then don't even bother with the other elements of branding. Purpose helps you to define who your target customer is and what they need. Lots of people may buy you but there will be one type of person, or rather one mindset, which will be most receptive to your sense of purpose – it drives what you want to be special and different for in their minds (the 'positioning' of the brand). It drives the personality of your brand.

Much of branding is emotional, the establishment of a 'relationship' with a customer psychologically, based on a perception of their own self-image. You create that image through the way you look, talk and act. So personality (tone of voice, visual style, sales environment, packaging etc) is critical. Specifically, it informs your choice of a protectable, relevant and appealing brand identity. That is the only way that customers can actually find your brand, buy it and recommend it. It is the most important legal asset you will own. We constantly talk about the 'branded customer experience'. It means making sure that the valuable experience you give to customers is so distinctive and unique to you that your customers associate it with you and no one else!

Apple's insight was that computers would become media devices for personal pleasure and enrichment. Steve Jobs famously declared in 1977 that in the future everyone would have an Apple computer. And in 1983, he gave a speech in a small room in California in which he described that insight in terms of a vision of what the future would be. The tape of that speech was

found in 2012 and uploaded to the internet. It is remarkable in the accur
its predictions.

That insight into people's desire for empowerment and creativity through
knowledge drove the purpose of the brand. And that purpose informed the
choice of name as well as a trademark look and feel for graphic, product and
retail design, communications and marketing. An apple is fresh and zesty,
as well as being associated with breakthroughs in human knowledge and
empowerment.

Purpose defines how far your brand can stretch and whether you will
want or need to create sub-brands or other brands. Disney knows that the
purpose of its brand is to make people happy; it does so by promising magical
family entertainment targeted at the child in all of us. It has the production
capacity also to make films that are not 'happy' movies, but it makes them
under a different brand, Touchstone Pictures. This protects the integrity of
the Disney brand for both the customer and the business.

Purpose drives the culture and processes you develop internally and thus
the choices you make to 'deliver and live' your brand externally. Steve Jobs and
his team were zealous about communicating internally. They even changed
the design of their head office to allow people to 'bump' into each other, so
facilitating more natural, intuitive and creative conversations. Johnny Ives, the
UK designer given much credit for Apple's success, insists that though Steve
Jobs was demanding, it was because he believed passionately in Apple's purpose and so he was very clear to everyone what was expected from Apple.

Robert Stephens explains how 'purpose' drove culture and customer experience at Geek Squad:

> 'For me, purpose acts like a lighthouse, but the light shines at a certain
> wavelength that only attracts a certain kind of person. The kind of people
> you want; it helps keep the others out. The purpose of the Geek Squad
> is to help ordinary people do extraordinary things with technology; a
> squad of people who combine their individual talents within a team to
> provide a service for the public. What they fix, whether it's PCs or tablets
> or phones, will change as technology changes, but how they serve
> customers will never change.
>
> 'That's what the Geek Mobiles did for us. You know, people think the
> uniforms and the cars and our branding were some kind of marketing
> gimmick. Not at all, in fact they weren't even really for the public. They
> were for our people. I needed those people to believe that they are the
> nearest living things to James Bond, five times a day. Take the uniforms:
> there are a lot of tech people who look at that uniform and say, "I'm not

n tie." That actually becomes a litmus test for humility and *out. So purpose acts as the lighthouse that draws and*

ust be what you measure business performance against. whether you are doing what you said you would do and ...other that is converting into the customer and financial performance you want. Most measures are generic and every company looks at them. There are the lag measures (which tell you how you've done) such as sales, market share, profitability; and the lead measures (which tell you how you might do) such as brand opinion, brand image and net promoter score (NPS). What is more important, however, is to identify the specific measures that determine whether your customers are getting the experience that your brand is promising. For example, telco O2's purpose is to connect customers with the people and things they want, so a key measure is how many 'dropouts' (ie losing a signal during a call) customers experience. If you are a priority customer trying to book your tickets to a big gig at the O2 arena, for example, you are going to be fairly angry with O2, the network operator, if half-way through booking you lose the connection and have to start all over again.

Being purpose-led is vital for businesses who want to succeed, who want to win and retain customers and talent, and who want to progress with a 'licence to operate' by all stakeholders in society. And to be truly purpose-led, you need to have insight into the world they live in, and *will* live in, and what needs and wants they have and will have. And that insight can often come from being aware of yourself and the things that are affecting your own life.

One example of a brand that was conceived around a purpose and that has been led that way ever since is giffgaff, a subsidiary of O2 but about as different as you can get from most telecom brands and, indeed, the parent company.

giffgaff – a purpose-driven company

The mobile network run by you

Tim Sefton, director of strategy and new business development at O2

I was appointed to the UK Board of O2 with a remit to champion the strategy that had driven our growth in previous years – to be customer-led. The nuance was that by this time the UK market had reached maturity and total revenues were declining year on year. This meant that there was a clear need to create new revenue streams away from the core business.

We spent a fair amount of time analysing alternative strategies because we knew how many other corporates had tried and failed to create new business from within. We also learned from our previous experiences as a business and from others about what it takes to give new businesses a chance to succeed within a corporate environment.

One key insight that emerged was that it was essential to give them an arm's-length relationship with the core business so they could be incubated and nurtured. Another was that if you decide to go down the path of creating new revenue streams, you have to commit resource to making it happen.

With the UK board fully aligned behind the strategy I built a new business development team, drawing talented people together from across functions – strategy, marketing, commercial finance, IT, HR – with a remit to create a pipeline of new business opportunities and to win board approval for financing them.

One member of this team was Gav Thompson who had the role of Head of Brand Strategy – his brief from me was simple... to apply the types of thinking that had created great brands in the past and come up with one amazing idea that would get funded and had the potential to 'move the needle' every year...

Gav Thompson

My real insight came because I was going through a midlife crisis.

I had just started riding a motorcycle and didn't know anything about how to fix the bike or tweak it. So at night I'd go onto web forums asking questions about how to change the suspension settings. I would get really good quality answers from strangers around the globe, for free, in minutes – in fact, better quality answers than I was getting from the BMW dealer.

And I thought, 'Well, this is amazing. There's so much goodwill around the internet and people sitting in their bedrooms willing to share it. Why don't we capture the knowledge of a bunch of people who, without trying to disparage them, are probably geeks who knew about phones and technology and how, for example, to get your photos from an iPhone onto an Android or to get your music from an Apple laptop to a PC? Why don't we harness that knowledge and goodwill and launch a business that would share that knowledge and empower those people? In doing so, we could actually create a brand that was more appealing to this segment of people who were a bit underwhelmed by O2 and all big telcos.

And so, whilst daydreaming about motorbikes during a Web 2.0 conference in San Francisco in 2008, giffgaff was born – a brand where marketing and customer service is provided by the customers. Customers are more engaged because they are helping you run it, it's cheaper to run and you are hitting the segment that normally wouldn't have been that interested in O2.

Stand up – purpose driven

giffgaff, which is an ancient Scottish word meaning a mutual gift, was built around a one-word essence, 'mutuality'. That word popped into my head when I first came up with the idea. I wrote it down as an original scribble in my notebook and to this day that simple essence of mutuality has informed everything the business has done and how the business should behave, through to pretty much every decision the business now makes.

The idea was in the back of my mind, when I was working for O2, having worked for 18 months as head of brand strategy. O2 was undoubtedly the best telco in our market, but there were a bunch of people who, because they were digital natives, probably thought that O2 and all the other big telcos were just a bit too corporate, a bit too glossy, a bit too complicated. They just wanted a good quality, cheaper telco that they could engage with online on their terms. They wanted more of an equitable relationship, not the kind of classic big brand telling you what to do. 'You've got to come to our shop and you've got to buy this phone'; so, a far more open, transparent relationship.

Our manifesto, which is on the website to this day, says we're about mutuality. We have a charter of eight points: it starts with mutuality; second, it's got to be a great deal; third, members need to be involved in running the company; fourth, the business wants to do stuff for the collective good of the

Image 1.2 giffgaff's purpose – mutuality

community; fifth, it's got to be simple and less complicated than most telcos; sixth, it's got to be an online only business – no shops and no sales people; seventh, it's got to be independent from the parent business; and eighth, we've got to do our bit for the environment.

When you have that kind of manifesto from day one, you can't just change it further down the line. And when your purpose is mutuality then you always have to think about what's best for the community, because the customers are the community, and the community is your business.

This means that when giffgaff's managing director Mike Fairman and the management team needed to put up our prices, because the cost of running the network had increased, that decision was put to the members to debate, to discuss and, ultimately, to take a vote on it. It was debated for a couple of weeks on the members' forum. Then, through the members, we got to a series of choices and then put it to a vote with the caveat that the guys running the business would get the casting vote. But it's never been the case that we've had to go against the will of the members.

At the end of the debating process, the goodwill of the community was higher than before. So the prices went up and everyone was happy as a result, which was a bizarre state of affairs.

With mutuality comes a notion of a sort of socialism and total transparency, which, when you're in a very competitive business like mobile telephony, creates a dilemma. You can't just put all your information up for anyone to read because it means that our competitors will either try to copy us or mirror us or steal our customers. So, although mutuality comes with this notion of socialism and openness and transparency, that's not at the expense of doing what's right by all stakeholders in the business.

A sense of purpose allows you to make some tough decisions as long as you can join up the dots.

If we put prices up, or, choose not to stock handsets, the logic flows back to the purpose. It's like having a kind of conscience operating all the time. If any member of the management team were to be stopped by a member in the street, or if we had to explain a decision on the forum, how do we make the link between mutuality and what we've chosen to do?

Here's a great example; giffgaff is one of the few networks still to have unlimited data usage but it was getting to the point where a certain number of members were using so much data that the rest of the members were getting reduced service. So Mike and the management team had a debate with the members about members who were taking the piss, by using so much data. The debate was: 'Shall we let them carry on doing this or shall we restrict them or shall we kick them out?' The view from the people was to *kick them out because their selfish behaviour was getting in the way of what was good for the membership.*

Sure, sometimes we make mistakes, but our clarity of purpose allows us to take tough decisions and recover from those mistakes relatively easily. As long as giffgaff remains about 'mutuality', I can't see it going too far off course.

Note

1   http://blogs.wsj.com/moneybeat/2015/02/23/apple-is-now-more-than-double-the-size-of-exxon-and-everyone-else/.

Chapter Two

Chapter Two
Purposeful leadership

'There's always a little element of bravery when you start a new project. It's a bit like jumping in the deep end in a way. You don't know exactly where you'll come out so you need to stay true to your core purpose – it becomes the compass that guides you.'

SONU SHIVDASANI,
FOUNDER, SIX SENSES

It takes conviction

Purposeful leadership takes courage and conviction. It has two main responsibilities. The first is that leaders must be clear and committed advocates of the purpose in their public and private words and deeds. The second is that they must take decisions for the business that are in line with the purpose. The second is probably harder than the first for many executives who, however committed personally to a sense of higher purpose, are under pressure to show results in the short term, either to shareholders or to the city. But it is business-critical for leaders because purpose drives company profits.

Leaders who display a profound commitment to purpose do not have to be as charismatic or as high-profile as Richard Branson or Steve Jobs, or as controversial as Robert Stephens (Geek Squad) and John Legere (T-Mobile) – we shall hear more about them later. In this book, for example, we have included examples and case studies of companies who are not well known other than to the customers they serve. But their businesses are purposeful and the leaders are enthusiastic and committed to their purpose, whether their business is connecting people, laying floors or running a hotel. They all 'declare a future that others commit to' but only because they commit to it too. It therefore follows that the most important quality that any leader must have above all else is authenticity – a genuine belief in the purpose to which they are asking others to commit.

Daniel Pink in his book *Drive* (2009), which looks at motivation within organizations, argues that wages are not the main motivator for most – if not all – people. 'The best use of money as a motivator is to pay people enough to take the issue of money off the table,' he argues. 'Pay people enough so that they're not thinking about money and they're thinking about the work.'

He goes further and gives a clear warning to leaders who focus on the short term and on that other 'p' word:

> *'When the profit motive gets unmoored from*
> *the purpose motive, bad things happen.'*

For example, one of the big news stories of 2012 was Hurricane Sandy. This 'storm of the century' caused 85 deaths and left 8 million people on the eastern seaboard of the United States without power for several days.

It was interesting to see how brands responded to this event. Some, such as the fashion retailers American Apparel, Gap and Urban Outfitters, saw this as a sales opportunity and quickly launched a campaign. American Apparel targeted customers in the nine stricken states who were 'bored' at home and invited them to visit American Apparel, offering a 20 per cent discount, saying *'In case you're bored during the storm, 20 per cent off for the next 36 hours'*. Not unsurprisingly, consumers reacted with anger at this commercialization of what was a terrible event for many people, and Twitter and other social media channels were buzzing with outraged customers voicing their opinions about the apparent lack of sensitivity.

However, some other organizations chose to respond differently. For example, two of the P&G brands, Duracell and Tide, found ways to help consumers in their hours of need and, in so doing, created goodwill for the brand.

P&G's purpose is 'to touch and improve more consumers' lives with more P&G brands and products every day'. Here's how they brought this to life during the crisis. Duracell sent mobile charging stations to Lower Manhattan so that people could charge their mobile phones and connect with loved ones. Tide loaded a truck with 32 washer/dryers and sent it out on the streets so that people could wash their clothes. A cynic might argue, however, that this was just another form of marketing. That might be true in terms of the long-term effect but the fact is that the first response of these brands was to ask what they could do to help, rather than what they could do to sell. They behaved in a way that was motivated by purpose rather than profit.

As we cited in the Introduction, the annual Edelman study on trust has found that consumers are increasingly inclined to favour those brands that have a social conscience and are prepared to give something back to the world: 66 per cent will recommend or buy from a brand that supports good causes. However, the study also found that customers were more influenced by how these brands behave in their everyday business operations rather than the extent to which they might donate to good causes. So, being purposeful is much more about the choices and decisions that you make as a company than having a CSR policy.

It is more about behaving in a purposeful way than 'doing good'

Consumers will also 'vote with their feet' when a brand that they admire in every other respect is found to be doing the wrong thing for society. A perfect example of this is the 25 per cent boost in sales for Costa Coffee that parent Whitbread announced in 2013 as a result of consumers boycotting Starbucks after it was revealed that the brand had paid just £8.6 million in UK corporate tax for its 750 stores since 1998.

Mitch Markson, chief creative officer of Edelman, said this in their report:

'Purpose is now the "fifth P" of marketing. It is a vital addition to the age-old marketing mix of product, price, place and promotion.'

Many would argue that purpose is the sixth 'P' of the mix because 'people' are the fifth 'P', but this does not negate his conclusion. Those brands that are transforming their markets through the customer experience share a common approach to business; they have a purpose beyond merely making profit – and their leaders are making decisions based on fulfilling that purpose.

Sometimes, leaders force themselves to 'go back to' a sense of purpose. When organizations grow, particularly at a fast rate, that growth can come without intentionally focusing on purpose. While that is good in the short term, it poses a dilemma in the long term and sets up a potential crisis of identity for the brand. The result of this can be for a company to effectively create a generic market that lots of competitors come into, 'stealing' their clothes, aping their proposition and eventually undermining their growth. It is therefore vital to a branded business to stay true to its purpose as it grows so that it remains differentiated in the eyes of consumers from the competition it creates.

The Nando's fast food chain, which specializes in Mozambique-style chicken, is an example. In 1987, Robbie Brozin and Fernando Duarte borrowed money from friends and family to buy a cafe called Chickenland, which sold Mozambique-inspired cooking in Johannesburg, South Africa. They renamed it Nando's (after co-founder Duarte's first name), and began to grow a global brand. They now have more than 1,000 outlets in 23 countries as diverse as Namibia and Bangladesh, and their famous Peri-Peri sauce can be found all over the world. In 2010, they were identified as one of the 30 hottest marketing brands by the magazine *Advertising Age*. Their culture has always been brand and people focused, with a spice to it that reflects the vibrancy and piquancy of its signature Peri-Peri chicken dish. This includes a list of 'Ten Don't F... Withs' that is core to the running of the global franchise and it includes the logo!

Nando's is famous for its product. But its founders are very conscious of its purpose and, as the brand has grown, they became concerned that a sense of purpose was being overlooked. Brozin told the marketing magazine *The Drum* that 'as the brand took off, South Africa became irrelevant in the Nando's world', which he described as 'the saddest thing that we could do'. Brozin continued, 'For me every brand needs a soul and [although] our brand heritage is in Mozambique the first restaurant was in South Africa and from here it went global. It's actually very easy to lose your heritage as the business gets bigger and you can lose a sense of purpose. For me, any business needs a strong sense of purpose, and it would be so sad if we had a business that was successful but never had a purpose, and that purpose is really the soul of Africa to a certain extent.'

In 2015, Nando's undertook major new investments in its store experience as part of its next stage of growth and has decided to go back to its roots and celebrate South African design. It launched a 'Heartfelt Celebration of South African Design' project at the core of its refurbishment. This produced a collection of items such as chairs and tables made by 12 South African designers showcased in its stores globally. It has also launched the 'Hot New Designer' competition in South Africa. Any designer, amateur or professional under the age of 35, competes to develop a pendant light to be displayed in its restaurants globally.

The investment in these activities, and their introduction as part of enhancing the customer experience, will reinforce for both employees and customers the distinctive promise of the Nando's brand and communicate a sense of its higher purpose to bring South African culture to the world.

Stay true to your purpose as you grow

Purposeful leaders are constantly obsessing about this subject. They recognize the dilemma that happens as you grow quickly, in that growth can be so fast that it can obscure your purpose. Soon you become just another one of the 'big guys who run the market' rather than the cool guys challenging it. It's a dilemma that Innocent foods faced when they were acquired by the Coca-Cola Corporation (CCC). How could this cool, quirky little brand whose purpose was to put 'the best food and drink into the most people and places' survive when it was gobbled up by the sugar-loaded, carbonated soft-drink global behemoth? Some people predicted that having sold its soul it would lose its appeal to consumers. Richard Reed, one of the co-founders of Innocent, saw it differently. He argued that the decision to sell to Coca-Cola was exactly in line with the brand's purpose. What was the best way for Innocent to fulfil its purpose? Was it from a small factory in west London, where it was headquartered? Or through one of the world's largest food and beverage distribution systems, which is what CCC offers? The answer is clear when you look at it that way.

As Angela Ahrendts, the former CEO of Burberry and now senior vice president of Apple, said:

> *'There is always this balance between hard and soft strategies, investment and intuition, but if you have a greater purpose, it becomes relatively easy to make those calls.'*

Robert Stephens faced a similar dilemma to Innocent when he sold his Geek Squad to Best Buy. His sense of 'greater purpose', as Ahrendts put it, helped him to decide what to do, as he explains here:

> *'It seems there's always this paradox: either you're small and you're loved or you're large and everybody hates you and you lose your soul.*
>
> *I thought, what about if you had a vision around growth and you really do care about the customer, why can't you do both? So that was the goal I set when I sold the Geek Squad to Best Buy. I talked to other business founders and asked "Should I sell my company?" and they said, "No, you'll hate it, you'll quit the company." But I decided to defy that advice. Just because you're a founder doesn't mean you can remain the CEO beyond a certain point, so I stayed with Best Buy to find out what makes a top company perform.*
>
> *'I'd go and sit in meetings – way too many meetings – and try to figure out, why are these meetings not really going anywhere, why aren't they talking about what's important? At first I assumed, "Well, they're smarter than I am and I have a lot to learn." Then after a while I came to believe something different. I don't really think they have a compelling purpose here. There are just competing political priorities. So I stayed to make sure that Geek Squad didn't die. I stayed 10 years and we expanded into the UK and went into China. People ask me if I regret doing it, and I say no, because there is not another Geek Squad out there. There's no one else of our scale.'*

Purposeful leaders show the way

One of the most important ways that people learn what a leader's true motives are, is by what they see him or her do – not just say. This is a principle summed up by Carlos Ghosn, the CEO of Nissan, one of our featured case studies:

> *'Don't believe what I say; believe what I do.'*

Herb Kelleher, the former CEO of Southwest Airlines, a company that remains the 'gold standard' case study for customer-centricity, was also unusual in that he was famous for behaving in ways that were 'on brand'. Herb used to fly as often as he could on his own planes or, if he wasn't travelling, he would meet passengers when they were boarding or leaving the planes. He would share a joke with them or a drink but always he would be asking them about their experience, which helped him to understand how to improve it. Southwest Airlines featured Herb in many of their adverts: reinforcing their key messages, showing the connection of the leader to his customers and always with the company's customary sense of humour.

https://www.youtube.com/watch?v=HCoTICEbJrc

Leadership at Procter & Gamble, as you would expect of one of the world's most successful consumer goods businesses, is religious about its purpose. When AG Laffley became its CEO in 2000, he faced a crisis. P&G had announced that it would not meet its profit target and the share price had tanked, falling by almost one-third in one day. When Laffley later discussed how he diagnosed the problems facing the company and turned the business around, a core theme was the importance of getting 'up close and personal' with consumers – a leadership behaviour that he himself demonstrated by visiting the homes of consumers and inviting them in to P&G laboratories and workshops. This is Laffley explaining those twin responsibilities in a *Harvard Business Review* article he wrote, entitled 'What only a CEO can do':

> *P&G's purpose is to touch and improve more consumers' lives with more P&G brands and products every day. Of all our stakeholders, both outside and inside, the primary one is the consumer. Everybody knows that the customer is king; we knew this in 2000 as we know it today. But we*

were not acting on what we knew. That had become apparent to me in 1998, when, as executive vice president, I returned from an assignment in Asia, where we didn't have reams of research data on consumers and markets. In China, for instance, we had no choice but to visit consumers where they lived and observe them where they shopped. Coming home to our global headquarters, in Cincinnati, I was struck as I walked the office halls by how many employees were glued to their computers and how much of each day people spent mired in internal meetings with other P&Gers. We were losing touch with consumers. We were not out in the competitive pressure cooker that is the marketplace. Too often we were working on initiatives consumers did not want and incurring costs that consumers should not have to pay for. Everywhere I go, I try to hammer home the simple message that the consumer is boss. We must win the consumer value equation every day at two critical moments of truth: first, when the consumer chooses a P&G product over all the others in the store; and second, when the consumer or a family member uses the product and it delivers a delightful and memorable experience – or not. Almost every trip I take includes in-home or in-store consumer visits. Virtually every P&G office and innovation centre has consumers working inside with employees. Our employees spend days living with lower-income consumers and working in neighbourhood stores. At our global headquarters we replaced dozens of paintings by local artists with photographs of everyday consumers around the world buying and using P&G brands. All these efforts keep the two moments of truth foremost in the minds of P&Gers as they work.

Laffley retired as CEO in 2009, having doubled P&G's sales to over $83 billion during his time there. Unfortunately, his chosen successor, Robert McDonald, endured a difficult time. The company struggled to address changing consumer trends towards value rather than premium products in a post global financial crisis world. McDonald stood down as CEO in 2013 and Laffley returned to replace him. In one of his first internal memos to all employees, Laffley reminded them of where true leadership lay: 'the consumer is boss', he wrote.

Laffley's words illustrate the importance of a leader doing 'small things people notice' such as replacing the office art with pictures of consumers, of visibly role-modelling behaviour by visiting consumers himself. He insisted that in-home visits with consumers be arranged for him in whatever city he visited. Executives at P&G realized that if the CEO could make time to visit consumers in their homes, so should they.

What you believe in and what you demonstrate determine what kind of leader you are. In 2014, Howard Schultz, the CEO of Starbucks, was named one of the world's great leaders. His face appeared on the cover of *Time* magazine, an iconic symbol of fame and achievement. Starbucks opens a new store somewhere in the world every 12 hours and serves around 44 million customers per week. But it was not for the sales growth or profits that Schultz was honoured; it was for his qualities as a leader. He was voted into a list of world leaders compiled by *Fortune* magazine that included Angela Merkel and was topped by Pope Francis! Schultz has championed an empathetic style of leadership that puts his people and his customers ahead of profits, since he first began steering Starbucks as an 'experience', not a coffee shop.

Speaking about his leadership style, Schultz said the following:

> *'The currency of leadership is transparency. There are moments where you have to share your soul and conscience with people and show them who you are and not be afraid of it.'*

Schultz wants his people to care passionately about each other and the customer, which is why he is so insistent on talking emotionally and showing empathy. He demonstrates the brand he wants customers to experience. It's why he called his book *Put Your Heart Into It*. As we said earlier, though, even Starbucks was found wanting when it came to paying a fair share of taxes in the UK, as perceived by customers, which goes to show that purposeful brands have to achieve this delicate balance between doing the right thing for customers, for employees, for shareholders and for society at large. No easy task.

Robert Stephens cites T-Mobile's CEO as another example of a purposeful leader taking decisive action in line with a customer-driven purpose:

> *'My favourite CEO in the world right now is John Legere of T-Mobile: irreverent, maverick, a rebel. Now, you can be a crazy guy, wearing the T-shirt and wearing the brand and, you know, that lasts for about 10 minutes, but why is he my favourite CEO? It's because he seems to naturally, authentically blend enthusiasm for his job. Authentically he's himself. He doesn't have any social media handlers. He's on Twitter. He's one of the few CEOs who is on a major social media channel and is engaging.*

 http://mashable.com/2015/02/17/john-legere-spoiled-ceos/

'What he did is to simplify the data plans and policies for T-Mobile. He did what every carrier should have done, what every retailer should have done, and what Best Buy still hasn't done, which is simplify the policies.

'And not just because that's a great headline, but because it actually saves money in the business, because if your policies are simpler, guess what? You need to spend less money on training. There's less customer misunderstanding. If you have complex policies, the employees are probably going to make mistakes, so you've got to pay money to train them and write manuals, and you have to audit those people to make sure they're doing it.

'But John Legere comes in and says, "These data plans are too complex. Let's simplify them." Done. And that's why if you're in third or fourth place, you've got far more to contribute to the world than if you're in first place, because you've got less to lose, so you should be taking more chances, you need to be even more bold as a challenger brand.'

For an interesting LinkedIn article on Legere see: **http://linkd.in/1Lf4fSg**.

Throughout the books we have written, we have featured the visible habits of leaders that show their true motivation. Here are just a few of them:

Virgin: Richard Branson has reaffirmed his intention of being aboard the first Virgin Galactic passenger flight into space, despite the tragic accident in 2014.

John Lewis: managers have particular responsibility for their 'buddy stores'.

Harley Davidson: managers must ride with their customers.

Procter & Gamble: managers visit consumers in their own homes.

Amazon: an empty chair is included in board meetings to represent the customer.

JCB: Sir Anthony Bamford personally inspects the vehicles as they are coming off the production line, and orders adjustments according to customers' needs.

Carphone Warehouse: management sit not in the head office but in the Sales Support Centre.

Umpqua Bank: CEO Ray Davis answers the phone just like every other employee with the words 'Welcome to the world's greatest bank'.

Purposeful leadership is about behaving, not saying

So what are the competencies that make leaders so effective in creating a purpose-driven organization?

Think about a positive experience that you recently had with a company. Why was it positive? You probably felt that the person at the other end really cared about your concerns and had the power to do something about your situation. Most times, great customer experiences worth talking about are associated with 'going the extra mile'.

How can leaders within companies create cultures that support a purposeful brand and deliver great customer experiences?

First and foremost a leader must create 'a foundation of care' according to Claudio Toyama, a leadership coach (and also a TED Fellows coach). Claudio explains this concept:

> *Purposeful leaders create cultures where employees fully engage with the company, its purpose and its customers. Employees must FEEL like they matter and what they DO matters.*
>
> *Care creates commitments – and when employees care, they are committed to serving the customer in the best way they can. This, in turn, causes employees to act in ways that positively impact the customer experience.*
>
> *Southwest Airlines is an example of how care translates into great customer experience and decades of consistent profitability in an industry that has been hit by high oil prices, recessions and cut-throat competition. This US-based no-frills airline provides services that are efficient, safe and fun, and they have a reputation for going the extra mile to make the customer's experience enjoyable.*
>
> *Care per se is not enough to create great customer experiences. Leaders and employees must also have the necessary skills and competencies to deliver great customer experiences that are on brand and on purpose.*
>
> *But building this kind of culture is not easy. There are certain essential competencies that leaders must demonstrate. The Leadership Circle® found two primary leadership domains: creative competencies and reactive tendencies:*[1]
>
> > ***Creative competencies** – these include skills such as bringing out the best in others, leading with vision, behaving authentically, acting with integrity and courage, and focusing on 'whole-system' improvement and community welfare.*

Reactive tendencies – *the self-limiting traits that emphasize caution over creating results, self-protection over productive engagement, and aggression over building alignment. These styles focus on gaining the approval of others, protecting oneself, and getting results through high-control tactics.*

Whilst the above may seem obvious (and similar concepts have been discussed at length in leadership books for years now), why is it that so many leaders are still driven by the reactive rather than the creative? And when the leader is reactive, the culture becomes reactive. Purpose doesn't stand a chance.

In our many years of experience of helping brands implement customer experience and driving purpose throughout the organization, we know the one thing that is guaranteed to see the initiative fail is lip-service leadership, ie leaders who 'talk' creative, but behave reactive.

Organizations can however nurture great leaders by promoting and teaching the creative competencies and helping leaders let go of their reactive tendencies. But it starts with leaders opening themselves up to a 'warts-and-all' self-assessment and a readiness to embrace the idea of personal development. (So often leaders are the first to advocate a training solution for the management team and front line, but the last to accept that they themselves may need further skills development or training).

A good first step is for the leader to take a leadership assessment and work with a mentor to gain a true understanding of their creative competencies and reactive tendencies – and how these impact the culture and delivery of the brand purpose and customer experience. This enables a very personalized and tailored approach to coaching the leader in the specific competencies that he or she needs to create a true 'culture of care' and a purpose-driven organization.

Behavioural change does not happen overnight and must be constantly reinforced. For this reason, the third step is often executive coaching. Coaching helps the leader to get in touch with what he or she cares about, to see possibilities for action where he or she didn't see them before and to get the support needed to implement changes.

The leader as coach has become a popular theme in business. This does not mean that the leader has to be all 'soft and cuddly' or so consensual as to seem indecisive. It does mean that the primary job of a leader is to provide clear direction, to encourage his or her people to excel in pursuit of the purpose and to give those people 'every chance to succeed and no excuse for failure'. That requires, as Claudio says, the ability to 'listen'.

Captains of ships have known through the ages that the way to navigate through dangerous waters is to have a clear course to steer – one that leads to the ultimate destination whilst avoiding immediate hazards. Unless 'captains of industry' have this same clarity of purpose they will find their organizations continually tossed about in the continuing turbulence ahead. Customer experience innovations that are disconnected from the brand purpose become mere marketing gimmicks. Nor can you navigate your business solely through your profit and loss account, NPS or any other metric, because they are essentially a record of where you have been. You also need a compass to know where you are headed too. That compass is your purpose and it is evident to consumers which brands have one and which do not.

One industry where differentiating by creating meaningful experiences for customers is becoming increasingly important is hospitality, particularly the hotel sector. There are so many hotel brands all promising similar things that it is only by having a strong sense of purpose that leaders can begin to create a culture that drives a different kind of guest experience.

Image 2.1 citizenM logo

A brand that is challenging the way that this sector operates and is doing so with a strong sense of purpose is citizenM. Founded by Rattan Chadha, it opened its first hotel in Amsterdam in 2008 and has since opened hotels in Rotterdam, London, New York, Paris and Glasgow. CitizenM's purpose is to offer affordable luxury to its target customers, defined as 'mobile citizens'. It is a great example of a brand driven by purpose that is winning a growing legion of fans. Here, Rattan explains how he had his insight into founding a purpose-driven brand and how he has been zealous in ensuring that the brand stays true to its purpose.

Rattan Chadha – citizenM chairman

The insight

The idea for citizenM started when I owned the fashion retailer Mexx. We had 1,200 stores in 56 countries. It was a big business and by the time I left it was turning over more than €1 billion per year in sales. I had about 100 designers working for me in fashion design; they were all in the age range of 25 to 40 years old, from 26 different countries. I insisted that they travel every month – to New York, Paris and London to look at the new trends and absorb whatever they could in order to create differentiated and desirable collections. Every year my design director would come to me and say there was a hassle with hotels, because these kids didn't want to stay in bland, boring budget hotels and we couldn't afford to let them stay in five-star hotels because they were travelling so often. They refused to stay in a Holiday Inn Express or a Ramada Inn or a Travelodge, which is what the budget allowed for, and so they always found some bed and breakfast somewhere far away and then spent more money on taxis. Some of the places they were staying in were not in safe areas.

So that planted something in my head about the absence of 'hybrid' hotels. I experienced hybrid in almost everything else I was doing. For example, I wear an Armani jacket with a shirt from Zara or Gap. It doesn't mean that I don't have money; it's a choice. And that choice didn't exist in hotels. I finally said 'I've got to take this on, this whole idea of a hybrid hotel.'

I actually recruited all the senior team before I had a site, before I had the name. We had nothing except about 12 to 15 people on the payroll. I spent millions at that time just figuring out how to design a hybrid hotel. What are the things that are important and what things are not important? We looked at the current hotel industry and asked ourselves 'How can we change all this and cut the waste?' We did about 500 interviews with travellers around Europe. I did many of those interviews personally.

We heard the same story every time. A traveller goes to a city for business. They go to the hotel and dump their bag and check in – single occupancy for 80 per cent of the time, usually people travelling on business. They run out of the hotel, do their work, come back in the evening at 6 o'clock and then have a shower, do some e-mails in their room maybe, come down to the bar, have a drink while they wait for people to take them somewhere for dinner. Then they would come back to their room, watch TV and get a good night's sleep. And the same pattern the next day or they would leave. And that pattern was consistent.

We added our own frustrations of travel into the story. For example, arriving in Hong Kong and waiting in a queue behind 20 Japanese tourists to fill out this silly registration form; the hotel has all my details, I've stayed in the hotel five times before, but I have to fill out my name and address and sign here, sign there, do this, do that. So the whole idea of self check-in came from the frustration of standing in a queue to check into a hotel. I also noticed that most people working on reception and at the concierge desk do not ever step out from behind their desks. As a customer I have to go to them and stand in a line to ask for their help. But half the time the concierge is on the phone and I have to wait. What the hell do these guys do? The other crazy thing about five-star hotels is that before I get to the hotel I've carried or wheeled my *suitcase all the way from Amsterdam to Hong Kong; I've been wheeling it through airports and into taxis but to get it from my taxi to my room I suddenly need help according to the hotel. I just stayed in a Four Seasons Hotel in Paris where you pay €1,200 per night for a standard room. The guy who took my bag was wearing an immaculate uniform that must have cost at least €1,000. He dropped my bag and then stood there for that extra five seconds and that killed the entire experience for me. How much shall I give him, €50 because I don't have change? Should I ask him for some change back? Shall I tell him I'll pay him later? Such a frustrating experience. Hotels insist on giving you what you don't want rather than what you need.*

Stand up – purposeful leadership

We took a clean sheet of paper and said 'I want this price.' We started with the price because we want people to be able to afford it. Then we said 'I want a hotel that I will not be embarrassed to tell people that I stay at. It has to have great style, great design and have all the things that are critical to my stay. I don't care about the rest.' The third starting point was the people working at the hotel. We said they are not to do any functional jobs; they are there for the customer, nothing else. Everything else we will outsource. So that created the blueprint of what we were trying to do.

That led us to work out how to make it affordable for this kind of customer. For example, I don't need a wardrobe large enough for me to stay for two months; I carry one suit when I go for two days or three days to a city. So we thought how we could use space more effectively. A lot of the people told me we were crazy, because we should build more rooms and make the lobby small. I said, 'But the lobby's my living room. When I go home how much time do I spend in my bedroom? I go to my bedroom, I dump my bag and maybe I change and then I come down to my study or my living room, somewhere I can relax or work. Why would I stay in my bedroom? Why should a hotel be any different?' So we created the lobby as a living workspace and we said, 'Let's extend the public space for people to relax and work.'

We have tables, computers, TVs, fireplaces and books on display because I want it to feel like it's home, not a hotel. We have hundreds of books; I want people to use the books but people say that guests will steal them. You know, guests in my house may also take books away; I don't care. The experience for me is more important than worrying that the guest might take a book home; I want them to feel at home.

Rattan's last point goes to the heart of what is wrong with so many brands and why, as the Havas survey shows, 73 per cent of them could disappear and people wouldn't care. Brands are too often built with the business in mind rather than with the consumer or customer in mind.

Our vision would have been easy to realize if it was a five-star hotel, but it was difficult to achieve because it had to be done within our target budget. That meant that staffing had to be very low. We couldn't afford receptionists. We couldn't afford a concierge. We couldn't afford housekeeping if the room was complicated to clean. I wanted a maximum of 10-minute clean-up per room because that means the room costs me £5 to clean instead of £25. So everything was driven from that desire to make it affordable, because as soon as you let that vision go it becomes too expensive to make the concept work.

We wanted everybody to be a concierge. That became the idea of our ambassadors; everybody's equal, everybody does the same thing. One of the things we recognized early on is that the single most important thing for me in a hotel is if I can recognize a person or they recognize me. If everybody is available where the guests are, they get to know the guests. When I'm check-ing in it's the same guy; I go and get a coffee, it's the same guy; I need help, it's the same guy. I figured they will be much more in contact with guests if they are floating around at what I call the 'moments of truth', the interaction points – they will get closer to the customer. If you look at TripAdvisor they say the 'service is fantastic'; actually we do nothing, we're just there standing next to you. We don't fill out forms, we don't fetch you a cup of coffee, we don't even get you a glass of water; you do it yourself. And yet we rate a consistent 9 on TripAdvisor.

I want to be the Starbucks of hotels because it gives you easier operations, so it is very cost-effective. Second, it gives you brand building; you'll be a dominant force. So when you go to London, if I have one hotel you might not stay because it might not be convenient for you, but you cannot escape me if I have six. Remember, a citizenM hotel has only a few hundred rooms, and I believe we have many more mobile citizens who would like to stay with us. I can't build a hotel of 2,000 rooms on one site but I can build 2,000 rooms across multiple sites – it's a question of having the rooms to satisfy my customers.

The key is to do one thing and try to do it right. Stick to who you are. I'm the brand director here, 100 per cent. I say 'This is not right for citizenM'. I said no to so many locations. Great financial deal, but I'm not touching it. Why not? Because my customers are not going to come here, this is not coherent with what citizenM is all about.

It needs a lot of discipline to build a brand. I've learnt that the hard way. It takes a lifetime to build a brand, to build a true brand. In fact citizenM, the *brand book, was ready before I had the first site: the entire brand book, including room design, the living rooms, everything. I imagined a hotel and from that I decided what it was going to look like; this is what the mattress is going to be like; this is how dark I want the room. The people who don't get our DNA think our coloured lighting is a gimmick – and copy it, but what they don't realize is that it's not about the f*****g lighting – it's about the whole concept, the citizenM DNA.*

Note

1 http://leadershipcircle.com/wp-content/uploads/2012/02/
   Bowling-Green-Validity-Document-Final.pdf

Part Two
Stand out

We have our purpose. So all we need to do, then, is to communicate it. That is often the attitude of many organizations, particularly if their agency has been instrumental in helping to write the purpose. But this would be the worst thing to do. Let's put ourselves in the shoes of a typical customer to find out why.

A customer's perspective...

I remember it well.

1995, and the Seattle Coffee Company had just hit the streets of London. A ray of light shining out amongst the grey, soulless London cafes strewn across the capital.

The smell of freshly ground coffee, the mellow jazz, the warm welcome, the theatre of the barista and the thick dense foam swirling on the cappuccino. But above all, I remember the feeling that the people who worked there really cared about me. Every time I walked through those doors, I felt uplifted because they greeted me personally and remembered my favourite drink. It was my temporary escape from the world.

For me, it was the beginning of a new way of thinking. Coffee was no longer an instant brew, it was a fulfilling experience. Did the brand have some kind of purpose statement, guiding everything it did? I don't know. But it fulfilled a real purpose for me.

Sadly one of the big brands came along (Starbucks), took over the company and gradually the personality died and a little part of my daily life died along with it. Sure the coffee was good, but the soul had gone.

Now 20 years later, and we're seemingly in the 'Age of Purpose'

I hear that many brands have a purpose now. According to the experts, it's the meaningful way of 'engaging with us customers emotionally' and 'turning us into brand advocates'.

But I'm not really sure I care about their purpose. I am more concerned about mine.

My bank is telling me that their purpose is to 'help people fulfil their hopes and dreams and realize their ambitions'. But I'd far rather that a person, and not a machine, answers the phone when I call them and that they don't put me on hold for 40 minutes, subjecting me to phone 'music', before eventually connecting me to someone in a call centre whose accent is authentically different, but totally incomprehensible (HSBC).

My mobile phone operator also now has a purpose. They say they want 'to empower everybody to be confidently connected'. I say, just give me a reliable mobile signal, whenever I want to use my phone – and I'd be happy. Unfortunately, half the time I can't get a signal at home and they can't tell me why (Vodafone).

As far as I know, my local convenience store doesn't have a purpose. But it's always open when I need it. They always deliver friendly service and never overprice anything. They are there for me when I need them and so I make a point of shopping there.

Don't get me wrong, I'm not 'dissing' 'purpose'. I would always prefer to deal with brands that had an ethical purpose or some kind of social conscience, but I above all want to do business with brands that first and foremost care – yes, genuinely care – about their customers.

And I want them to prove it.

Just give me a great experience first – and then maybe, just maybe, I'll care about your purpose.

Robert Stephens told us that 'a cynic is a romantic with higher standards'. In other words, we all hope for the best but are frequently disappointed. We shouldn't be surprised if customers are as cynical as the real customer quoted above. Brands bombard them with promises that they fail to deliver, offers that turn out to be spurious and service that is grudging. So, whatever you do, don't decide to communicate your brand purpose in some way on your website or allow your agency to put it into some folksy story unless you have first ensured that you are delivering it.

So far we have argued that it is important for organizations to *stand up* for something; to have a purpose beyond profit. But this is just wishful thinking unless this purpose is evident to customers and employees. The most inspiring purpose in the world counts for naught unless people are clear about it and unless it serves to differentiate you in some meaningful way from competitors, be they in the general market or the employment market. That's where *stand out* comes to bear. It is the process by which you make tangible your purpose. It is manifested in three ways: through the way you communicate, the way you deliver experiences that create value for target customers and, finally, the way that you innovate in order to continue to be the brand that you want to be.

Chapter Three
Infectious communication

nfectious communication is the result of creating such compelling experiences and content that your customers enthusiastically become your best advocates. It involves any method through which your message is conveyed by willing and (usually) unpaid intermediaries. It can cover everything from word of mouth to shared media such as TedTalks, for example. Success is when things go 'viral' and develop a life of their own beyond your control, scary though that may be.

More and more organizations see the benefits of infectious communication. Brands such as Burberry, LEGO and Apple are moving most of their marketing activity to social media platforms. Unfortunately many others are simply applying old rules to new media. You see it on websites that are clunky to use and therefore deliver poor user experiences. You see it with demeaning pleas for customers to 'Like us' on Facebook, or worse still, the purchase of followers and fans from sweat shops in India. Why do some organizations simply not get the power of infectious communication and how to achieve it?

Marketing should be a verb, not a noun

The answer to the above question is that in many organizations marketing has become a noun, a set of processes and a function. Instead it should be a verb, a set of behaviours and everything that an organization does. When John Lewis, Arthur Guinness and Conrad Hilton started their brands they saw marketing holistically. They believed that it was how they treated their customers and ran their companies. But, perhaps, because of the introduction of the scientific view of management largely founded by Frederick Taylor and continued by Alfred Sloan in his time at General Motors, fuelled by the rigour of P&G's approach to brand marketing in the 1960s and 1970s, and reinforced by the plethora of MBA programmes since then, marketing has become a function supported by its own set of rigid principles not dissimilar in their rigour to finance. But this is changing.

The advent of social media has opened up so many communication channels that are beyond the remit of traditional 'above the line' marketers. The ways in which consumers form impressions of brands are so much richer than advertising alone that marketing activity has become an experience in and of itself in many organizations. Adam Greenwood, a teen 'vlogger', discovered that there was no loo paper available when he used the toilet on the Virgin Train from Euston to Glasgow so he did what any good millennial would do – he tweeted Virgin HQ about it. Virgin picked up the tweet and within a few minutes a Virgin employee was knocking on the door with a roll of toilet paper to rescue Adam from his predicament. That tweet and its follow-up story have been 'liked' and shared by over 6,000 people.

http://www.huffingtonpost.co.uk/2015/01/06/
toilet-paper-delivery-twitter_n_6423760.html

Is this story about customer service? Is it about complaint resolution? Or is it about marketing? The answer to all of these is 'yes'. The fact is that 'above the line' is now 'below the radar' for many consumers.

Research by Thales S Teixeira for a *Harvard Business Review* article revealed that the percentage of ads considered fully viewed and getting high attention has decreased dramatically, from 97 per cent in the early 1990s to less than 20 per cent in 2015.[1] In 2013, the average American was exposed to about 52,000 TV commercials. So it is no surprise that, in these days of remote controls, TiVo and digital video recorders, consumers vote with their fingers and skip the ads – unless they are entertained. The most powerful way to entertain people is to engage them emotionally through storytelling. At Christmas 2014, the supermarket brand Sainsbury in partnership with the Royal British Legion released a moving video that celebrated relationships forged in the First World War. Despite it being 3 minutes 40 seconds long, nearly 17 million people have viewed it on YouTube.

http://youtu.be/NWF2JBb1bvM

Tell a story that people care about

John Lewis Partnership released its own Christmas ad, also celebrating relationships, in this case featuring a penguin. It has been viewed nearly 23 million times.

http://youtu.be/iccscUFY860

Neither of these ads promoted a brand or a product. They told a story that was emotionally engaging about a higher purpose – being with people whom you care about at Christmas.

So we have two interesting but opposing trends: one is the decline in consumer attention to traditional advertising and therefore the increasing cost of buying awareness; the other is the increasing trend for consumers to willingly view marketing material and even share it if it strikes a chord. How much would John Lewis have had to pay to air their ad on prime-time television to attract 23 million viewers, we wonder?

Some brands go even further. LEGO's purpose is 'to inspire and develop the builders of tomorrow' and it does this through its range of plastic building blocks but also increasingly through its social platforms and media activity. In February 2014 it released *The LEGO Movie* to critical and consumer acclaim. By September 2014 the movie had enjoyed sales of $468 million and LEGO was reporting a shortage of product. The trailer has also been viewed over 27 million times on YouTube. If you are one of the apparently few people that haven't yet seen it you can do so here.

 http://youtu.be/fZ_JOBCLF-I

Think about that for a moment. LEGO has earned nearly $500 million in income by enticing consumers to sit through a 98-minute advertisement for the brand. A very high proportion of those viewers were 'highly qualified prospects' in the jargon of marketers – kids, to you and me. LEGO achieved this by creating marketing that is so infectious that their target consumers are willing and enthusiastic participants.

Bigger is not better

One of the things about infectious communication is that it is a great leveller. You don't need to be a large corporate or spend mega-bucks to get your message across. In fact, the less you can spend the more likely it is that you will hit on something that really works because it forces you to be innovative.

For example, Air Canada staged an experiential event in a bar in London called 'The Maple Leaf' – which is popular with Canadians – in order to highlight its London to Canada service. A pilot and flight attendants visited the crowded bar and gave away free tickets so that expat Canadians could be with their families at Christmas.

 http://youtu.be/r5YvVB1FJrs

First Direct, the online bank owned by HSBC, went out to 580,000 of their customers and asked them what they liked most about the brand. Their answer was that being able to engage with a real person rather than an interactive voice response was really important for them. So First Direct said, 'Great, would any of you like to be in our ad?' Hundreds of customers said, 'Yes!' and so First Direct's advertising agency created a number of advertisements featuring customers speaking about their First Direct experience. One, named 'Call Centre', featured a customer speaking about her experience of calling First Direct and being able to speak to a person to get help any time of the day or night. The ad was shot in a bare room with the customer speaking to a single hand-held camera. She is nervous and stumbles over her words, but her enthusiasm for First Direct is clear. The simple treatment, engaging tone and authenticity are estimated to have produced £3.8 million in incremental revenues for First Direct – the ad cost next to nothing to make. This was probably one of the first examples of crowdsourcing, and First Direct has continued to engage with its customers since then. It now has a section of its website called 'Lab', which tests new product and service ideas and invites customers to try them and give their feedback. First Direct has won numerous awards, including Best Banking Brand by *Which?*, and it remains the most recommended bank in the UK[2] – achieving an NPS rating of 62 per cent in an industry that scores an average NPS of 0 per cent, according to Satmetrix Systems UK research. First Direct's score is remarkable for any brand, let alone a bank.

Traditional marketing can be costly, slow and unengaging. Robert Stephens, founder of the Geek Squad, says, 'Marketing is a tax that you pay for being unremarkable.' There is a great deal of truth in Stephens's comment; it often seems that the more boring the brand, the larger the marketing budget.

The average marketing campaign can take months to plan and execute, with all the risk that by the time it is aired circumstances have changed. For example, AT&T, Accenture, Gatorade and Gillette all dropped Tiger Woods from very expensive sponsorship and advertising campaigns in 2009, when he was involved in a car accident following a row with his wife and disclosures of infidelity.

The benefits of infectious communication, by contrast, include cost-efficiency and speed. Infectious communication allows you to be 'in the moment' and communicate something that is topical and relevant. But you have to be clever and you have to be fast. In 2014, Nissan produced an ad just seven minutes after Clarence House announced that William and Kate, the Duke and Duchess of Cambridge, were expecting their second child. Featuring the Nissan X-Trail, the company tweeted a picture of the interior of the vehicle with a crown on each seat. The message accompanying the image was 'It could be triplets and there would still be enough room for the Queen.'

You also have to be prepared and organized to take advantage of opportunities. In 2013, during the third quarter of Super Bowl XLVII, a power outage at the Superdome caused the lights to go out for more than half an hour. Within minutes, Oreo cookies tweeted an ad that read 'Power out? No problem' with a picture of an Oreo and the caption, 'You can still dunk in the dark.' The message was shared 20,000 times on Facebook and Twitter and gathered 525 million earned media impressions (five times the number of people who actually watched the Super Bowl (and its ads) on TV). Despite the fact that it was a spontaneous, unscheduled tweet on social media, *Adweek* voted it one of the Top 5 ads of Super Bowl night. Oreo achieved this because they had a 15-person social media team ready to respond to whatever happened at the Super Bowl within 10 minutes or less – and they were aware of a survey that showed 36 per cent of the Super Bowl audience would be consulting a second screen while watching the game.

The effects of infectious communication are long lasting. If you Google Oreo Super Bowl even now, you will find a plethora of references and links to it. But the important thing is to ensure that your social media message is consistent with what your brand stands for.

When infectious communication goes wrong

When you let the 'genie out of the bottle' and invite customers to share their views and participate in brand communications, then, of course, things can go wrong – as the condom brand Durex discovered. They launched a social media campaign for a new brand called SOS condoms. They invited customers to visit Facebook and vote for which cities should get SOS condoms first. They imagined that it would be the cities of romance: Paris, New York or Rome, perhaps? The answer, thanks to pranksters, was a place called Batman located in a conservative Muslim province in Turkey. Not the result that Durex wanted.

 http://youtu.be/LJxSRZMgP1s

We used to estimate that a dissatisfied customer would tell 9–10 others. In today's socially connected world that has multiplied several-fold. Convergys, the contact centre company, found that the average detractor tells 45 friends via a social media site.[3] However, that figure hides a wide range of potential impact. Dave Carroll, a United Airlines customer, created a YouTube video of himself and his band singing a song called 'United Breaks Guitars'. His song relates the story of how, whilst travelling on United Airlines, his guitar was damaged and, despite all his efforts to claim for the damage, he was unable to get United to listen to him. Finally, in desperation he wrote a song about his experience and posted it on YouTube on 6 July 2009. United was quick to respond via Twitter and offered to compensate him, but by then it was too late – the damage was done. By the end of July the video had been viewed 4.5 million times and, as of January 2015, over 14 million people have viewed the video, with thousands more posting comments about it. It is impossible to gauge the damage this has done to United's reputation, but imagine how much the average company might need to spend in order to create and air an advertisement that attracted that many viewers.

 https://www.youtube.com/watch?v=5YGc4zOqozo

The other problem is that social media are a channel open to everyone in your organization, not just your marketing department. As a result, your employees can send messages that have the power to undermine your brand and in this case infectious communication can work against you.

Some companies have had to dismiss staff for comments they made on social media. Marks & Spencer disciplined 76 staff for participating in a chat forum where they described the firm's customers as 'idiots' and 'cheap little b******s'. Virgin Atlantic sacked 13 crew members who posted remarks calling passengers 'chavs'. The results of a recent survey reported by Chadwick Lawrence, a UK law firm, and compiled by a recruitment agency, showed that 40 per cent of UK employees admitted to criticizing their employers on social networking sites such as Twitter and Facebook. In fact, 20 per cent of employees admitted that they had 'lambasted' their employer online at least once.

The availability of social media channels provides the opportunity for employees to do much greater damage than in the past. This means that brands have to pay even more attention to ensuring that they hire people who fit the desired culture and then educate them to understand what the brand stands for and to behave accordingly. But we are getting ahead of ourselves because that is where *stand firm* comes in, which we discuss in Part Three.

How do you engage in infectious communication?

Central to infectious communication is the plethora of social media. There are just too many social media platforms to describe here, and by the time this book is published undoubtedly there will be a lot more, but in searching for definitions online we came across this handy little primer of the main ones:

Image 3.1 Social media primer

So what are some innovative uses of social media? To answer the question we turned to Alison Battisby, an expert on all things digital. Alison speaks and writes about social media and advises clients how to use them most effectively.

Social media offer brands the tools to reinforce their customer experience through rich media including imagery, video and real-time interactions. They are also the only communication channel that allows customers to have a one-to-one conversation with a brand, in a very public forum. They can also be an extremely powerful tactic for businesses to build a loyal community of customers who are willing to recommend, defend and champion their beloved brands. Because of all of this, social media are therefore an excellent indicator in understanding whether a brand has an authentic sense of purpose.

Jimmy's Iced Coffee, a British family-run company, has created a seamless experience for its customers across social media, which has helped them to stand out against their giant competitors Nescafé and Mars. Founder Jimmy Cregan's purpose is clear: he fell in love with iced coffee whilst travelling in Australia, became obsessed and wanted to start selling the drink in the UK. The brand's purpose is to bring proper off-the-shelf iced coffee to the people of the UK and beyond. Now Jimmy's Iced Coffee is stocked in Waitrose, Tesco Express and BP. So how have social media supported its growth?

From the early days, Jimmy's Iced Coffee has featured the brand motto 'Keep Your Chin Up' on its packaging. This happy ethos reminds customers that things could be worse, and to concentrate on the positive things in life – such as their tasty refreshing drink. By understanding how Twitter, Facebook and Instagram support the use of hashtags, Jimmy has managed to translate the motto perfectly into social media, as #KYCU, and now includes it in almost every post.

A key part of how the company has grown in social media is by encouraging their customers to tag posts, images and comments in social media with the hashtag #KYCU. Similar target audiences to their own then see these posts, as social media platforms such as Facebook make it easy for brands to target friends of their fans.

The active community very much feels like an online fan club, and the company has successfully reinforced this through their online shop, which sells merchandise such as hats and stickers featuring #KYCU. This motto helps Jimmy's Iced Coffee remind customers why they exist, and what they stand up for.

Jimmy Cregan's social media posts follow the company's adventures during their first few years of trading, and are all written in the first person. This really helps to support the fact that this is his mission to supply those with similar iced coffee cravings as himself with the sweet drink. His enthusiasm for life, and the coffee drink, is infectious and this is obvious from his happy-go-lucky tone of voice in social media. Often he will include personal detail in his posts, such as the arrival of his new baby, his sister's engagement, or his regular morning snaps of the seaside in Dorset, where the company is based. Customers who have been following the growth of the company relate well to these posts as they make the brand more human, and reinforce the company's values as being British and family run.

https://www.facebook.com/jimmysicedcoffee/posts/
876749095688853
http://instagram.com/p/x_sKplxeKF/

Jimmy Cregan has spoken about the fact that his social media have been a success because he is honest and open with his customers, about every detail around the business. In an interview with Enterprise Nation, he said: 'I run my brand like we're on The Truman Show by showing our community everything that is going on in the business. It's important to keep your customers entertained by talking about your life and not just about the products. I even recommend letting people know about the mundane things – for example, share pictures of you out at meetings with potential buyers and get your community involved when you're brainstorming new ideas. Getting support from your followers at pivotal points in the business will encourage a deeper level of loyalty.'

https://www.enterprisenation.com/blog/posts/jimmy-
cregan-s-five-steps-to-building-a-brand-that-customers-love

Joining Jimmy's social media community gives the customer an insight into the growth of the business, and he will often invite customers for feedback or the chance to help decide on big decisions. Questions he has put to the community in the past include deciding on the colour of packaging, which festivals they should take their promotional stand to, and feedback on merchandise. He even announced the day when the company was finally debt-free – to his social media community of 30,000 plus.

http://instagram.com/p/ubFRqGxeD1/?modal=true
http://instagram.com/p/hNx-YnReJb/?modal=true

Go Pro

Go Pro is a fast-growing brand with an army of passionate followers. It makes small but incredibly powerful video cameras that people can use to record activities. It is a fantastic example of a brand that is using social media to reinforce their authentic sense of purpose. The company states on their website, 'We dream. We have passionate ideas about what's possible in this world. Our passions lead us to create experiences and realities that expand our world and inspire those around us.' They continue with their purpose: 'Go Pro helps people capture and share their lives' most meaningful experiences with others – to celebrate them together.'

http://gopro.com/about-us/

Go Pro is popular with active customers who have an interest in adrenaline sports, including snowboarding, surfing and mountain biking. Instagram is a popular social network with these groups of people, who find that the photography filters and short-form video features are a perfect way to share their experiences, and to inspire others.

For this reason, Go Pro has adopted Instagram as its primary social media channel to highlight some of the creative and interesting ways their customers are using the product, as part of their active lifestyles. The Photo of the Day feature allows the brand to post images of their creative, fearless community.

Go Pro is actively monitoring brand mentions on the platform, as well as welcoming customers to submit photos via their website, and is sharing their customers' content on to their channel, with the label Photo of the Day, which is featured to over 4 million subscribers. This results in a colourful, interesting community, which appeals directly to their target audience and reinforces the brand purpose of dreaming of what is possible in this world.

http://instagram.com/p/yASxx8Lf0W/?modal=true
http://instagram.com/p/xZqQZmLfya/?modal=true

Go Pro was an early adopter of short-form video content, which has risen in popularity with apps such as Vine, Snapchat and Instagram's video offering, and is set to be a large trend for 2015.

Facebook now auto-plays video content as a user scrolls through their newsfeed, and Go Pro Facebook has adapted its posting strategy to ensure there are at least three videos posted a week to the channel. The content posted is usually unique, capturing the viewer's attention, and encouraging them to share with their peers.

> **https://www.facebook.com/video.php?v=10152816196466919 &set=vb.50043151918&type=2&theater**

It is interesting to note that both these brands focus heavily on the use of visual content in social media. Not only are the brands using photos they have taken themselves, but they also include user-generated content in their social media posts.

Both of the brands have carefully considered which social network they are using for every piece of content, playing to the strengths and themes of each to reinforce their purpose and positioning.

How to use infectious communication

We have a mantra about brand purpose that works equally well for infectious communication: 'You can't force it, fake it or fudge it.'

By 'force it' we mean imposing your communication on people whether they want to hear from you or not. In the good old days the only choice viewers had was to go and make a coffee when your ad came on TV; now we can tune out at the click of a mouse on the 'unsubscribe' button. You have to earn the right for people to consume your marketing and you do that by being entertaining, educational or empathetic. So the rule is to whisper, not shout, and, if they are like all good whispers, they will be passed on.

When Innocent introduced their quirky tone of voice a number of other brands followed suit. When Robert Stephens started the Geek Squad and made a feature of his people, a number of computer repair firms tried to copy his model. They failed. Why? Because infectious communication only works when it is authentic and stems from your purpose. So don't 'fake it'.

Don't 'fudge it'. When your actions fail to live up to your brand purpose or marketing promises you are fudging it. Anyone can create great copy, but your customers will soon find you out if your deeds do not match your marketing. You only need to look back at the huge losses suffered by BP as a result of the Gulf of Mexico oil spill in 2010 and its failure to deliver on its promise of being the environmentally friendly energy company to see that fudging is a short-sighted option.

When Tony Hayward gave his final press briefing shortly before departing as chief executive of BP he said that BP had shown itself to be 'a model of corporate social responsibility' but it was 'not a great PR success'. On the face of it BP had done most things right: they managed to cap the worst of the spill, they managed to keep most of the oil from washing up on the beaches, they paid millions of dollars in compensation to the US locals whose livelihoods were affected. So why, then, the furore and criticism heaped on BP and its CEO?

We believe that the failure was one of authenticity; a failure on the part of BP leaders, past and present, to be authentic in their delivery of the brand purpose. BP, although embracing 'green' credentials and purporting to be the fuel brand most closely identified with sustainability, when put to the test drilling for oil off the Florida coast seemed to act first and foremost as an energy company concerned with maximizing its profits rather than concerned with sticking to its purpose.

Let's look at an example of a brand that not only sticks to its purpose but one that has used infectious communication very successfully.

Stick to your purpose

In the 'Stand up' part of this book, Part One, we advocated that you 'stick to your purpose'. In a photo shoot for British Airways *High Life* magazine, Sugru inventor, Jane Ni Dhulchaointigh (pronounced nee-gull-queen-tigg), managed to combine (and dramatize) both of these principles at once by sticking herself to the ceiling of her offices in order to demonstrate the effectiveness of her product.

So what is Sugru? In its own words, 'Sugru is the world's first mouldable glue that turns into rubber.' The brand says on its website: 'Our dream is to make fixing, modifying and making things easy and fun for anyone, and Sugru is our solution.'

The name, Sugru, is the Irish word for 'play', which seems appropriate when you see some of the wild and wacky uses that its 1 million users in over 160 countries put it to.

Image 3.2 Jane Ni Dhulchaointigh
Source: Image by Charlie Clift

A quick browse through the many videos and photographs uploaded by customers to the company website (**https://sugru.com/about**) will reaffirm your belief in the ingenuity of people when they buy into an idea. But lest you think that Sugru is just a toy, the product was named as number 22 of the 50 greatest innovations of 2010 by *Time* magazine... the iPad was ranked 34.

It starts with insight

It was while Jane Ni Dhulchaointigh was studying for an MA in Product Design at the RCA in London in 2003 that she had an idea: 'I don't want to buy new stuff all the time. I want to hack the stuff I already have so it works better for me.'

That notion led to experimenting with various substances, culminating in a mix of smelly silicone caulk and wood dust called Formerol – but it worked. It would stick to anything yet remain as flexible as rubber when dry. It was waterproof, dishwasher proof and heat resistant and could be moulded into any shape. It was high-tech and even more useful than the ubiquitous Duct tape.

Have a bold purpose

This was when Jane got excited:

'This was bigger than just me. I got out my sketchbook and started imagining a world where this material existed. I knew that, by tapping into people's innate creativity, all kinds of products could be transformed and improved. I knew that we could adapt and improve almost anything mass produced.'

This book is about those brands that have a 'purpose beyond profit'. They are all commercially successful yet this is not what drives them – they exist because they are passionate about making a difference in their world.

It was Jane's purpose that led to her putting a team together to develop the product, finding funding and setting up distribution channels. Discussions quickly followed with major glue manufacturers, because Jane's assumption at that time was *'a small company can't build a household brand'*. She was wrong – because with infectious communication you can.

Don't force it, fake it or fudge it

The pace of development with the large partners was very slow and Jane felt that her vision and sense of purpose were being compromised. She began to question her assumptions:

> *'I started to feel that maybe we could build our own brand. A friend told me "Start small and make it good." The dream started coming back.'*

That dream led to three years of effort and 8,000 hours in the lab to perfect the user experience so that the product smelt good, looked good, felt good and worked great. This effort meant that the company nearly went bust several times over but eventually, in November 2009, working night and day for a month, the company made its first 1,000 packs commercially and shipped them. Then their world changed.

Infectious communication

They sent a trial pack to the *Daily Telegraph* magazine and columnist Harry Wallop gave it 10/10 in his article. *Wired* and *Boing Boing* magazines picked up the story and linked it to their websites. The first 1,000 packs sold out in six hours. Sugru had arrived.

One of the remarkable things about the brand is the way that customers have embraced the idea of hacking their stuff to make it better and have contributed hundreds of stories, photos and videos from all over the world to show other users how they have done so. The user community has expanded to over 500,000 customers who subscribe to the brand purpose, 'The future needs fixing'. But it isn't just about fixing, it is also about improving and making things better. Much better. James Davis, the youngest member of the British Olympic fencing team, used Sugru to personalize the grip of his foil handle before competing in the 2012 London Olympics.

http://sugru.com
https://www.facebook.com/pages/Sugru/118586600911

If you look at the Sugru website or Facebook page you will find hundreds of ideas contributed by customers showing the power of infectious communication when customers really embrace an idea. Increasingly, brands and products will be 'owned' by their consumers who will contribute towards product development, promotion and technical support.

For example, Jane received hundreds of e-mails asking for the product in other colours. In April 2012 Sugru was launched in all the primary colours and in 2014 a further five new colours were added to the mix, so some customers are now using it to model things and create works of art – not just to fix things.

Purpose driven

Jane Ni Dhulchaointigh started with a clear vision of what Sugru could be: 'I pictured it as a kind of space-age rubber – super easy to shape, sticky and durable. I knew it needed to feel gorgeous and that, if I cracked it, it would have a million uses.'

Her purpose has sustained her through the bad times as well as the good, and it was that purpose that persuaded her to build her own brand and to do it in her own way. It seems to have worked. In September 2012 she was awarded 'Design Entrepreneur of the Year' at the London Design Festival and CNN voted her one of seven tech superheroes to watch in 2015. In July 2015, Sugru set the record for attracting the largest single investment of £1 million and raised £3.5 million in just six weeks through crowdfunding via 2,700 investors. Such is the power when people buy into your purpose.

giffgaff

Another brand that has really embraced infectious communication is giffgaff. In Part One we showed how the brand was built around a purpose. It was also built from a basis of enthusiastic advocates in the target customer base.

Mike Fairman, the 'Gaffer' (an old English term meaning the 'boss'), tells the story.

On the day that we launched giffgaff, we turned the website on at midnight. By 5 am the next day we had 'super-users', two or three of them, who had spent the night reading our terms and conditions, got to know the site, and were there at 5 am answering questions that had been posted by other people who had come across the site. We were just blown away by that and to this day we've never had an issue with getting people interested enough to help contribute.

We pay cash to contributors in the community. If you're on the top rung of involvement in the community, you might earn £100 a month. But it is not just about money, they do it because they believe in what we're doing; they believe that giffgaff is a movement, as do the people who work at giffgaff, because what we do is, I think, quite special. They do it for the love of it. My big learning is that if you genuinely set out to do something different and you are customer focused, then people will cooperate with you in a way that you might not think they would.

giffgaff 's infectious communication

This mutuality is what makes giffgaff different. It's a belief built around working closely with the member base and offering them ways to help the business run and operate and grow. We were very conscious, however, that it's very easy, when you start a community, if you get it wrong, for the community to die very quickly. In our case if we had launched with a community that died very quickly, then the business would die along with it, so we came up with the idea of launching the community before we had a SIM product to sell. It was based on a promise to say we're going to do mobile differently, we're going to do it working with our members, and we want to involve you early to get your views on what we should be doing.

We went to look for help in other communities, such as Yahoo Answers, where people were helping each other with mobile phones. We said, look, here's another thing that's going to come along, are you interested in just having a look?

We were able quickly to get a community of interest going, and at that point we realized we would need resources to manage it. We hadn't thought that it would take a huge amount of time. We realized that there would be some discussions going on in there and we would need to be involved and contribute – but not to the level that became apparent. I remember, we had one lady who was our CRM person, who was busy trying to design the entire customer communications programme for the business, and we just gave her this job on the side. Very quickly it started taking up half of her time as well as her boss's. So, we employed a community manager from the gaming industry, because gaming businesses have huge community management teams.

You don't really see much of the community managers publicly; they make the odd contribution, and they will start some threads, and then listen to the discussions that go on, but a lot of their work goes on in the background, private messaging between them and the individuals in the community that make it tick, making sure that they are kept happy and have the information that they need.

Through a combination of that management and the super-users themselves, the community becomes self-policing. The antithesis of that is YouTube and Facebook, which are free for all communities, in which it is very difficult to have a positive atmosphere largely because there is no way of communicating privately with the less friendly members and to educate them how to contribute in a more positive way.

We work with our members, and we believe that we are better off working together, and if we do that, every time and through every decision that we make, then it just turns you into a very, very, customer-focused business. It makes you laser-focused on the community all the time; it's like having about 10,000 community members watching over your shoulder and looking at what you are doing; and if you get something wrong, or make a decision that they don't like, you just know about it instantaneously.

For example, we took a finance decision, which we thought was a very low-level inconsequential decision – Maestro cards are being phased out, and our payment provider needed us to do quite a lot of work in order to keep them going on the website. We had very few people using Maestro cards, so we said, 'We're going to stop supporting and taking payments from Maestro cards.' And there was an uproar in the community because we hadn't consulted them on it, as we thought it was too small an issue. So, we went back to the payment provider and we switched back on Maestro cards, until they naturally just expired. When the last card runs out of its date, then that is when Maestro will disappear from giffgaff. When we reversed the decision, the community were absolutely delighted because they said, 'Wow, that's an example of a business that actually listens to its members.'

We are a budget brand and so the principle behind our pricing strategy is we get help from our members to keep our cost base lower and we plough that back into our products and have keen prices as a result. So pricing is a critical activity for us. For example, we were in a position where we had to raise our pricing because we had made some wrong initial assumptions about how many minutes, text and data would be used by customers in the bundle that we were selling. People were using more than we assumed. So, when we looked at the costs, obviously the inter-connect costs and all that stuff for those minutes, the profit and loss (P&L) wasn't shaping up in the way that it should, so we had to change the pricing. These decisions come along at mobile companies all the time; you go through a big research process, you have a pricing manager that works out what the price should be, what the advantage is of putting it up, how many people you're going to lose, you work out what the financial impact is going to be, and finally you tell your customers that you're going to put prices up. What we did is very different. We said, 'Okay, we think we know what we need to do; it's a case of putting up the price for the minutes and texts that you use outside your bundle.' But instead of actually just doing it we went out to the community and we explained to them why we needed to do this. We said, 'Look, if you want giffgaff to survive in the long term then we need to be profitable – because we are a business, we're not a charity. You're using more of the free minutes than we thought – which is great for you, but it's not great for our P&L, and if we carry on like this then we won't achieve our numbers and that will threaten the future of the business, therefore we need to put our prices up. We've thought about it, this is what we think we need to do, but there are other options – tell us what you think.'

We've done this twice now; the first time we had a good response in the community, something like 5,000 people contributed towards the discussion. What is really surprising is that you get very mature conversations taking place. You get some people saying, 'Oh, you're awful, you can't put prices up, that's terrible, you know, we want more stuff for free'; and then other people will come in to the community and say, 'Well, hang on a minute, be sensible about this; they are a business, we want them to be around next year and the year after that, they've told us that they need to do this, so what do you want: do you just want to make a quick buck now and then they disappear, or do you want them to be around?' Then you start seeing contributions that are more practical, such as, 'Have you thought about doing this... have you thought about doing that...?'

So we had a proposal as to what we were going to do with the price, and actually, we ended up amending our plans a little bit; some prices went up a bit, some prices went down a bit; and we were able to say, 'Okay, with your help we've now decided that we're going to do this...' And the remarkable thing is that when we did that we had 55 per cent positive sentiment, which was just remarkable.

Purpose creates true advocates

The thing is, this community may only represent a relatively small proportion of your base, 20 per cent, say, so that still means that 80 per cent of people don't know about what is going on. But when you do actually put your prices up, more of them visit the website, and if you have consulted beforehand, then what happens is you've got advocates already in the community who will be able to explain 'They consulted on this; this is the reason why they've done it, don't be so upset.' And of course those people, those same people, are also active on external communities; Facebook, Twitter and whatever else, and will just as readily jump in and defend you there as well as on your own community. So you get double benefit – a community that will communicate complex or unpopular messages, but also will defend you in public spaces where you haven't got the tools to do it otherwise.

An interesting example of this is the handling of outages. In 2012 we had two major outages: one was a complete service outage for 12 hours; the other was for six hours. Not good at all, and on the second occasion we decided that we needed to offer a gesture of goodwill.

Now, what O2 did, on the first outage, which had also affected them, is they offered a 10 per cent rebate on the monthly bill and free accessories for everyone. What we did was to say it's fair that we need to make a gesture of goodwill, but actually, we want to offer our members a choice of how that money is used. So, we made our apologies and said, 'Look, we want to make a gesture of goodwill, there's a pot of money that we're going to put up for doing this. If you were affected by the outage, because obviously not everyone was, then you can come to us and you can say, "Right, I want a share of that," or, you can say, "Keep the money and do something good for the business in order to improve the customer experience."' We didn't tell them how big the pot was, we didn't set expectations about how much they would get, but we actually had a pot of £350,000.

Interestingly, 80 per cent of the people who voted wanted the money themselves, but 20 per cent said, 'No, you keep it and do something good with the business.' We had hundreds of thousands of people responding. So, that was really interesting, because what we were able to do with the 20 per cent of £350,000 that was not required was to create some member service tools that only those people who voted to invest can use. So, they got a reward for being altruistic with their choice.

We ran a survey and we asked questions about what people thought about that approach, and some of the feedback we got was, 'I trust you more now'; 'I didn't trust you because the service went down, but the fact that you've handled it like that, makes me trust you more'. So we turned what was a very bad situation into something genuinely positive. We even had some members saying, 'Well, the fact that you care what we think about what you did just underlines why I love you as a business.'

It continually amazes me what you can do when you actually engage with customers.

Notes

1 Thales S Teixeira, The rising cost of consumer attention: why you should care, and what you can do about it, *Harvard Business Review*, January 2014.

2 From February 2014 to July 2014, 63 per cent of First Direct current-account customers had recommended their bank in the last year. The closest brand over the same time had 48 per cent recommend their bank. Source: Charterhouse Research Customer contact survey covering nine major banks in England and Wales, based on 16,466 contacts.

3 Convergys 2010 Scorecard Series.

Chapter Four
Distinctive customer experience

Standing out isn't just about infectious communic
barded with marketing messages that we often bec
them – even if they are engaging. Actions speak louder t
is that more important than when it comes to brand
experience. It is easy to claim that you stand for som
to behave in a way that supports that claim. As Gav Tho
says: 'Don't tell me how funny you are; make me lauç

It is even harder to make your customer experience come alive in such a way that customers 'just get' what your brand is all about. The challenge is about standing out, or differentiating your brand, in a way that is meaningful and valuable to target customers but when you do the results are dramatic.

IBM and Ogilvy conduct an annual survey called BrandZ, which measures those brands that have strong relationships with customers.[1] They found that when brands create an emotional connection to customers, as opposed to a purely functional one, cross-sell ratios increase from 16 per cent to 82 per cent and retention ratios rise from 30 per cent to 84 per cent.

The more multi-sensory the experience, usually the more memorable it becomes. We call this 'dramatizing the customer experience'. It means looking for moments along the customer journey where you can demonstrate what your brand really stands for in a compelling way. There are two types of activities: 'brilliant basics' are those things that you have to deliver consistently to satisfy customers; 'magic moments' are those things that you may only do occasionally or at certain hallmark touchpoints. These are the most powerful and create the 'wow' moments that customers tell others about. These touchpoints can be formal, as in the case of O2's 'Priority Moments' when customers get invitations to see their favourite bands, such as the Rolling Stones, or their favourite sports teams, as a thank you for being loyal to the brand. Or they can be very informal, when one of your people does something that creates a mini-experience for customers that epitomizes the brand values.

For example, there is a story that Linda Moir, who was formerly the director of customer experience for Virgin Atlantic, tells about the days before seat-back entertainment, when airlines would have a drop-down screen in the main cabin and schedule movies to follow the meal service. Virgin Atlantic decided to make the experience a proper movie experience and serve ice creams, just like at the cinema. That was a magic moment at that time because no other airline served ice cream on their aircraft due to the lack of freezers on board. Virgin solved the problem by packing the ice cream in dry ice.

A Virgin cabin attendant by the name of Sue Rawlings took the creation of this unique, memorable customer experience one stage further. In the galley, before serving the ice creams, she would smear some ice cream around her she walked down the cabin with the ice cream tray, she would say so that people across the cabin looked up at her: 'People tell me these creams are delicious, but I'm on a diet and never touch them. Enjoy!'

As passengers looked up, they saw the ice cream around her mouth and the smile on her face and a ripple of laughter would follow her down the aisle. Other passengers looked up to see what people were laughing at and joined in the laughter too.

The passengers who experienced Sue Rawlings's 'Virgin flair' told their friends and family and the story rippled around the world, becoming viral. People who had never flown Virgin heard about it. And when they had to book a transatlantic flight and had to choose between Virgin and their competitors, they went for Virgin because they wanted the ice-cream experience.

How much does an ice cream cost compared with a new aircraft? How much did that viral story cost compared with a glossy advertising campaign? Consumers remember an emotional experience more than a functional one and people trust referrals from other customers more than they trust a marketing message. It was a great manifestation of Virgin Atlantic's brand values of 'Fun, entertainment, irreverence, innovation' and serves to reinforce the brand positioning.

Compare this to Singapore Airlines, for example. Wonderful airline though it is, you could not for a moment imagine a Singapore Airlines flight attendant doing anything like that because that is not what the brand stands for. Singapore Airlines is positioned as the airline that consistently provides state-of-the-art air travel; 'the journey is the destination' as their famous advertising slogan expresses it. It dramatizes this by investing billions of dollars to be the launch carrier for new aircraft, such as the A380, so making a very public statement about how its brand drives its choices for the customer experience. Consistency of delivery, down to the smallest detail, is key to its brand. This includes its world-famous flight attendants, particularly the female ones, immortalized over decades as the 'Singapore Girls'. The recruitment and training of the staff are conducted with rigour and discipline to ensure that the appearance, attitude and behaviour of the 'Singapore Girl' are almost predictably consistent on every flight. Little is left to chance. In contrast, at Virgin Airlines or Southwest Airlines the flight attendants are encouraged to 'improvise' and bring their own personalities to the job. These brands tend to be lower-cost airlines and use the personal engagement of their people as a competitive advantage.

We must stress that there is a world of difference between dramatizing the experience and providing service gimmicks. The former is absolutely aligned

Image 4.1 Innocent foods' promise is simple and memorable

with the brand promise and desired experience; the latter is something designed to differentiate but without expressing what the brand really stands for.

Innocent is a great example of getting this right. Innocent smoothies have become a case study in how to differentiate a commodity (fruit and yoghurt drinks) in a crowded market by creating a brand and associated tone of voice that tap into people's emotions. Innocent's brand promise is 'tastes good. does good'.

Okay, so we get the 'tastes good' part, but how do they dramatize 'does good'?

First, 10 per cent of all profits are donated to good causes. Second, they are scrupulous about sustainability in the supply chain. Third, they involve their customers in doing good together with them. Every Christmas, Innocent launches the 'Big Knit' where they invite customers to knit little woollen hats to decorate the bottles. The decorated bottles are marketed at a slight premium and, for every one sold, 10 pence goes to the charity Age Concern. Last year 862,763 hats were knitted and sold. This is not only a great example of infectious communication (see this link **http://www.thebigknit.co.uk**), it is also an example of 'dramatizing the experience' because the little woollen hats decorating the bottles serve to remind consumers about the feel-good factor of the brand. 'Buy innocent smoothies because they taste good and do good'.

Any other beverage maker could copy Innocent and decorate their bottles in some way and, perhaps, even donate something to charity. But would it have the same impact? Probably not. In the first instance we doubt that nearly a million customers would voluntarily give their time to making it work (customers need to have an emotional connection with a brand before they will be willing to invest effort in supporting it); and second, we wonder if the end result would be seen as authentic in the same way as Innocent's 'Big Knit'. Remember, from the last chapter, you can't fake it, force it or fudge it.

Fix it or feature it

Some other 'F's to think about when creating a distinctive customer experience are, 'fix it or feature it'; this is a mantra of Greg Gianforte, founder of RightNow Technologies. It means either improve something that creates hassle or dissatisfaction for customers, or turn it into a benefit and then feature it as a selling point that becomes a hallmark for your brand.

Guinness is a great example. You need to wait for Guinness to be poured in two stages and then wait for the foam head to form, which takes time. Usually, waiting for your pint to be poured is a pain for the customer and a chore for the barman. But if you want that rich creamy head that is so distinctive to Guinness there is no avoiding the two-step pour. It cannot be fixed, so Guinness features it as part of their proposition using the tagline, 'Good things come to those who wait.'

For Guinness advocates, drinking the black stout through the creamy white head is an intrinsic part of the brand experience. 'The wait' as Guinness marketing people call it, is part of what makes ordering Guinness in a bar or pub unique; the wait was turned from being an inconvenience into the notion that good things are worth waiting for and, therefore, Guinness must taste better than the competitors. This taps (pardon the pun) into the emerging feeling among consumers in recent years that too much of life is a rush and that moments need to be savoured.

One of our all-time favourite ads is this Guinness one that hallmarks 'the wait':

 http://youtu.be/tf47teVn6Zl

The great thing about Greg's phrase, *fix it or feature it*, is that it helps you to home in on every aspect of the customer experience and make a decision about each one. This analysis of your product, service or experience in a forensic way – deconstructing the experience so you can examine the detail – is a powerful discipline for ensuring that everything about your customer experience that is in your control is examined and a decision is made about it.

Can we fix this issue so that the customer is not even aware of it, or do we turn it into a 'brand hallmark' that differentiates us from competitors? IKEA's infuriating requirement for customers to navigate their way completely around the store before finding the checkout is not only a fundamental part of their business model but also a hallmark of their brand experience. IKEA displays its products in complete room settings rather than by category, unlike most of its competitors. The customer is forced to visit each room in turn rather than go to the bed department, for example. This is a brand hallmark. It can be an irritant to some people but it is what makes IKEA, IKEA.

There is another application of *fix it or feature it*. It is one that can damage your brand if you don't deal with it in the way we are suggesting. If your product or experience contains a feature that is in serious need of fixing and you ignore it, then your competition can feature it in their own ads as a way of attacking you to win market share. EasyJet attacked Ryanair by offering better service and the opportunity to reserve seats, which forced Ryanair to follow suit.

Traditionally, marketers communicate the obvious benefits of a product or experience, downplaying features that are harder to interpret as an advantage or that can be seen as a weakness. The *fix it or feature it* mantra is a powerful reminder to think about creating an experience that is memorable for all the right reasons and that becomes particularly important in a crowded or commoditized market.

Create a multi-sensory experience

Holidays are the time of year when many of us buy gaily wrapped gift packs of toiletries for relatives who will probably never use them. The products are often of poor quality and only cost as much as they do because two-thirds of the cost is in the packaging. But there is one brand – Lush – that boldly challenges this traditional practice and dramatizes its purpose and business model through a multi-sensory experience.

If you are ever lucky enough to receive a Lush bath bomb as a gift we encourage you to try it. The vibrant colours, wonderful smells and fizzing effects will convert you to the world of cosmetics Lush-style. Co-founder, Mo Constantine OBE, invented the original bath bomb in 1989 and, ever since, Lush has continued its exploration into the world of bath-time innovation and successfully exported its unique customer experience across the globe. Lush currently has over 900 shops worldwide and is present in 49 countries, with manufacturing sites across the world.

Lush was formed in 1995 and since then has spent years developing what they call 'naked' products that work really effectively. Why? Because these solid products don't need preservatives or excess packaging, which is altogether kinder for the environment and allows the brand to invest 100 per cent of the cost of production in using better ingredients. As they say in their promotional materials, 'Simple really'.

You can find out about the Lush purpose and beliefs via the following link:

http://www.lushusa.com/A-LUSH-Life/
lush-life,en_US,pg.html?fid=a-lush-life

The stores are just as distinctive as the products themselves. As you walk along the high street and pass a Lush store, your senses will suddenly be bombarded by the smells, colours and hand-written notices calling your attention to the products that are displayed in all their 'naked' glory. Think of a fruit and vegetable stall in a market and you might come close to visualizing a Lush store. Handmade, natural and fresh merchandise; butchers' blocks of soap; a myriad of orb 'fizzing bath ballistics' that are presented like perfectly round apples; chilled fish counter-style cabinets displaying Bio Fresh face masks; prices by weight, greaseproof paper wrapping (if any wrapping at all) and best-before dates. But what was the stimulus for such an innovative approach?

Creating a distinctive customer experience

Mark Constantine OBE puts it simply: 'I've always loved the way fruit and vegetables are displayed in a grocery store.' Lush started with the metaphor of a fruit and vegetable stall and this remains at its core. It is able to afford the extra cost of using natural ingredients because of the savings from eliminating packaging. This is a fundamental principle of creating a distinctive customer experience: divert funds away from the things that customers don't value to the things that they do. This allows you to differentiate without having to charge a higher price point. The brand is therefore able to stick with its principles and remain purpose driven in the face of pressure from competitors who are less differentiated and compete primarily on price:

> 'Freshness is intrinsic to Lush – it's at the heart of our philosophy. It means we can minimize the use of synthetics and it means that we can create wonderfully effective products when the ingredients are at their most potent. When Lush products reach the customer, they are literally weeks, days or even just hours old. No product in any of our shops is more than six months old. We've been working with fresh produce for many years and have vast experience in how to formulate products that incorporate whole fruits and vegetables. At Lush, we believe that using the whole fruit or vegetable is infinitely more beneficial than isolating a property and removing it from a fruit, vegetable or natural material and adding it to a cosmetic product to try to recreate its function.'

Image 4.2 Bath bombs

This unique approach leads Lush to squeeze the following fresh ingredients every year: 25 tonnes of organic fruit and 50 tonnes of fresh fruit and vegetables; the oil from 20 million lemons, 6 million fresh bergamot fruits and 900,000 Sicilian mandarins; 10 tonnes of fair trade and organic cocoa butter; the juice of 90,000 zest lemons and 33,000 fresh oranges; 8,000 bunches of fresh flowers; and 20 tonnes of olive oil. For an innovative manufacturer and retailer like Lush you would expect that their focus lies solely on the product. You would be wrong: according to Constantine, 'You build a brand around people.' We shall say more about this in Part Three of this book (Stand firm).

The Lush approach seems to work. The Consumers' Association – Which? – surveyed 12,504 of their members in 2014 to find out the best and worst shopping experiences in the UK. Once again, the top-rated brand was Lush with more members rating their last experience in terms of satisfaction and likelihood to recommend the brand than any other.

Involve your customers in improving the experience

History tells us that most new products fail. So how do you ensure success when you are changing 30 per cent of your products each year? Mark Constantine OBE of Lush says:

'The key is making sure the customers clearly understand what you're doing and debating with them beforehand to make sure the product does what they want it to do at a price they are willing to pay.'

Sometimes this approach leads to dropping a product, a move that makes every kind of sense – except to the customer. For example, Mark Constantine says:

'We sell millions of pounds' worth of toner every year – you're buying some lovely essential oils, maybe a few other elements but basically it's water and preservatives and packaging. We would like to eliminate all preservatives and packaging in the next couple of years from all of our products. So, we invented a toner tab: tiny little tabs that you dissolve in water when you want to use it. It lasted a week. It was a much nicer toner than you could make in the traditional way. There's no preservative or packaging and the price is substantially lower as a result. Everything about it was perfect except that the customers hated it because it was less convenient. So, we continue with the bottled toner because that is what our customers want. When you get yourself aligned with the customer, it isn't about profit and loss or pushing your product. It's about producing what your customers want to buy.'

Reinventing your industry

It is relatively easy to create affection for a smoothie brand or a retailer but what about if we were to take the most disliked sector of all? Banking. On 5 March 2010 the Financial Services Authority gave Metro Bank the first full-service banking licence granted in the UK for over 100 years. The bank launched with one 'store' (it thinks more like a retailer than a banker), grew to four in the first year and by 2015 had over 31 stores located across the south of England, with 10 more due to open as we go to press. It grew deposits by 118 per cent in 2014 alone and is currently planning a £1 billion flotation.

http://www.telegraph.co.uk/finance/newsbysector/
banksandfinance/11547670/Metro-Bank-plots-1bn-
London-float-next-year.html

Metro Bank's co-founder and chairman is Vernon W Hill II. He is often credited with reinventing US banking as he is also the founder and former chairman and president of Commerce Bank, which like Lush has gained a reputation for achieving high levels of customer advocacy. Metro's purpose is to 'Amaze the customer'. Vernon Hill explains it in this way:

> 'Amazing the customer means providing unparalleled customer service, making sure every transaction goes quickly and smoothly. It means fulfilling customer needs, even anticipating them. More than that, it means turning customers into fans. We want them to tell their family members, friends and business associates about the products and superior services we provide.'

'Fans, not customers' is so core to how Vernon Hill thinks that he wrote a book of the same title in 2012. This belief has propelled Hill into the *Forbes* 20-20-20 club. This is the group of CEOs who have held the top job for 20 years, at a company with publicly traded shares for at least 20 years – and have presided over at least 20 per cent annual return on share price during his or her tenure. Just seven CEOs make the list and Vernon Hill sits in fourth place with an annualized return of 23 per cent over 30 years.

Metro Bank is still relatively small in terms of market share but is growing rapidly, unlike most of its high-street rivals and, more importantly, is achieving 'mind-share'– a brand that is talked about for positive reasons. The fact is that consumer expectations are shaped by what they read and hear and so inevitably, small or not, banks like Metro and First Direct, which provide a best-in-class online and telephonic experience, influence what a banking experience can be like and set the benchmark for others. Perhaps it is no surprise, therefore, that Metro Bank scores the highest net promoter score (NPS) in the industry of 78.9 per cent, with First Direct following at 62.3 per cent (Satmetrix Account opening survey 2014). RBS makes do with a score of –6.3 per cent. No wonder, then, that the big five banks are closing branches.

We interviewed Vernon Hill to find out what makes Metro Bank different and how it has achieved such impressive results.

Metro Bank is the fifth new bank I've started from scratch. I started my first bank when I was just 26. Somehow they gave me a banking licence, opening with one office, nine people and $1.5 million in capital. At the time there were 24,000 banks in the United States and we were number 24,001. So I wondered how were we going to take this no-name, no-capital, no-brand retail bank and turn it into something special and a growth business? When we sold it in 2007 we had became the eighteenth largest bank in the United States, with 500 locations and $48 billion in assets – and we achieved that purely through organic growth rather than acquisition.

Early on we decided that this was a retailing concept that happened to be a bank, and that the customers cared more about service and convenience than they did about price. This is a non-price-driven model. Some would say that we learned to decommoditize a commodity business. We gave the consumer and the businessman a completely differentiated experience. You don't buy iPhone 6 because it's the lowest-price handset; you buy it because it is an entry into the Apple world. Well, we learned to deliver the Commerce Bank world.

When we sold Commerce Bank in 2007 I had nothing to do for a week. A business contact of mine in the UK had been on at me to bring this idea to Britain so I got on a plane, arrived in London and mystery-shopped the big five banks. When I stopped laughing I went to see the government. They indicated that there hadn't been a new high-street retail bank licence issued since 1840. So I said, 'Alright, it's time to start a new bank in Britain.'

Metro Bank is based on the Commerce Bank model from the United States, but everything we did in the States actually works even better in Britain because British customers have not had a choice up until now. The big banks take them for granted; they see them as a target of opportunity for the next product; they think they are doing customers a favour by letting them bank. That is compounded by the fact that they have IT systems that are about a half a step up from a quill. They must be the world's best bankers if they can operate with their IT. Finally, they have operated a cartel – and cartels typically overcharge, underserve and underinvest in the business.

As my book says, our objective is to build a business that builds fans. Fans join you, they stay with you and they bring their friends. You cannot have a growth company without building fans. And that certainly is a foreign concept in the banking business in Britain and not that common in the United States. So we set out to build this bank from scratch with modern IT and a fresh slate. I was taught at Wharton Business School that it's easier to build a brand than it is to fix a brand, and I think there's a lot of truth to that. As we moved from market to market, they used to tell me, 'Oh it's different in this market.' When I decided it wasn't different, that our model worked in every market, that's when the growth curve went straight up.

What entrepreneurs do for a living is entrepreneur. We want to prove that our model is better. We want to attack the establishment and we believe that creating wealth is not the object of what we do but the result. I believe that if we create value for our consumers, they will create wealth for us.

We're delivering the best service and convenience by every channel for business and retail consumers. It's the way we deliver; it's the hours; it's never just one thing. It's all the points of touch, not the one point of touch.

*Our seven-day-a-week branch bank opening hours makes a tremendous state-
ment to the consumer. If you were to ask customers about Metro Bank they
would say this is the bank that opens seven days a week and we are the bank
that welcomes dogs in the branch. The British public, more than the US public,
believes that if you love my dog, you must love me too.*

Quite coincidentally, at this point in our interview the door opened and a small
dog came running into the room only to bound into Vernon Hill's lap where it
stayed for the rest of the interview.

Image 4.3 Vernon W Hill II and Sir Duffy II

*Say 'hi' to Sir Duffy. Sir Duffy tweets every day and people tweet back to him
too. Some people think this is a marketing gimmick. It isn't. Great brands create
an emotional attachment with their customers and that's when I believe you
create real value. We do this through things like killing all the stupid bank rules,
and letting our customers bring their dogs into the bank. This isn't about
marketing; it's about how you run your business.*

**https://www.metrobankonline.co.uk/
Discover-Metro-Bank/About-Us/**

We have three main elements to how we run Metro Bank. First, you have to create a differentiated business model where the customer sees clear value. Second, you have to build a culture to match your model. We see so many businesses where the model and the culture are opposed to each other. And then, finally, you have to fanatically execute the model. The number that used to scare me the most in the United States was that we were getting 21 million in-store visits a month from customers. Think about that number. That's like one-third of Britain walking through our doors every month. How do we make 21 million people happy and, if something goes wrong, how do we make that person more of a fan by the way we respond?

Let's take our differentiated business model. Our competitors are busy closing branches whilst we are opening new ones. Our first job is to get people to switch banks and we're just passing the 500,000 level this week. Every survey, and my experience, tells me that the branch is the public face of the brand and where the account switching happens. But once you've switched, we have to deliver to you the best experience across every channel – online, mobile, telephone, ATM – and we have to let you pick the channel. But the growth numbers we've seen in Britain prove that the branch is your public face. It's for the same reason that Apple built stores.

The culture is designed to deliver the model. And if your model is superior service and convenience, you have to recruit, train and manage people to deliver uncommon service and convenience. We have a few little things we use as part of our recruitment. If you're applying for a job and you don't smile during the first job interview, you're out. It's not that hard to train people to deliver retail banking. It's the way they deliver that is important and that comes from within. Remember, we are selling essentially a commodity product and we have to turn it into a non-commodity product. So we recruit, we train, we manage, we promote, to bring out the best in people.

Train, train, train and train some more. You simplify the delivery. When you're at a branch you've got 19-year-olds opening accounts. So our philosophy is that we can't have a rule that we can't easily explain to an 18- or 19-year-old. You try opening a bank account in the big five in Britain – there is so much mumbo-jumbo that you don't know what the hell is going on. So first of all your model has to be clear, it has to be simple and then you have to reward people for executing it.

British banks have morphed into a product sales channel. Their customers are targets of opportunity for the next sale. The only performance they measure is product sales. We don't sell products. If you ask us for one we will provide it, but we reward our people for delivering service and convenience. We mystery-shop our stores physically every other day. We report net promoter scores both at the store and the corporate level. We also measure deposit growth per store, not sales per store, deposit growth.

The final part is execution. Our job is to deliver this unique service and convenience experience and to comply with the rules. And there is an endless amount of rules and regulations and they are going to get worse. So our management job is to comply but in a way that doesn't degrade the customer experience. I'll give you a simple example. Every customer thinks that if they wish to switch banks they need to show proof of ID, as well as proof of their address, their utility bill etc. There's no truth to that whatsoever. You need one form of photo ID by law. With modern IT you can check all the other stuff. We can open your current account in 15 minutes. You walk out with your debit and credit card printed and your PIN number. Our competitors struggle to open an account in 10 or 12 days. If you have designed your business around service and convenience, you have to do all the other things, make money and comply with the regulations but not degrade the customer experience. It's very easy. When Commerce Bank got very big, I spent half of my time making sure we didn't become a bank – because I wanted to deliver a fun retail experience. I want to build fans and I don't want to let any of the endless regulations I have to comply with degrade my service experience. For example, security is a big deal but you don't have to let it inconvenience the customer. Our mobile app has a cute little feature. If you lose your card tonight, you can turn your card off. And when your wife finds your card tomorrow morning, you can turn the card back on.

All of these parts have to work together. Our first job is to get you to switch. Then it's to deliver the best experience. So it's all of the touchpoints. You can't look at one. You have to look at all of them. And then it's building the culture and finally executing every day. We have centralized the brand but decentralized the delivery. We have four or five regions now. The regional manager is a captain running our ship in their region. It's their job to deliver it, it's their job to be the Metro Bank in south London but they're not allowed to change the model.

We serve business customers as well as consumers. On the commercial side, customers want a banker. Business people want a banker who can handle their £5 million loan, who can take care of their mortgage for their house, can give their son or daughter a car loan, can solve their cash management problems, and if something goes wrong they can call and, if they're not happy, they can call me. That has totally been lost out of the British banking system. I'll give you a clear example. When you're applying for a commercial loan, you meet the lending officer who really has no authority; it's the credit officer who actually approves it. The British banks have a rule that the credit officer *is not allowed to visit the borrower. We have a rule that the credit officer must visit the borrower. That's the two sides of the same coin.*

Now, when we do something wrong, how we respond is very important. When we do something wrong we've got to make that customer more of a fan after we solve it. So we have to solve it right. We have a rule that says that it takes 'One person to say "yes", two people to say "no". Now, that is a powerful statement. If you go downstairs and ask one of our store people a question, they've got two choices – 'Yes sir, let me take care of it for you,' or 'Let me go and find somebody that can solve it for you.' In other words they are effectively not allowed to say no. And we reinforce the message that they get in more trouble for not waiving a rule they should have waived instead of not enforcing it.

As I think about the future, we have to service our customers' banking needs in whatever channel they want, in whatever way they want. The business hasn't changed fundamentally: we take deposits and we make loans. It's how we deliver these products that really matters. Your number one objective is to create a business model that creates value for your customers. And if you get that right they will create wealth for you.

So Metro Bank has thought about each touchpoint in the customer journey and where they can most effectively deliver their purpose, 'To keep the customer at the heart of everything we do'. But note that Metro Bank does not try to compete against the high-street banks at every touchpoint of the financial services experience, just those that they have decided to play in.

Don't 'flat line' the customer experience

This takes us to our final 'F', which is to avoid 'flat lining' the customer experience. When we work with organizations, one of the key steps we take is to research the current experience at each touchpoint. This creates a curved line that we like to call our heart line or ECG graph (EKG in the United States) because, like a real heart trace, it has peaks and troughs, and it is vital to avoid a flat line! A flat line at the bottom of the satisfaction scale means that you are performing very poorly and therefore unlikely to survive against better competitors. A flat line in the middle means that you are undifferentiated and likely to be mediocre in terms of customer satisfaction and loyalty, a flat line at the very top of the satisfaction scale is very difficult to achieve consistently and very expensive if you do. There are a few brands, such as Ritz-Carlton for example, that excel at most touchpoints. Of course, the pain is then experienced when the customer comes to pay because it is only by charging a very high price point that the organization can afford the level of investment required to resource these touchpoints. Don't gold plate your customer experience. Customer experience is a neutral term and does not imply gold-plated service. Ritz-Carlton offers a great customer experience but so too does Premier Inn in the midscale sector. Their business models and price points are very different and delivered in distinctive ways. So be careful not to upgrade your customer experience beyond the point that target customers want and are willing to pay for.

For most brands it is about deciding where to 'over-index' and that depends on their strategy and their brand promise. Taking IKEA as an example, the pleasure of the helpful room layouts and affordability of the well-designed products is paid for by the 'pain' of the inconvenient store layout and requirement for self-assembly. But this is what makes the brand different and memorable. If you are a target IKEA customer (typically young couples equipping a home) you will love it, and if you are not (typically more affluent, older people with limited time), you will hate the experience. But love it or hate it, IKEA stands out from the crowd. It is this 'light' and 'shade' that create the memory of an experience. A play or book that generated exactly the same emotions in every scene would soon become boring. The ancient Greeks and Romans would design slight imperfections into their art because perfection and complete symmetry were considered boring. So, too, a customer experience that is the same at every touchpoint becomes unremarkable.

Pain is good

Sampson Lee published a brilliant book in 2015 called *PIG (Pain Is Good) Strategy*, in which he explores this concept in some depth and even takes it a step further, arguing that the greater the distance between the pleasure peaks and the pain troughs, the more memorable the experience becomes. So, for example, Ryanair dramatized their very low prices (pleasure) by some very unfriendly customer policies such as charging large amounts for forgetting to print your boarding card, for example (pain). There is no doubt that customers who were subjected to this policy had a very clear memory of their experience and what the brand stands for. We do not go quite as far as Sampson; we believe that satisfaction has to be at a base level in order to avoid irritating customers, but we certainly subscribe to the view that you have to be remarkable at some things and it is perfectly all right to be just okay at others.

So how do you determine which touchpoints to over-index?

Where do you over-index?

It depends on your brand purpose and promise. Understanding what your customers truly value and what you stand for as a brand becomes the lens through which to design the experience. For example, some years ago we did some research for O2, the mobile phone company. We identified that their most profitable customers were worth several times more than the average customer but received exactly the same service and were not valued in any formal way. As a result, the brand took the bold decision to significantly reduce marketing budget in order to free up the funds to invest in putting more staff into the retail stores and building a dedicated contact centre for high-value customers. They also launched their highly successful 'Priority Moments' proposition, which values loyal customers. O2 chose to over-index in the retail, contact centre and customer engagement touchpoints because this was consistent with their brand purpose and what customers said they valued. They under-indexed against their competitors' spend on marketing and head office functions, but this was something that the customers didn't notice.

Felim Mackle, the UK sales and service director for Telefonica UK, explains by saying:

> 'Being in business and doing well means you have to invest. And that's a very big management decision because, when times get tough or when you're actually carrying out financial reviews, it would be oh so easy to cut the things that you can't absolutely, explicitly link back to a financial return. One of the things I think O2 has done very well is to take those big decisions and make them in a very holistic way. We said, actually, that this is part of the O2 experience that we need to keep investing in.'

There is not space here to go deeply into the psychology of the customer experience, but for those who are interested we recommend reading Daniel Kahneman's behavioural research into the 'peak–end' experience, where he discovered that our memory of an event is highly influenced by the peak of pleasure or pain and how the experience ended.

http://www.ted.com/talks/daniel_kahneman_the_
riddle_of_experience_vs_memory?language=en

Kahneman draws the comparison between the 'experiencing self' and the 'remembering self' and makes the point that what we remember can be very different to what we actually experienced. Our memory is coloured by the highs and lows and the most recent events. This suggests that the experience we design should intentionally create some hallmark moments associated with our brand purpose and promise, avoid undermining our brand promise by having hassle associated with it, and ensure that we finish strong (most organizations do the opposite: they typically start strong with marketing and sales activity and finish weak at the point of purchase or problem resolution).

We use this principle when designing a new experience for our clients. For example, we found that one of our software clients delivered a good sales experience but a very poor technical support experience. They also failed to communicate with enterprise customers after the sale to check on how satisfied they were with the product's performance. No surprise, therefore, that the advocacy of customers was poor as measured by NPS, and their renewal rates were low.

We designed a new experience to over-index the web experience to make it easier for customers to get information about the product. More importantly the 'Get Help' touchpoint was emphasized, so that when business customers called for technical support it was fast and effective, because when business customers have a technical issue they want it resolved immediately. We also engineered a new touchpoint called 'Product Value', where an account executive would contact the client on a quarterly basis to find out if the product was performing to the customer's requirements and what else could be done to create value for the client. The result was a 'peak–end' experience that increased the perception of value of the product, improved satisfaction with the account relationship and led to higher renewal rates (Figure 4.1).

Behavioural scientists Richard Chase and Sriram Dasu identified five simple rules to ensure that you design an experience that maximizes the pleasure and minimizes the pain.[3] We have listed these in the box below. For the sake of illustration and simplicity we have focused on the hotel industry – with a bit of creative, bold thinking, the same principles can be applied effectively to any sector.

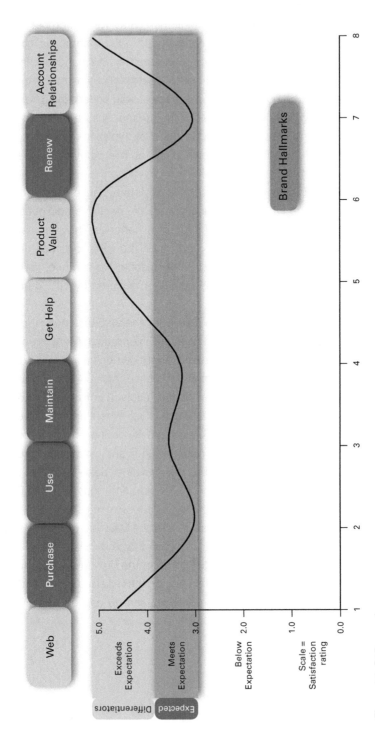

Figure 4.1 B2B experience curve

Five simple rules to create a memorable customer experience

Finish strong

Finish on a high – do something unexpected at the end of the experience, for example, a small gift given at the point of checkout. This helps to create a positive moment at the very point you are asking the customer to part with their cash.

Get bad experiences over with early

If customers have to do something onerous, get it out of the way as quickly as possible. In the case of hotels, pre-register guests online so that their first experience of the hotel is not one of lining up at the front desk and filling in a registration form with exactly the same information they provided when they booked or stayed last time.

Segment pleasure, combine the pain

Spread the pleasure along the touch-line. So provide those little touches of fresh cookies served with coffee, cold face towels on the beach etc. They cost very little but create 'spikes' of pleasure. Combine the 'pain' by bundling internet and other facility charges into the room rate so that you experience them in one step rather than every time you wish to use them.

Build customer commitment through choice

Give guests full information about your charges (such as water sports) on your website so they are transparent and expected. Guests can then make informed choices about the package they need and, most importantly, will not be surprised by them.

Stick to rituals

Create on-brand rituals that customers associate with their stay with you. For example, a trait of the Banyan Tree Resorts is to leave a little locally made, handcrafted gift as part of the turn-down service rather than the ubiquitous chocolate. Not only does this create a little moment of surprise but also serves to highlight their support for the local community and the environment.

Of course all of this is becoming increasingly more complex because the consumer has multiple channels to deal with. They can choose to interact with the brand in store, online, via the contact centre, via social media etc. All of these channels need to convey a consistent tone of voice so that the perceptions of the brand do not change from one channel to the other. Brands such as Burberry have done an amazing job of melding these channels so that they become 'one pure customer experience'.

We had the privilege to work with Burberry on their 'Burberry Experience'. We identified that a common weak area for many luxury fashion brands is the 'experiencing the product' touchpoint before purchase. In stores this is generally the fitting-room experience and online it is the ability to really learn about the product and interact with it virtually. Burberry did a fabulous job of bringing 'online in store' for their new flagship store in Regent Street in London so that the experience became seamless. Radio-frequency identification (RFID) devices in the products 'light up' plasma screens in the fitting rooms to play videos of the products being made or shown on the catwalk. Sales associates with iPads show the customer complete 'looks' and find out exactly what the availability of stock is, bringing items to the fitting room for the customer to try and even ordering items for collection later or home delivery. There is not a cash register or formal point of sale; instead, the sales associates take payment wherever the customer happens to be, sitting on soft couches to do so.

So the 'peak–end' experience is quite different in Burberry's flagship stores than in those of their competitors. Burberry is now taking this experience even further into the digital domain by creating experiences via social media and smartphones. In the words of Angela Ahrendts, their former CEO, Burberry has now become 'mobile first'.

 http://youtu.be/LpV8Cd_dKgY

Ahrendts is now the senior vice president for retail and online sales for Apple, so you should expect some amazing things in the next generation of Apple stores.

So what are some key considerations when designing the end-to-end multi-channel experience? Tim Wade was formerly the director of marketing and e-commerce at Best Western, the world's largest hotel brand, and was responsible for driving growth in the brand. Best Western has a great many advantages as a brand but it also has a major disadvantage when compared with corporate hotel brands that own their own properties. Tim used the principles discussed in this chapter to take on the market-leading hotel brand – and win.

The brand purpose Tim defined was *'To make life more enjoyable'* and he set about delivering this through a completely new guest experience.

Image 4.4 Best Western hotel brand

Best Western – 'Hotels with personality'

In 2009 PricewaterhouseCoopers (PwC) published their latest hotels report predicting the future prosperity of the UK hotel market in the forthcoming years. Contained with the report were comments from participants in the research that:

'The budget sector will do well.'

'The luxury sector will see growth.'

BUT... 'The mid-market is getting killed.'

Now imagine yourself as a mid-market hotel brand building your strategy and budget for the coming year. This was Best Western, by number of hotels the largest hotel brand in the world, but firmly planted in the mid-market in Britain with around 280 three- and four-star hotels – and firmly predicted to 'get killed' in the toughest economic conditions for decades.

Best Western is made up of over 4,000 independent hotels around the globe and whilst each hotel has to meet strict quality controls they are free to express themselves and run their business as they see fit. In Britain, Best Western was struggling to have an identity; its brand tracking showed a mediocre and stagnant performance whilst the budget and luxury sectors expanded. In Britain, Best Western was stuck in the middle of the road, undifferentiated and in danger of getting run over by the budget hotel train. People just weren't talking about Best Western!

From a brand perspective this is an interesting challenge; brands traditionally have been defined as a promise consistently delivered. With 280 independent hotels, from 12th-century castles to rambling country houses and contemporary city-centre pads, consistency is a challenge. Certainly with such diversity it is not possible to have consistency of the physical aspects of the experience. This is exacerbated further when Best Western doesn't employ the people that work in the hotels and Best Western doesn't take the financial decisions about investment in hotel assets.

So, product inconsistency was perceived as our biggest weakness, but the fact was we couldn't fix it because of Best Western's membership model; so we decided to feature it instead.

As always there are different perspectives and with inconsistency lies a real way to stand out from the monolithic corporate brands. As the growth of budget hotel brands rocketed, the hotel market was becoming a sea of sameness, where it wouldn't matter which town, city or region you were in, everything was the same. This has the benefits of reassurance and predictability, which for many customers is desirable, but for those frequent travellers – those people staying in hotels week in week out – these hotels can be dull, boring and soulless. Best Western saw a great opportunity to stand out.

Focused on a core group of customers, the independently minded frequent traveller who is bored with the formulaic experience – Best Western created a new brand position and strapline. As a way to celebrate its own 280 independent hotels and the independent thinking of its customers, Best Western created 'Hotels with personality' – three words that were to transform the fortunes of a mid-market brand stuck in the middle of the road. This was more than just a new strapline, it was a whole new way of thinking. It was about celebrating the independence of the hotels and differentiating Best Western from all other hotel brands. It built on the brand heritage, the diversity of the hotels (and the fact that so many are historic), and the characters who choose to work in that particular hotel rather than working for a corporate brand.

Realizing that 'Hotels with personality' had to be more than just a strapline Best Western knew that to truly differentiate it had to be delivered through the customer experience – in fact the brand had to create the 'personality experience'.

The customer experience has become omni-channel

Travel is always one of the key things that customers search for and talk about online and this means that, as with many other sectors, customers are adept at moving between digital, social and physical environments. In fact they do it with such ease that customers pay little attention to channel and just do what is natural and easy at that moment in time.

For Best Western the challenge of how to bring alive the 'personality experience' through the digital, social and physical experiences so that it differentiates was tackled in five key steps.

1 Bring the story alive

The benefit of having 280 eclectic and independent hotels is that each has a story to tell. These stories included wonderful history: the oldest purpose-built hotel in England, a hotel where allegedly Henry VIII had built a secret passageway to hide an illicit affair and stories of hotel ghosts that haunted corridors; hotels that make their own craft beer and grow grapes to make wine; and, of course, stories of wonderful characters within the hotels. It is these stories that create the personality, it is these stories that create the anticipation of a great stay and it is these stories that make Best Western stand out. So we employed a team of journalists to go out and capture all these stories from every single hotel. This created a giant storybook, which we used to power the marketing activity, social media and internal communications. Stories were our way of connecting with people no matter what channel they chose to use.

2 Empower people to tell the story

As humans the experiences we crave and remember are those human-to-human moments, so the hotel teams needed to be empowered to bring alive the story and experience for guests through their own behaviour. Rather than create robotic service procedures and scripts, we allowed people to celebrate their independence and trained them how to demonstrate this using branded experience training. This equipped them with the skills to bring their personality to work, to find and share the stories in around the hotel and get up front of any issues.

3 Engage the customer and make them part of the story

With TripAdvisor being the biggest travel site in the world, hotels cannot ignore the power of the social consumer. By bringing alive the story for guests, and focusing on the customer experience, we brought the customer into the story and encouraged them to share it socially so that they became part of it.

4 Make it personal

Travel is a very personal thing and each customer has his or her own story to tell. The key was to use technology to make the journey personal, so we connected the data and the channels together to create a single view of the customer and create bespoke communications and experiences so that each guest's journey was unique.

5 Have some personality

Having a personality and tone of voice is vital. Humans don't talk in corporate speak so why do brands? A 'hotel with personality' needs to be fun and enjoyable *and everything needs to reflect this. Life is too short and busy for boring hotels, boring communication and the usual dreary monologue of marketing messages. So we aligned our marketing, our advertising, our behaviour and our measurement around the 'personality experience'.*

Best Western created a pilot of the programme in six hotels and achieved impressive results, which featured in a Forrester Case Study in 2014.[4]

- *Net promoter score increased by 7.4 per cent.*
- *Employee engagement increased by 346 per cent.*
- *TripAdvisor comments improved.*
- *And, importantly, financial performance improved.*

In 2014 Best Western rolled out the programme to all its hotels and the brand continues to outperform the market.

    http://www.bestwestern.co.uk

Notes

1 Source: IBM/ Ogilvy Loyalty Index/ BrandZ survey.

2 Sampson Lee (2014) *PIG (Pain Is Good) Strategy: Make customer centricity obsolete and start a resource revolution*, iMatchPoint, Hong Kong.

3 Richard B Chase and Sriram Dasu (2001) Want to perfect your company's service? Use behavioral science, HBR OnPoint © 2001, Harvard Business School Publishing Corporation.

4 https://www.forrester.com/Case+Study+Best+Western+Great+Britain+Wins+Validation+For+Customer+Experience+Strategy/fulltext/-/E-res116862.

Chapter Five
Continuous innovation

'History has shown that many of the innovations that we have come to take for granted were a result of entrepreneurs, pioneers and early adopters willing to invest their own money, and sometimes lives, in a big idea.' **RICHARD BRANSON, FOUNDER, VIRGIN GALACTIC**

Richard Branson wrote those words some years ago, little realizing that on 31 October 2014 his comments would, sadly, come true. His spaceship, VSS Enterprise, suffered a catastrophic malfunction leading to the total loss of the aircraft and the death of co-pilot Michael Alsbury and serious injury of pilot Peter Siebold.

Recognizing that his vision was putting other people's lives at risk Branson wrote: 'I found myself questioning seriously for the first time, whether in fact it was right to be backing the development of something that could result in such tragic circumstances. In short – was Virgin Galactic, and everything it has stood for and dreamt of achieving, really worth it?'

He goes on to report: 'I got a very firm answer to that question immediately when I landed in Mojave. From the designers, the builders, the engineers, the pilots and the whole community who passionately believed – and still believe – that truly opening space and making it accessible and safe is of vital importance to all our futures.'

Bill Bernbach, founder of the celebrated ad agency Doyle Dane Bernbach (DDB) was fond of saying '*A principle isn't a principle until it costs you something.*' Similarly, we believe that the true test of purpose is if you stick with it in the face of adversity. All too often, organizations define some uplifting purpose, or conceive some great customer innovation, only to dump it as soon as they have to invest substantially in order to deliver it. The true test of Virgin Galactic and Sir Richard Branson's dream is how they deal with the aftermath of the VSS Enterprise tragedy and whether they continuously innovate until they achieve their dream.

We often run workshops with executive groups to help them define their purpose and we test commitment to it by identifying what we call 'the sticky moments'. What are those things that are likely to happen that may cause the executive group to gulp and waiver in their resolve?

We were running a workshop for Premier Inn, the hotel brand, to help them define their purpose of '*Making guests feel brilliant through a great night's sleep*'. We invited the executives present to identify their 'sticky moments'. One plucky regional operations manager piped up and said, 'We have thousands of old rooms without adequate sound proofing or air conditioning. What will our people say when we announce this purpose and they are still dealing with guest complaints?' The room went quiet and then Patrick Dempsey, the Premier

Inn managing director, asked the question, 'How much will it cost us to fix it?' The answer was in the millions of pounds. Right there, the executive group decided to invest in upgrading those rooms. It was in that moment that the Premier Inn purpose moved from being a set of words to a mobilizing force in the organization.

Let's face it, most companies wouldn't innovate if they didn't have to. It's not that people hate new things, it's just that innovation is often risky, expensive and fraught with failure. There is a well-known phrase: 'if it ain't broke, don't fix it,' which probably sums up many people's views about innovation.

But the fact is that innovation is necessary. We would not have any of the technology we enjoy today without it. We would not be able to drive, fly or even catch the train, things we now consider commonplace. Yet way back when these technologies were being developed they were considered just as risky as space travel is today. It is bizarre to think that just over 100 years ago the 'Locomotive Laws' required a person to walk in front of the newly invented automobile carrying a red flag to warn pedestrians of the danger posed by a vehicle that was restricted to a maximum speed of 4 mph. In 2014 the UK government passed a law allowing the use of driverless cars from 2015; Google has been testing driverless cars for some time in California and Nissan has introduced driverless features into its vehicles, such as 'park assist', where the car literally parks itself at the touch of a button.

The need for innovation is accelerating. Increasingly, customers are demanding more from their brands. What was innovative yesterday is commonplace and expected today. The cycle of product replacement is ever shorter. The first Apple iPhone 1 was released on 29 June 2007. By 2014 they were on version 6. That's six versions in seven years. When the first iPhone was released it was revolutionary; today, it seems like commonplace technology. This inflationary effect keeps raising the bar and fuelling the need for new, different and better approaches to business.

Digital, mobile and web technologies have increased the rate of consumer demands and the speed of response they expect from companies. Time has never been a friend to the business person but it is now openly hostile. New products have an increasingly limited window before being replaced or copied. In fact they are often superseded, imitated or hacked while they are still in development. Competition is everywhere and accelerating the rate at which people can find and buy almost whatever they want whenever they want it.

One problem for many organizations, when they think about innovation, is that typically they focus on the product. However, we know that customers form relationships with brands, not products. And we know that the areas of that relationship that are often given least attention but which mean most to the customer are in service, sales and support. According to Peter Fisk, founder of Genius Works (@GeniusWorks), whereas the vast majority of innovation efforts by companies have been linked to product, the biggest returns on investment have actually been in new business models (eg online shopping) and in the customer experience. Think of brands such as Google, Facebook and Alibaba: they are among the largest brands in the world in terms of capital value yet they didn't exist 15 years ago. They do not manufacture products, they do not find scarce resources, they do not bring vital new drugs to market, they simply connect people digitally to things made by others and yet the returns for their founders are huge.

Constantly innovate in both large and small ways

Purposeful organizations are possessed by a relentless commitment to improvement, to seeking a better way. Sometimes it can be a huge game-changing innovation, as in the case of Virgin Galactic. But often it is just the everyday focus on innovation in many small ways throughout the business. Just so long as they make things better for customers.

A problem with innovation is that many business people are obsessed with 'the big idea'; they want 'game changers' and are constantly poring over customer data to try to come up with the 'killer app'. Of course, if you can come up with a game changer, then that is great. The reality, however, is that this may only buy you a short-term advantage because of the tendency for brands to rapidly first play 'catch-up' and then 'leapfrog' in terms of technology. It wasn't so long ago that Nokia was the leader in mobile phones. Where are they in 2015? The brand has been acquired by Microsoft and has, for most practical purposes, ceased developing its own technology. So even more important than these big things are the little day-to-day things that make an enormous difference to consumers and employees – that earn their advocacy and loyalty, cost little but reap financial reward and demonstrate your commitment to creating value for customers.

Purposeful organizations understand that 'little things have a big impact'. They are often obsessed by detail and are endlessly curious about even the smallest aspect. Whether it is digger manufacturer JCB's chairman Sir Anthony Bamford personally adjusting the hub cap on a backhoe digger because he noticed it wasn't quite right, or smoothie manufacturer Innocent's annual 'Big

Knit', they are all manifestations of the fact that a small action can have a big impact on the perception that customers have of you. Zappos, the online retailer, understands this perfectly. One of their core values is to 'live and deliver WOW'. They believe that creating moments of 'WOW' have a huge impact on creating a distinctive customer experience. These 'magic moments' form an essential ingredient in customer experience design.

Drive innovation from a deep understanding of what target customers value

As we already mentioned in Chapter 4, history tells us that most new products fail. So how do you ensure success when you are changing 30 per cent of your products each year? To restate Mark Constantine of Lush: 'The key is making sure the customers clearly understand what you're doing and debating with them beforehand to make sure the product does what they want it to do at a price they are willing to pay.' Sometimes this approach leads to dropping a product, which makes every kind of sense – except to the customer. Again, to restate Constantine: 'When you get yourself aligned with the customer, it isn't about profit and loss or pushing your product. It's about producing what your customers want to buy.'

This was a principle used to good effect when Sonu Shivdasani and his wife Eva were planning their luxury hotel brand, Six Senses, in the Maldives; they called up tour-operators and travel agents and asked them what customers complained about: 'There were things like "the lack of fresh food: everything was imported and tinned"' he said. 'So we developed our own organic garden, which means we could actually offer our guests much fresher and more nutritious salads than they get in London.'

It is also important to understand that what you sell is not necessarily what customers are buying. RayBan thought they were selling eye protection; Chilli Beans, the Brazilian retailer, realized that customers were buying a fashion accessory. This insight led them to create a business model that produced sunglasses of good quality, but exceptional variety – 10 new product designs are launched in over 500 stores and franchises every week! Because of this, a typical customer will own three or four pairs of Chilli Beans and visit the store weekly to see the latest models.

http://www.chillibeans.com/sunglasses.html

Use your purpose to drive growth

Umpqua Bank is a community bank based in the Midwest of the United States. It has created a reputation and enthusiastic following for its innovative approach to banking. By calling its branches 'stores', recruiting its people from retailers and using innovative marketing techniques that it calls 'handshake marketing' that is so personal you can almost shake the hand of the customer, the bank seeks to deliver on its promise of being the world's best community bank. One example of this approach to 'handshake marketing' was its use of an Umpqua-branded ice-cream van, which drove around the streets of California to create brand awareness in this new and important market.

Ray Davis, the CEO of Umpqua Bank, says:

> 'Innovation permeates our organization at all levels. To me, that's the most important driver of our organic growth. The second route to growth, of course, is through acquisitions. The reason that we've been so successful with acquisitions is because we've created a very unique culture that aligns our people with the Umpqua strategy and brand.'

So having a clear sense of what you stand for not only helps you to stay ahead of competitors through being more innovative but also helps you to acquire other organizations and meld them into your own. It is interesting that so many companies conduct due diligence to explore the economic benefits of making an acquisition or merger; they investigate the pension plans for compatibility, they compare customer lists looking for revenue opportunities, they overlay distribution maps to identify supply chain synergies. But how often do they compare their organizational purposes or what their brands stand for in order to ensure a good cultural fit?

Use innovative technology and processes to support the delivery of a superior customer experience

Umpqua, LEGO, Chilli Beans and many other brands use social media and their websites to create customer communities. Burberry uses 3D high-tech broadcasting of their runway shows; and Chilli Beans uses music and events to involve customers in the Chilli Beans world. O2 drives innovation through continuous customer feedback by involving them in events and their participation in customer communities such as giffgaff, its 'people powered network'. First Direct uses its online 'Lab' to generate customer feedback.

But the technology does not have to be digital to support an innovative idea. Six Senses refuse to fly in any branded bottled waters to any of their properties. Instead they invest in their own water filtration and mineralization plants at their resorts to bottle and sell their own water; 50 per cent of the proceeds of these sales go to a water charity to provide clean water in places such as India. The environment benefits, as do the customers. As Sonu Shivdasani, founder of Six Senses, says:

> *'You need to stay true to your purpose –*
> *it becomes the compass that guides you.'*

Six Senses' purpose is 'intelligent luxury', by which they mean environmentally sustainable.

Encourage your people to demonstrate superior skills and capabilities

Sir John Hegarty, the founding creative director of advertising agency BBH, says:

> *'When you are in a [creative] environment such as ours, it is fundamentally important that the creatives feel that what they do is the most important thing in the company; that they are being encouraged to do what they want to do. If you don't have that, you won't get them pushing themselves to create the kind of work that they want to create. So it is fundamentally important that I encourage an environment of constant innovation, and that they know that when they do creative work, I am going to take it seriously and I am going to sell it as best I can.'*

This should remind us of the final point that all these companies realize about innovation: in the end, it is only important if it is going to make a difference to delivering your organizational purpose and, ultimately, value to customers. Moreover, if it is going to make a difference, it has to be sold to customers or consumers with passion and with the conviction and commitment that it will be delivered. That is where having a purpose really helps. It keeps you focused on the things that really matter.

Focus innovation on the things that make you different

In Chapter 4 we looked at how to differentiate the customer experience through creating brand hallmarks. We advised over-indexing on those things that drive value for customers and the brand, and accepting that it is okay to meet basic satisfaction levels on the things that do not. If you do this, it

Source: http://www.amazon.com/b?node=8037720011

Image 5.1 Amazon's drone delivery

presents you with a very focused agenda for innovation because you know exactly where investment is required to accentuate what your brand stands for and increase your differentiation. A good example is Amazon Prime Air. This is the innovative service that Amazon is developing that is designed to get a package into the hands of the customer in less than 30 minutes. The high-profile manifestation of this service is a drone that delivers your package to your door. The regulatory challenges, the logistics and the costs are significant, so why bother? Because state-of-the-art convenience and rapid deliveries lie at the very heart of the Amazon DNA and their differentiation. The drone dramatizes what the brand is all about.

So let's look at some inspiring examples of innovation in customer experience.

Umpqua Bank

Umpqua Bank has a promise of 'being the world's best community bank'. This means not only being deeply rooted in the community, but also going above and beyond customer service and transforming the mundane task of banking into an unexpected, engaging experience.

An example of their approach in thinking of innovative ways to help people switch banks is in their choice of three different media venues that are a more interactive, tactile and stirring delivery method than the usual banking choice of TV and advertising. Here's a quick introduction into what they are doing.

Bank account-moving day

Umpqua think of themselves as the community's best friend. And what would a best friend do? Help you move. Umpqua transformed an old moving truck into a one-of-a-kind bank account-moving truck. To take the hassle out of switching, the team drove all around the US north-western states taking all the heavy lifting out of moving customers' accounts to Umpqua. The truck comes equipped with ready internet-access laptops, enabling customers simply to step into the truck and switch banks there and then using an e-switch kit.

Switch-kit-in-a-can

One of Umpqua Bank's goals was to engage potential customers into switching their bank accounts in a fun and unique way. So they introduced completely customized vending machines and stocked them with free bank switch-kits-in-a-can, symbols of a refreshing change, and placed them in all types of locations in the north-western states.

Locally grown community kit

For Umpqua to be seen as the world's best community bank, it recognized the need to be informed, take action to inspire, protect and develop members of their community. So Umpqua developed the Locally Grown Bank Accounts programme that focuses on empowering the local community. Umpqua showed their support by appearing at all sorts of community events, from farmers' markets to fairs. Their farmer market stands are fully stocked with fresh Umpqua blend coffee, wildflower seed packets, authentic market bags and the handy switch-kit-in-a-can.

In keeping with this, they issued guidance to all staff to act as people, not as bankers (easier said than done)!

LEGO

LEGO has pioneered innovation driven by its customers. It has not just listened to its customers, it has actively encouraged them to collaborate, co-create and customize the experience of 'play'.

In 1997, the LEGO Users Group was formed by a couple of enthusiasts on the internet and quickly grew. It enabled LEGO to make the simple observation that its customers were not only children; a large part of its fan base was adults. Moreover, the adults were often the most passionate users of the brand. The company eventually gave these super users a name: 'Adult Fans of LEGO' or 'AFOLs'. The company began to tap into the insights and experiences of these AFOLs. Through basic digital channels such as e-mail, they were able to share insights as to what made a great LEGO experience and ideas for new ranges. They discovered that among their users were doctors, architects and designers. These were people who could not only suggest an idea for a range (ambulances, for example) but also give valuable insight and practical detail as to how to make the suggested range as authentic as possible.

The user group evolved and with the advent of social media and the expansion of digital technology it became an even more populous and creative community. So valuable were these super users in both product development and brand advocacy that LEGO named them 'ambassadors' and created the LEGO Ambassadors programme for them.

Listening and working with them, the company understood that its brand was not restricted only to real 'bricks'. The essence of LEGO branded product is not the brick but the 'shape' of the brick, a distinctive visual style that actually translates well into digital design because of its slightly 'pixellated' appearance. And the essence of the brand itself lies in the unlimited imagination of constructive play. Users would make their favourite superheroes or famous people out of the bricks and then plunge them into an exciting world of adventure. This world might look like the kitchen table to you and me but to the user it is a plateau of fantasy. So it did not take too much imagination for the company to realize that its customers would appreciate LEGO versions of superheroes and villains and electronic games in which they could play. The franchise deals that the company made with Star Wars and Harry Potter not only fuelled sales; they also brought the brand into the modern era.

In 2014, the company redeveloped the Lego Users Club into a new type of network community whose aim would be more explicitly to create, collaborate and share ideas. The new 'LEGO Ambassadors Network' even has its own 'charter' with the following purpose and objectives:

Purpose:

A community network for both the LEGO Group and influential adult fans of LEGO (AFOLs) to provide valuable dialogue and initiate activities of relevance to the success between the LEGO Group and the AFOL community.

Objectives:

1 To provide a central communication network for the LEGO Group and user-group ambassadors to: 1) collaborate and share information with the wider AFOL community; 2) to strengthen best-practice sharing within the AFOL community.

2 To provide a point of contact between the recognized LEGO User Group and the LEGO Group in all support programmes and related activities.

3 To be task oriented, by having clearly scoped activities and discussions that benefit the LEGO Group and AFOL community.

4 To provide valuable insight on ad hoc business decisions and intelligence.

You can find more about it here: **http://www.brickwiki.info/wiki/Ambassador**.

An early example of how LEGO collaborates with its customers was its Mindstorms range. Mindstorms was conceived as a way of offering electronic LEGO to a new generation of children who were growing up in a world dominated by electronic gaming such as Nintendo Game Boy. Mindstorms, developed together with the Massachusetts Institute of Technology (MIT), were LEGO bricks containing software and sensors that allowed customers to programme their creations to move – effectively creating LEGO robots. Within weeks of it being launched, an estimated 100,000 people had 'hacked' into the software and were reprogramming it. LEGO understandably feared that this illegal hacking would be malicious, aimed at disrupting the programmes or stealing the software codes. In fact, they soon realized that these 'hackers' were intent not on destroying the product but on improving it: 100,000 LEGO fans with software program skills had spontaneously collaborated to create an even better experience for themselves and for all LEGO users. Think of that: 100,000 computer programmers working for free to build you a better product. It was one of the earliest examples of open-sourced innovation. And LEGO has continued to embrace this mindset of openness to direct customer creation of the experience in all its developments since.

The latest innovation is called LEGO Fusion. It responds to the twin trends of increasing digitalization and desire for personalization (see Image 5.2 opposite). It allows you to take your favourite LEGO toy – your own creation from real LEGO bricks in the real world – and then to scan it digitally and upload the image into a world of gaming. The 3-D image of your toy then becomes a 'lifelike' character in a virtual world, interacting with other pre-existing characters or ones created by other customers.

LEGO's closeness to its customers and its openness both to listening and to allowing customers to create their own experience have helped drive business growth. By September 2014, LEGO had become the world's number one toy maker, with just over $2 billion of sales globally in the first half of that year alone.

KPMG and McLaren

It is not just in the world of consumer products that exciting innovation can happen. It can happen in the business-to-business (B2B) market. It can even happen in the field of accounting audits and business advisory services.

McLaren Motors is one of the leading brands in motorsport. Dynamic engineering and rigorous technical expertise drive its high-performance technology. Data analytics are key to everything it does. Every element, every

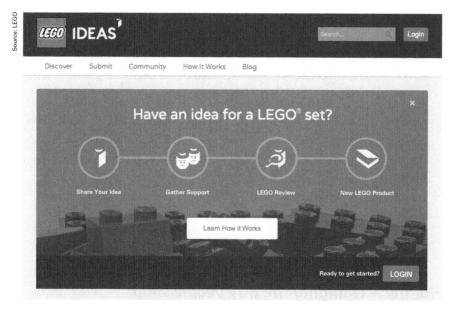

Source: LEGO

Image 5.2 LEGO encourages anyone to come up with an idea for a product

detail of every aspect of its Formula 1 cars, the drivers and the crew are meticulously analysed and that analysis is translated into real-time information that improves performance, often shredding valuable micro-seconds off the time it takes to complete a lap.

McLaren makes money from multimillion-dollar partnerships with business-to-business (B2B) and business-to-consumer (B2C) brands that want the awareness and image enhancement that come from association with Formula 1 globally. Household brand names such as Diageo's Johnny Walker whisky, Vodafone and Santander benefit from the excitement, thrills, sexiness and raw drama of the track.

KPMG is one of the leading accounting and management-consulting firms. It is also a partner of McLaren's. However, their partnership is a unique and innovative one. KPMG's purpose is '*To turn knowledge into value*'. So, rather than simply benefit from the glamour and high-performance image of an F1 team, KPMG use the access to McLaren's technology to benefit their customers' experience.

In November 2014, KPMG and McLaren announced a 10-year strategic alliance whereby KPMG will have access to McLaren Applied Technologies (MAT) predictive analytics and technology programmes. This can be used to improve the quality and impact of auditing and of business advice. Businesses who have large mobile workforces where speed of response is important (such as telecom firms or utilities companies whose employees are often driving around cities and towns in vans) can benefit from the kind of predictive analytics that help McLaren to turn around their F1 vehicles in pit stops within seconds.

Simon Collins, UK chairman of KPMG, said of the deal:

> *'Our alliance with McLaren gives us the opportunity to accelerate the transformation of our audit and advisory businesses. McLaren has honed sophisticated predictive analytics and technologies that can be applied to many business issues. The same is true of our advisory services, where we believe applying McLaren's predictive analytics and know-how to, for example, a complex international supply chain, could help our clients make a step change in the service they provide to their customers.'*

Formula 1-powered accounting? Now, that is innovative.

Hointer – changing the way people shop

One of the most innovative brands we have come across in a while is the Seattle fashion retailer Hointer. The brand's purpose is to change the way that people shop. The company's CEO, Dr Nadia Shouraboura, is a retail revolutionary. She has extensive retail experience and was the former head of supply chain and fulfilment technologies for Amazon.com. She melds these experiences into a totally new concept in the Hointer brand.

 http://youtu.be/O_G8m4FLk6g

Let's hear the story in her words.

Our purpose is to change the way people shop in physical stores. I think it is long overdue. We have made enormous progress in online in the last 15 years, but very little has been done in physical stores. I am actually more excited about physical stores than online, because our community is bigger.

Stand out

For many years I have been reinventing the e-commerce experience, and I thought it was the answer to everything. I was absolutely convinced that we can get online experience to a point where you don't need physical fulfilment at all, you just click and you are done. It was only when I encountered apparel that I started to think that it would be nearly impossible to create a phenomenal customer experience online for apparel, or some of the other products that we want to touch and feel. So I started to think about the perfect shopping experience, and that brought me back to the physical store.

It is very easy to say that you are going to be great at everything. But it's just impossible because you don't know what to focus on. I think just as important as thinking about who you are, is thinking about who you are not; what you are not going to be good at, because you cannot be great at everything. You cannot be great to your customers, to your employees, to your suppliers, to your shareholders and to the community. So you need to decide who is your primary focus, whom do you care most about, and what is your primary purpose? After that, everything becomes very simple. It's not that you physically want to suck at some things; it's just that you prioritize them below other areas, so they are not your strengths.

Distinctive customer experience

We put the customer experience above all. For us, employees are definitely secondary, and we all know that. Let me give you an example. If it is midnight and we just realized that we missed a customer order, the question is do we wait until the morning, or is one of our employees going to put it in his or her car and deliver it? We consciously make a decision that for us the customer experience is the most important priority, so yes, we will do things like that.

Also, what we don't do is put technology first. We actually don't think about technology at all, even though we are a technology company. We first think about the experience. How do we really want our customers to shop? What do we want to happen when you come in? How do you want to search for your products? Where do you need information about a product? What is the easiest way to request a different size? So we write down how we want the experience to be, and then we try to make it happen through various means. It can be technology, it can be the process, it can be employees, and it can be even be via robots. It can be whatever it needs to be, but it's definitely not the technology.

Continuous innovation

We try to make sure that our mobile experience looks and feels very much like our in-store experience. Our in-store actually looks a bit like the website, so when you tap an item when you are in store, you get information and you get pictures, you get exactly the same thing when you shop from home. Then we try to make sure that when you shop in the store, we learn as much

Image 5.3 The Hointer retail experience

from your shopping experience as possible. When you shop from home using your mobile experience, we use that information. For example, we show all the items that you viewed in store, those that you liked and those that you didn't so you can recall your experience. If you are trying to buy items online that you already tried in the store in the past and didn't like, we will remind you of that.

We continuously experiment with our displays; it is part of our innovation. We make sure it's easy for customers to look at displays, but what we try to do is make displays disappear so that customers really, really focus on the product. So when customers walk around, that's what they see. They don't really see displays, because they are so minimalistic. If you are a customer your focus is to buy the product, you don't have to look at the display. So, you want to see every detail of the product.

Infectious communication

We try to pool customer feedback on the product, and provide that to our customers. I think the reason it is very important is because when you are in a store as a customer, you have an experience with the product as it is now, but you don't know what is going to happen with it in three months from now, and customer feedback frequently gives you that. It tells you not only what the product is like now, but also how it has performed. So we are trying to get customer feedback online and make that available to customers in store. When you type in a product, you land on a product page and it gives you the information from the manufacturer but it also gives you feedback from other customers. You use the information in very different ways because you want the manufacturer to tell you what the product is made of, but you really want customers to tell you how it will perform a month from now.

Then we went even further and we started to integrate the customer feedback with social media. So for example when we added the 'Prince Harry' range, we added the most frequently pinned image to our product page, and for our docker pants, the most frequently pinned image by the customer community was Prince Harry wearing the product. The results were phenomenal. From being one of the least frequently tried products in the store it became the most frequently tried, literally overnight. Everybody wanted to try it, so I think the connection with social media in a physical store is very, very important because when I pick product images to show, I could be very wrong, but crowdsourcing the most relevant images works phenomenally well. We continue to double down on that, because it worked so well for us. We are spending more and more time trying to figure out the smart way to integrate social media content with our physical store experience.

Our purpose is not to sell jeans or groceries; our purpose is to change the way people shop. So for us, the fastest way to change the way people shop is to create the largest possible community of retailers who are innovating with us and using our technology. So, that is our business model.

Stand out – a summary

So what can we learn from these examples about how to *stand out*?

1 *Purpose driven*: you have to have a crystal-clear vision of your purpose and drive this through your customer experience ensuring that everything is aligned with it. Hointer is an example of a brand with a big idea.

2 *Purposeful leadership*: leaders have to 'walk the talk' if they are to make the tough strategic choices and appropriate investment in the experience, and also the conviction to instil the culture to deliver it. O2 did this by channelling investment to those areas that the customers valued most.

3 *Decide where to over-index your customer experience*: this is so that you create pleasure peaks associated with your brand promise. Making savings at those touchpoints that matter less to your customers or your differentiation can fund these. Lush did this by saving on packaging to spend more on ingredients and the store experience.

4 *Distinctive customer experience*: people do not buy Innocent
smoothies simply because of the woollen hats; Lush is not the most
highly recommended retailer simply because it doesn't use packaging;
Metro Bank providing dog bowls in the branches is not the reason that
people bank there; customers do not choose to stay in Best Western
purely because of their stories; consumers do not flock to Burberry
because of their fitting rooms, but these are the things that they
became famous for. All of these things are hallmarks of the brand and
a manifestation of their purpose. They serve to dramatize the
experience just as IKEA's inconvenient self-assembly reinforces the
consumer perception that what they are paying for is well-designed
furniture at a low price point.

5 *Ensure that the brand experience is consistent across all channels*:
so that irrespective of how the customer chooses to interact with you,
the hallmarks and their perception of the brand are the same, and the
experience they deliver is just as good. This requires a consistent tone
of voice and a single view of the customer across all channels. Best
Western ensured that the 'personality experience' was delivered
across all media.

Having looked at the elements of stand out, infectious communication, distinctive customer experience and continuous innovation, let's illustrate all of
these principles with a couple of example brands that have embraced most
of them.

We wrote a book a few years ago called *See, Feel, Think, Do: The power
of instinct in business* in which we argued that business was becoming too
formulaic, too left brain, too analytical and that it needed to move back to
being more visionary, right brain and instinctive. Tim Wade touched on this
when he spoke about Best Western and the 'personality experience'. Let's
return to our other hotel example – citizenM that we introduced in Part One.

Whereas Best Western has its origins in the United States – is large, long-
standing and has many old, individually owned properties – CitizenM is
Amsterdam based and is small, young and innovative. So, two hotel brands
with very different business models. This book is written on the premise that
starting with your brand purpose (providing that it is unique) leads naturally
to creating a distinctive customer experience and a unique culture. Rattan
Chadra spoke passionately about his desire to create a new business model
for the hotel sector. But how do you go about translating that into a distinctive
customer experience so that you really stand out from competitors?

citizenM

Stand out

Let's hear directly from Robin Chadha, citizenMarketing.

We started by looking at the target audience. The people who like citizenM are people who are young at heart. They are very well informed. They have technology at their fingertips so they can compare prices very quickly. They know the value, say, of the dollar or euro or pound, and they are willing to pay for certain luxuries, but they are not willing to be taken for a ride.

We took a two-tier approach: first, what is their lifestyle? We were looking at other brands that they associate themselves with or the aspirational brands that they want to be associated with. And then, second, looking at them in terms of the hotel experience. What do they like? What frustrates them?

These people are contemporary travellers. They know how to book a flight online. They get their QR code so they don't need to print out the boarding pass. They carry hand luggage only. They are not going to pack their large-size shampoo or water bottle, because they know they are going to get stopped at security. So it's all about speed and efficiency for these people.

When it comes to their lifestyle, it's a little bit of mix and match. People want to spend their money on certain luxuries, but for other things they prefer to buy what is smart and efficient. I describe this social group in this way: 'They travel by train but drink champagne.'

Out of all that data came the idea of these mobile citizens. So we said: 'Let's actually name the brand after our target audience: citizenM.'

Stand out – infectious communication

Then we started looking at how to communicate with them. When we first launched in 2008, a lot of the social channels weren't really there. So we did a lot of communication through our own channels, such as our own website, to tell the story. We made a brand movie to show this big idea: why we were doing this; not how good we are or how cool our rooms are or our technology, but why there is a need for this. Why this hotel is for you.

Social content is used to communicate why you should book citizenM. Genuine reviews from guests who have actually stayed with us are pulled in from TripAdvisor. We also have our citizenMag that is based on the target customer's lifestyle and what is relevant content for these people when they stay in different cities. What do they do there? Where do they eat? Where do they drink? Where do they go for a morning run? What is a cool little trail that only the locals would know? More and more people want this kind of local experience when they travel. We have customers who are contributors to citizenMag from all around the world; it's a platform for our customers to share.

The way that we usually run campaigns is to start with a teaser, often on Facebook, to engage with people. For example, when we came to New York, we had a campaign called: 'Letters to Locals'. We wrote a letter to famous New Yorkers in a very kind of naive way: we wrote to Andy Warhol, to Donald Trump, to JayZ. One of the letters was to Woody Allen asking him to make a little promotional film for our new hotel in Times Square: 'Something along the lines of your most famous film – Manhattan, not Antz.'

We're shooting a video with a very famous stop-animation artist called Pez who is making a one-minute movie for us about affordable luxury. He usually averages about 1 million hits per video. So we're doing a lot of things online just to get the buzz going. And it's measurable. That's the nice thing about online. I'd rather invest in that than putting a big billboard on Times Square, because how do you measure the impact of that?

Stand out – distinctive customer experience

We thought long and hard about our marketing communication: how do we advertise? How do we communicate? We came up with the idea of a tone of voice that is about communicating directly: 'citizenM says'. Our citizenM sayings are very, very strong and we use that as the basis for our communication platform. We came up with an idea to use traditional hotel clichés and

Image 5.4 citizenM marketing communication

exaggerate them to our benefit. In London our main tagline was: 'London, you look like you need a new place to sleep.' We also had taglines like: 'citizenM says: Death to the trouser press,' or, 'citizenM says: 'Why pay for bits of a hotel you don't need?' Then we pushed the boundaries a little bit more, so one said: 'citizenM says: Stay in a hotel that is 400 metres from here and a million miles from the Hilton.'

We rented a stretch limo in New York and had a huge poster stuck on the side that said: 'Luxury isn't a long car; it's free Wi-Fi and free movies on demand.' Then we took the car and took pictures of it in front of the Marriott and the Sheraton. The Marriott got angry with us. We actually wanted to park the limo and get it towed away. We also got the classic luggage trolley that bellboys use, and we put branding on it saying: 'Luxury isn't a bellboy taking your luggage up to your room, it's fresh cappuccino and free Wi-Fi.' We took the trolley to the other hotels and took pictures of it in front of them. All of this created great content for our own social channels.

We think about the complete end-to-end customer experience. The customer has been inspired through awareness to come to our website. Then comes the critical decision moment: why should I book citizenM? So you need to provide justification. Why is this better for you than staying at the Sheraton or the Marriott or some other hotel? Then comes the actual booking moment: how easy is your booking process? What happens after booking? What should the pre-stay communication be like? For example: 'Thank you for booking with citizenM, we're looking forward to receiving you on this and this date. You're staying in London. By the way, did you know that the Tate Modern is showing an exhibition by Roy Lichtenstein? Click here for discounted tickets, brought to you by citizenM. Borough Market is serving fantastic burgers on Saturday, you should check it out.' Pre-stay communication is very important.

Then of course you have the actual experience of staying at the hotel. I think that we have this down pretty well. But what happens post-stay? You've checked out, we should communicate to you right away: 'Thank you for coming.' Maybe get some feedback. Write a review. Or give the guest a special promotion for the next time they come. Inform them about our up and coming hotels that are opening. That means the next time they don't need to come in through the awareness channel. They come in straight at the booking stage.

We need to be up to date on what is happening. To be very well informed about what is happening in industries such as art and fashion and media and technology. To be aware as to where the customers' preferences are shifting and where the trends are going. I always put myself in the shoes of the customer and I speak to people in different industries just to keep my fingers on the pulse of what is happening, Otherwise how do you stay on top of the trends? You need to be relevant for customers going forward otherwise you die. Let's put it this way, if we had simply recreated citizenM Schipol in New York, I'm not sure if it would really still be innovative because we have taken the brand further. And of course the technology has improved. Our check-in is faster. We have the tablets in the rooms. We now have digital art screens in New York.

We are continuing to define the brand as we progress: for example, I'm busy creating a sonic identity; we are also creating a citizenM olfactive identity. The whole olfactive brand exercise is very interesting. I found a company in New York called 1229 and spent the whole day with the 'nose'. I wanted her to really experience citizenM, so she stayed in London for one or two days, and I sat down with her and spoke to her about the brand and then we did the actual exercise of the scenting.

She told me, 'Before we start, I'm not a psychiatrist. Don't tell me about your childhood memories when you smell these smells, but I want your emotional reaction to these smells. Do you think the smell fits with citizenM, yes or no?' It's very difficult to do but within 20–25 minutes she started to make me smell things that made me say, 'Yes, this is citizenM!' Finally, she says, 'I know what citizenM smells like. It smells like this. Maybe a little lighter.' All I could say is, 'Yes, you're right.'

I think technology is the key to our future. Take the whole online experience. How to make that as easy as possible? I really believe in a one-click booking. That would be fantastic. I could just go to citizenM and click. Don't worry about payment.

What keeps us focused is staying true to the reason of why we are doing what we're doing. Don't deviate from that, because along the path there will be a lot of people who are going to tell you, 'You can't do that, you can't do this, it's not possible. It's never been done before.' But as long as you stay true to what you are trying to accomplish, you will get there.'

Stand out – continuous innovation

We spoke to Lennert de Jong, citizenCommercial.

Rattan has this vision of changing the industry, it was his sense of purpose that drove us to challenge how the hotel business operates. Our model is anchored in three core pillars: first, the way you construct a hotel, the cost of construction, your carbon footprint while doing it, the amount of ground you ask mother earth to supply to your building all have an impact. We've only done modular buildings. For example, in Bankside we had the first plough into the ground in July 2011 and we opened in June 2012. It was a fully finished hotel, on budget and delivered ahead of time. This efficiency creates a saving for the consumer, so for the same amount of money others spend on a budget hotel we can make a luxury hotel.

The second pillar is the labour. Again it's a consequence. If you construct a smaller building you have less space for an office for the hotel manager, for the assistant hotel manager, for the director of sales, director of marketing, reservations manager, the telephone team. The labour and the third pillar, the way you sell the hotel, work hand in hand.

We said we are going to run it like a Starbucks, whereby the hotel team delivers the experience to the guests. In order to do that we have to be, not the headquarters, but the support office, so what we need is to hire experts who can take away the burden of running the functions from the hotels. By having a hotel team that is purely focused on guest satisfaction you eliminate a lot of duplication.

The fact that you do things smarter in distribution leads to the fact that you have fewer people and lower costs. But the thing that makes us really different is the mentality of our people. Our hotel managers understand most the people component, what makes a good team, what is a bad team and what makes a good interaction with a guest versus a bad interaction with a guest. Our people are available to do everything and anything. They will never say, 'It's not my job.' If you say,' I want a ticket for the tram,' or, 'Can you get me a taxi,' they will never say, 'Oh, ask the concierge.'

The check-in at a normal hotel is nothing about providing a service; it is all about performing a process. We give the responsibility for the check-in process to you. The ambassador is standing next to you, he doesn't have a task to perform; he's just there to make sure you're okay and that you're happy. I think that frequent travellers don't experience the human touch very often. I travel a lot and I see when people are process oriented, and when people are people oriented. I get irritated when people are just process focused and they don't look at me like a person, or treat me as an individual.

The third pillar is my area, the distribution cost pillar, or the way we sell. If an operator has a hotel with 200 rooms they start selling a year in advance to reduce their risk, because the main risk with a hotel room is that you don't sell it. It's like fruit, if you haven't sold it in three days it starts to rot; in a hotel it's more extreme, if you haven't sold the room today it's gone, you don't get the opportunity to sell it again.

So what do hotels do? Let's say the hotel needs to achieve an average rate of €100 per room per night. They have promised the owners a rate of €100 and an occupancy of 75 per cent. So they start with airline crews; they contract long term with KLM for a very low price, let's say €60, then they sell to tour operators who contract a year out at a discounted rate also. Let's say they block a certain percentage of rooms at €70 for the tour operators. Then they approach the corporates; let's say Microsoft because they are around the corner from the hotel at the airport, and they contract for a certain volume at €90. And then the remainder is filled up with people who they call 'traditional transient business'. These are customers who make their individual purchase decisions, like you and me; they don't have a contract, and they go online or they call you directly to ask for a room rate. This is the cherry on the pie; this is where hotels make their money; this individual doesn't have purchasing power, he or she needs the room on this date and you have one. This is the marketplace that you see on booking.com and others. But in order to achieve your average €100 rate you need to charge this guest €140 to €150. I was checking in to the Novotel in Bankside in London just before we opened. I got a deal for £225 at their friends and family rate. Checking in next to me was a French couple with a child and they were paying £80 in total for the night; so that's kind of the discrepancy we're talking about – you pay more the closer you book to the stay.

We said we're not going to do business with airline crews, we're not going to do business with tour operators and we're not going to do fixed corporate rates – for two reasons. First, we did not want to have to compensate for this business by placing more costs on our most desired segment. That is not good for us at citizenM. Second, it's not good for the people we're really after, those people that make online purchases. So we took a gamble and said, we can do this, we can live without 50 per cent of the normal hotel business, and just target the other 50 per cent. But we won't compete at €140 or €150, we start at €100 and we stay in this middle area. We used to call this the 'affordable luxury gap'; if you look at that area between low quality/low price and high quality/high price, we really want to be delivering higher quality at a lower price. Guess what? This segment is also the most likely to review your performance online, on sites such as TripAdvisor. It also gives us flexibility in managing demand because we are not locked into advance contracts. If demand is very low because of a terrorist attack or a crisis or whatever we can change the rates. On any day we have an answer to the demand that is there; sometimes it's a lower price, sometimes it's a higher price.

It is my job to maximize the citizenM proposition and its revenue potential, but I cannot mess it up. What I mean by that is if I charge so much that you have the feeling that you didn't get a good deal. We have to say, this is the maximum I'm going to charge. There's an annual convention in Amsterdam in the second week of September and hotels will charge up to €600 or €700. Our rates will go up and down, but not to the extremes you see with a lot of other hotels. With us the swings in Amsterdam are between €89 and €199. At the same time we were one of the first to provide free Wi-Fi and free movies. It is about removing the things that irritate the customers.

The hotel industry has consolidated so much that it seems like every hotel company has eight sub-brands and they are all based around one thing, their loyalty programme. But the game is changing, people no longer rely on the Holiday Inn logo, for example, to know that the hotel is good and of a certain quality – technology enables the customer to see on their phone or device what is a good hotel and what is a bad hotel; I think that this transparency is catching the top five brands with their trousers around their ankles. They have not invested sufficiently in creating a distinctive customer experience, they have not invested in the staff; they've invested in a loyalty programme that is costing them a lot of money. I think there is an opportunity for a brand like citizenM. The more transparent and bigger the portals like booking.com and others get, the more helpful it is for us, because they expose everyone who is not delivering the value that we are trying to deliver. That's where our opportunity lies.

Part Three
Stand firm

So far in this book we have talked about the importance of *standing up*, through having a clear sense of purpose, and *standing out*, delivering that purpose through distinctive marketing and customer experience. The third element to being a purposeful organization is the ability to sustain itself over the long term. What we call *standing firm*. We think there are three elements to this: 1) possessing a 'cult-like culture'; 2) creating a distinctive employee experience; and 3) measuring both the employee and customer experience to fuel continued improvement. While 'cult-like culture' may sound a bit sinister we mean it in the most positive sense. If you think of those communities that are strongest and completely aligned around a common purpose you will find that they have internal cultures that are unique and serve to protect and sustain the organization.

Take organizations as different as the United States Marines Corps, Manchester United Football Club or Disney and you will find common characteristics: a strong sense of why they exist, shared heritage, clear values and how these require the members of that organization to behave. You can almost see a thread that weaves from the purpose to the values to the behaviour. And if you were an outsider looking in and observing the ways that these organizations and their people speak, dress and behave you might conclude that they are, indeed, a cult.

Every organization has a culture, for better or worse, just like every organization delivers a customer experience, for better or worse. What matters is that it is the one you intend and that it serves to sustain your differentiation. Some writers suggest that a strong culture inhibits innovation because it seeks to maintain the status quo and discourages fresh thinking: so-called 'group think'. Others argue that if the culture is one that rewards the right behaviour then the culture becomes self-renewing. We would agree with the latter point of view. For us, a 'cult-like' culture is one that can be defined in much the same way as a distinctive customer experience – 'consistent, intentional, differentiated and valuable' – valuable in this context meaning that it creates long-term value for the enterprise.

In Chapter 5 we saw how citizenM has created an innovative brand that is built around purpose. How is it sustaining this through its culture? What is the link between purpose, culture and behaviour? We asked Michael Levie, citizenM's chief operating officer (COO), to tell us:

'If I look at the culture and DNA of our organization today we operate under some very simple rules; it's one team, one vision and we have very clear defined roles so that everybody understands what their job is.

'This attitude represents itself in the dress code because we're not very official. It's basically, be comfortable. You're supposed to be yourself. At the ambassador level, they may have a little tattoo or a piercing, or whatever, that's perfectly fine. Through their uniform we want them to show their own character. In the support centre, language is very loose, the word 'f..k is exercised frequently, it's a very direct, very open, very cohesive culture and one that people are comfortable with.'

Hospitality is quite a formal industry in many ways. Most of the senior industry figures have been trained in the great hotel schools in Switzerland. Their dress and manners are impeccable. There is usually quite a strict code of conduct. The hierarchy is almost military-like in its formality and a junior housekeeper would feel very uncomfortable speaking openly to a general manager. It is highly unlikely that executives would even dream of addressing the CEO with expletives. If you stay in one of the grand hotels of Europe you will feel this conservative culture wrapped around you like an invisible but cosseting cloak. Ritz-Carlton's company motto of *'We are Ladies and Gentlemen serving Ladies and Gentlemen'* epitomizes this old-school approach to hospitality.

CitizenM is quite different. Its business model is different. The guests are different. The customer experience is different. Its people are different. And because of this it needs to have a culture that is aligned to sustain that difference. We are not advocating that other organizations follow the example of citizenM or, indeed, that citizenM's approach is correct and Ritz-Carlton's is wrong; quite the opposite in fact. We are suggesting that 'form follows function' and that the culture you create must be appropriate for your brand, target customers and desired experience. It must be cult-like in being consistent, intentional, different and valuable to your brand.

Chapter Six
Cult-like culture

One of the brands that we featured in our book *Bold: How to be brave in business and win* was Zappos, the online retailer. The brand has established an enviable reputation for being purpose-led (delivering happiness) and delivering a distinctive customer experience (to live and deliver WOW), but it also has a very distinctive culture. Tony Hsieh, CEO of Zappos, says:

> *'A company's culture and a company's brand are really just two sides of the same coin. Brand is just a lagging indicator of culture.'*

Hsieh has continued to embrace innovation and adopt new business models; his most recent is to reconceive the organization in order to create natural sustainability. The concept is called Holacracy. The word comes from the Greek meaning 'one part of a whole' and it takes a very different approach to organizational culture. Instead of organizing around functions it arrays the business around shared purpose. Hsieh took his inspiration from the way that cities evolve and reinvent themselves quite organically:

> *'We want Zappos to function more like a city and less like a top-down bureaucratic organization.'*

Creating the purposeful organization

We asked long-term Zappos employee Christa Foley to tell us about this new concept and how it was conceived.

Our purpose is to inspire the world by showing that it is possible to simultaneously deliver happiness to customers, employees, community, vendors and shareholders in a long-term sustainable way.

An example of this is that we moved to Las Vegas from San Francisco. We knew that as the company continued to grow we were going to need kind of a campus environment. Tony Hsieh made the decision to move us into downtown Las Vegas into the former City Hall. It was, frankly, a bit contentious initially, because the downtown Las Vegas area – at least at that time – was not the best place to go. So Tony asked, 'How do I make this environment the best that it can be for Zappos employees? How do I make it safe? How do I make it convenient in terms of dry cleaning services, great places to eat, and all the things you need to make a neighbourhood great?' From there the concept really snowballed.

One of the challenges that Zappos has faced as we have got bigger is the slowdown of innovation and entrepreneurship that many companies face as they grow larger. They tend to stagnate and slow down. Yet cities seem to remain agile and vibrant as they grow. So, in addition to wanting to make sure downtown Las Vegas was a good place for Zappos employees, Tony started to see an opportunity. 'If I can help this community to grow by integrating Zappos into the community it will help us to become more innovative and entrepreneurial too.'

There's a strong desire to make sure that we continue to embrace and drive change, which is one of our core values, but we're highlighting that even more now. One of the ways that we're seeking to embrace and drive change is the move towards Holacracy. This is a new way to structure your organization. It takes away titles and managers, and really, flattens the organization so that people focus on the work that you need to do and what the purpose is. One of the major goals is to allow people to surface what are called tensions, which doesn't have to be a negative thing. It could be 'I have a great idea that we can do on the website,' for example. The structure allows employees to surface these ideas, or tensions, and have them acted on really quickly. It is about the spirit of innovation and agility and entrepreneurship.

The organization is formed of a number of circles that function around a particular purpose. And every circle has an individual purpose that supports the overall Zappos purpose. One of the circles that I'm a part of is Zappos Insights (www.zapposinsights.com); our purpose is to help external groups learn about the Zappos culture and how it is used to run a successful business.

There are two different kinds of meetings that happen in Holacracy. You have what is called a 'tactical' meeting on a weekly basis, and then a 'governance' meeting every other week. Tactical meetings are where tensions are surfaced. So, every week there is an opportunity for anyone in the group to bring up a tension. It doesn't mean you have to wait for a meeting, of course, you can do that via e-mail, or you can just walk up to someone, just like you would normally. But this gives everyone an opportunity every week to suggest ideas. Governance meetings are more about the work of the circle and the roles and accountabilities of the circle and the members.

Holacracy allows every single person in the organization to contribute to innovation. What we saw very quickly, within the first month, and we continue to see it every week, is the speed and agility with which we are able to move and shift direction.

I'll give you an example using the circle that I'm in. We initially were part of what was traditionally the HR group, but pretty quickly realized through these meetings that our work didn't really align directly with, or support, what HR was doing. And, so, I decided that I wanted to move our circle under a different circle, called 'Community'. If you think about moving a unit from a larger department into a completely different department at a typical organization, it would probably take four to five months of conversations to reach a consensus and a decision, whereas in Holacracy within 10 minutes of the meeting the move was made.

Leaders and managers no longer exist in Holacracy, because authority gets distributed across the entire organization. Each circle does have what is called a lead link, and they have very specific responsibilities, but they are not traditional manager responsibilities. They do get to decide who fills a role or decide if someone should be removed from a role, and they are responsible for the budget. But outside that, they are not responsible for performance management; they are not responsible for progression; it is really just about enacting the purpose of the circle.

The great thing about these changes is that they are about bettering our business and achieving our purpose.

Only time will tell if Holacracy is successful. It certainly has both advocates and its critics as you can read here:

http://qz.com/317918/holacracy-at-zappos-its-either-the-future-of-management-or-a-social-experiment-gone-awry/

It will be fascinating to see if an organization intentionally and entirely structured around purpose is a viable option for other companies.

Whilst the Zappos approach is unique, its desire to create a strong culture is not. One of the other brands we featured in our book *Bold: How to be brave in business and win* is the Geek Squad, the technology repair company. They promise to '*Save your ass*' and this irreverent approach is reflected in their language, their job titles (technicians are called 'Special Agents') and their uniforms. Even the 700 or so employees that work at 'Geek Squad City', the repair facility located in Louisville, Kentucky, wear the Geek Squad uniform every day although they never see a customer. Robert Stephens, the Geek Squad founder, has this to say:

> '*If the DNA is protected properly as the organization grows, it carries a copy of itself in every person. That's why it is so important to have a strong point of view, to have a clear vision that is unambiguous in its language, so that if competitors copy you, it's very clear whose DNA they've copied.*'

So the culture is carefully designed to reinforce what the brand DNA is in the minds of its employees and its customers.

Stephens's phrase '*it carries a copy of itself in every person*' is very interesting. This is Holacracy taken down to the level of the individual.

Chapter Seven
Distinctive employee experience

We have said that culture is a vital ingredient to sustaining success, but how do you create and then sustain the culture? The answer is through creating an employee experience that is a mirror for the customer experience. Ronan Dunne, the CEO of O2, sums this up well by saying:

> *'If you cannot turn your employees into fans there's no way that you will turn customers into fans.'*

Turn your employees into fans

We have found in our own research that there is about an 85 per cent correlation between the way that your employees think about your brand and the way that your customers do. It follows, then, that you need to make your employees your fans too.

Ronan Dunne's remark raises another interesting point – and that is the alignment between the kind of people your employees and your customers are. It is extremely difficult for employees to relate to customers from a completely different demographic and vice versa. You cannot always mirror these two groups, of course, particularly when you have lower-paid retail staff selling to high-net-worth customers who are probably considerably older. But if you can seek to hire people who relate to both your customers and the product you sell, it can be very powerful. Patagonia is a wonderful example of this. Its employees are passionate advocates of adventure travel who use the brand's products. These Patagonia ambassadors test the products and write about them in 'Notes from the field'.

  http://www.patagonia.com/eu/enPL/ambassadors

Ann Pickering, the HR director for O2, uses the same concept when hiring people:

> *'Take that cadre of people we call "digital natives" They have grown up with the internet; they have grown up with smartphones; they don't know what went before, that's just the way they've grown up, and they're our future. They are our future for O2 too because that's what our customer base is looking like now.*

'So we brought in these people who have changed our demographics. Our age profile now across the company is around about 40 per cent under 30. The average age used to be about 43. They learn differently, they crowdsource, they use websites and get their information in a very different way. So bringing them in and asking them to challenge the way we do things has really made a big difference, because they just think completely differently.'

Many organizations participate in surveys like 'Great Place to Work' and benchmark themselves very seriously against the other brands in the database.

http://www.greatplacetowork.net/home

We are strong advocates of this because we believe that engaged employees make for strong companies. However, having said this, as we have already stated, strong brands have unique cultures and whilst there are many generic attributes that describe a great employee experience – trust, pride, enjoyable work, among others – the mix will vary from brand to brand. Similarly, what employees value can vary from organization to organization depending on their generation, the nature of the industry and the brand. For example, Patagonia employees value the time and opportunity for adventure, Topshop sales advisors value their ability to buy great fashion at a discount, and Apple employees probably enjoy getting hands-on with the latest technology. For this reason, our Employee Experience Survey is built around our 'Organizational Alignment Model' (see the *On Purpose* toolkit). This measures both importance and performance of a number of attributes and compares the employee experience against what they value and what the organization is striving to achieve, allowing the context to inform the findings.

As we said earlier, Ritz-Carlton is a very different place to work than citizenM. It attracts different people, yet both provide great experiences. So let's hear from Michael Levie, citizenM's COO, as to how they create and sustain the culture through aligning the employee experience.

Having a strong purpose or being innovative is not enough; it's also about the people around you. So we have a very strict casting and immersion programme. You can build a hotel but no matter how pretty or nice it is, if it hasn't got a pumping heart it isn't going to live. We have found through our initial casting and immersion programme how to make the hotel come alive, and then, by having the right manager, make sure we sustain it.

Find the right people

Casting starts with social media; we usually gather a couple of hundred CVs, but it can be up to 800 sometimes. We filter this to the people who have done fun things or the people who look fun; down to 150 to 200 say and we invite those people for a casting day, which is a four-and-a-half-hour interview. We schedule this on a Saturday or a Sunday, which is a real shocker to people, and so out of those 150 to 200 that we invite we end up with 75 to 85 people on the casting day itself. As they come in, we take a photograph of them and then offer them great coffee and pastries. For the first 30 to 45 minutes we do nothing other than observe them. If we have chosen the right people then that first session becomes like a big club with people chatting to each other.

Then I welcome them. I explain who we are as a company and what it is that they are being interviewed for, and then we divide them up into four teams. The first team do one-on-one blind tasting. Imagine you and I have never met. You are blindfolded and I'm your partner and my job is to shove food into your mouth to taste. We've got to figure out real fast how we will work together! We observe that to see how fast they adapt, who is taking the lead, who is going first; you observe a lot of subliminal signals. The second test is making a collage with five people. It's an odd number to make a collage and so we look at teamwork; who uses their 'elbow' to make a point, who pulls in the quieter people, that type of thing.

Then they are put into groups of 15 for the third exercise, which is an 'elevator pitch'. In 30 seconds, using the metaphor of an animal or an object, they have to say 'who they are'. And the last exercise, once again in groups of 15, is to share with the group who their hero is, and why. So we observe the different social settings and in-between we have had coffee breaks and at the end we have a big sushi lunch; really an over-the-top lunch that they are probably not used to. Then I wrap up, I tell them: 'We're not making a judgement on who you are, or what you stand for, or how good you are, it's basically more of an alignment puzzle. We are looking for certain people, and the reason for these workshops is to align, as best as possible, the people who we feel will do well in our environment, and that we, as an environment, will do well for them.' Usually we have to push them out of the door by this stage!

The moment that they leave we lay out all the photographs we took to remind ourselves of the individuals and then there is a discussion about what they did well, what they did not do so well and then we come to a consensus. The team that we have selected are called that same afternoon and they are set up within the next three days for final interviews and then we hire them; the others are called and thanked for their interest. I think it is important that those who are rejected know it that same afternoon. As cruel as it sounds it is better to cut it short than to drag it out.

In-between the casting day and their hiring we get them on our premises with us. For example, we invite the new cast member, or the team, for a fun evening, and the purpose is just to meet each other. We go to a nice restaurant, usually a little aspirational that they perhaps couldn't afford themselves, and we have drinks and food. There's no speech; there's no formal welcome; there's just a high-five and a chance to spend time with them.

Start people in the right way

When we start the immersion programme it is a very serious intense first week where we get the culture across. That's when we introduce citizenM itself. Rattan talks about the brand and who we are and then I go into guest service and guest satisfaction. So the most important things are immediately nailed. We then get into the fact that, as ambassadors, they represent the company. We tell them we hired them because they are positive, spirited people, and what they need to do with that. The one thing that I don't care about is how 'good' they are technically; if they do not gel in our organization then it's wasted energy.

Because of the casting approach and resource elasticity that is achieved through this programme we are able to build volume quickly, and whether we do it in the United States, the UK, in Holland or in France, we see consistency in the performance of our hotels in outranking others in service because of our people.

Hire for DNA not MBA

Hiring the right people for your culture is vital. Robert Stephens said, 'I hire for the customer experience I want.' We have a saying when we advise clients: 'hire for DNA not MBA'. By this we mean find the people who fit your culture rather than the best qualified or most experienced candidate. You can train someone in what they don't know but it is much harder to get them to behave in a way that is alien to their personality.

We were speaking at a large financial services conference and asked the delegates to raise their hands if they provided customer service training to their people. All the hands went up. We then asked them to keep their hands raised if they felt their organization delivered a distinctive customer experience. Almost all of the hands were lowered. The point is that most organizations deliver generic service training, often delivered by the same training consultancies. No surprise, then, that the experience the customer gets is at best generic. When we work with clients we design what we call 'Branded Customer Experience Training'. In other words, training that has the purpose, brand promise and customer experience woven throughout it like a red thread.

Engage and inspire your people to deliver your customer experience 'on purpose' through branded experience training

Vanessa Hamilton has worked with Smith+co for 15 years and has designed branded experience training for many of the world's leading brands and so she has a definite point of view on what works and what doesn't.

After 15 years in the customer experience business, there is still one sentence that makes me want to run for the hills: 'We need a service excellence programme for our front-line staff.' You don't! You've probably implemented many perfectly good 'service excellence' programmes in the past. Any team member who has been in your company longer than 10 years might recall three or more of them. What does that tell you about how well they have stuck? About the impact they had? And about the difference they have made to your business?

That's because generic service training doesn't connect your people to your brand. It doesn't help them to understand what your brand stands for – and why that matters. It doesn't help them to explore how they can really bring your brand to life for customers through their actions and behaviours.

If you want your people to deliver a meaningful and valuable experience for your customers – one that differentiates your brand from your competitors and drives customer loyalty – you have to create a branded experience for them too. That starts with being intentional in connecting your people with your brand purpose. At the heart of every brand is a compelling story that people want to be part of. That's why every customer experience communication or training that you deliver should be able to answer – and keep answering – these three questions:

- *Why is this important?*
- *How will it benefit our company and me?*
- *What do I need to do additionally or differently in my role?*

Keeping these questions in mind throughout your training design process ensures everyone in your organization hears a clear, simple and joined-up message, and knows where and how they can play a valuable part in your brand's evolving story.

If you want to create a differentiated experience, create differentiated training. Our approach to branded experience training is that it:

- *Starts with ensuring your people understand, in depth, what your target customers expect and the value from your brand, what your brand promises to customers about the experience they can expect and what this requires from the people who deliver it.*

- *Engages your front-line teams in defining and designing the skills and knowledge needed to deliver your brand – they are closest to the customer in every sense and best placed to know what exactly your customers want. If new behaviours are to stick and become 'how we do things here', your people need to have a voice and a role in defining them.*

- *Is training created with people for people – not training done to people. Branded experience training is not about creating scripts for your people or prescribing exact behaviours for every single customer interaction. It is about freedom within a framework. Being 'tight' on what your brand stands for, and the customer experience you wish to create, but 'loose' in execution. It is about trusting individual staff members to use their initiative and do what it takes to satisfy each individual customer.*

- *Involves managers in 'owning' brand delivery and sustaining success. Managers – not HR and not your training team – are ultimately accountable for the customer experience that is delivered in their shop, branch, bank, site, hotel etc. Therefore, they are responsible for creating the workplace conditions for success through their leadership attitude and behaviours.*

- *Links recruitment, performance management and measurement directly to the customer experience you want to deliver – so you are hiring, developing, measuring and recognizing people who live your brand; and you're doing so 'on purpose'.*

This last item is a particular sticking point for many companies. They want their people to be welcoming to customers, to take time to understand their needs, to add value to customers through advice and recommendation and to make them feel positively about your company and what it stands for... but they still want to target and measure them on units per transaction (UPT), average transaction value (ATV), mix, call processing etc.

Purposeful brands approach this differently. They hire for attitude, train for skill and motivate for performance. I always remember a wonderful phrase that one of our clients used to describe their philosophy for hiring store associates: 'We want people with a bit of the barmaid about them!' This is referring to the ability of bar staff generally to make customers feel warmly welcomed into a convivial environment and to talk with them with a natural ease.

Purposeful brands, then, empower their people with the skills, information, authority and time to serve the customer well and then let them prove they can! When you demonstrate that you trust people – and equip and support them to do their jobs – they usually surprise you by just how much they can do.

What you get is real commitment to, and ownership of, the customer experience – and customer satisfaction, loyalty and profitable growth flow from that.

As Vanessa says, purposeful brands hire for attitude, train for skill and motivate for performance. We have discussed hiring and training so let's now turn to motivating.

Motivation is a poorly understood concept

One of our favourite TedTalks is Dan Pink's brilliant 18-minute speech, 'The Puzzle of Motivation'.

 http://www.ted.com/talks/dan_pink_on_motivation

Dan Pink makes the point that the things that most organizations believe motivate high performance are extrinsic or contingent rewards, incentives, bonuses etc. It turns out that they are much less powerful than we think. To really motivate high performance we need to use intrinsic rewards, things that are driven more by the satisfaction of the task itself. The three most powerful elements are: autonomy, mastery and purpose. Autonomy is the desire to direct our own actions; mastery is the desire to become better at what we do and purpose is doing whatever it is because it matters.

There is no greater proof of this than to motivate people to go to extraordinary lengths to provide an incredible customer experience for no pay at all.

But that is exactly what Linda Moir did as Director of Spectator Services for the London 2012 Olympic Games. The London Olympics were successful on so many fronts but one of the things most often referred to were the amazing 'games makers', that army of cheerful volunteers who created such a welcoming and distinctive experience. Linda was formerly Director of Customer Experience for Virgin Atlantic and so has customer experience in her blood, but how was she to create that kind of experience when the service providers were a group of unpaid and unskilled amateurs?

Motivating the greatest team on earth

The London 2012 Olympic and Paralympic Games saw one of the largest peacetime deployments of people the world has seen, from the front-of-house team who created the conditions for the athletes to perform to the legions of teams who worked away from the action ensuring that the London Tube ran smoothly. Whilst years in the planning, the Olympics were only fully operational for just over three weeks so there was little time for trial and error or for first-day problems. Teams simply had to come together across functions, organizations and countries to deliver the greatest show on earth, knowing that an estimated audience of 900 million people worldwide would be tuning in.

So how did this army of about 250,000 people, including around 70,000 volunteers, come together to be the games makers that made the London games one of the most iconic and memorable in history? The Spectator Services Team alone, who hosted over 9 million spectators at 36 competition venues, comprised 15,000 volunteers and 6,000 contracted safety stewards. Whilst the numbers were vast, the principles underlying the entire games maker experience were the same simple principles that leading service organizations apply to encourage passion and advocacy amongst their teams. Whilst I had never managed volunteers I had managed people before and took some advice from the team who hosted the Sydney Olympics and Paralympics of 2000. The Sydney team proudly talked about their high levels of volunteer engagement and retention. Our London games volunteers were at the heart of our operation so their motivation – and retaining them for the full length of the games – was a very high priority. The Sydney team said there were three simple golden rules to volunteer engagement and these 'rules' apply as much in the commercial world as in the games. Every step of the volunteer journey was mapped with the same care as the customer's journey:

- *Rule 1 – keep people busy*
  Our London volunteers made extraordinary efforts to get to their venues in time for the early starts and late finishes that were required. Many of them stayed with friends, camped or took a multitude of night buses to get there on time. Having made such Herculean efforts we made sure in the spectator services team that they were fully utilized. Not having enough to do is frankly boring and makes the day go slowly. So we looked carefully at our numbers and made sure we didn't overstaff.

- *Rule 2 – keep people rotated*
  We made the strategic choice to train our volunteers on a wide variety of tasks so that we could make sure that they had a varied and interesting experience. The spectator services team all commented that they really enjoyed the variety and the learning that the broad job roles offered. We made sure that each venue had a staffing manager whose job was to make sure the games makers had a rich and rewarding experience. One of the greatest lessons for me was never to underestimate the capacity and appetite of people from every background to learn. It was inspiring to see people start nervously then grow and develop and have fun with our customers.

- *Rule 3 – recognize people and their needs*
  Previous games had given their volunteers small 'shift gifts' as tokens of recognition. London also awarded small pin badges to games makers – bronze for their first shift, silver for half their shifts then gold when they completed all their rostered shifts. The usually reserved Brits wore their pins with pride and these are still treasured today. These 'low-cost high-value' gifts represented being part of a once-in-a-lifetime event and could be seen worn by the whole London team including the armed forces, the police, Transport for London staff as well as the games makers. However, these gifts alone were not the key in building real engagement; that came from the 'intrinsic' reward: the emotional connections that made this diverse group of people proud to be games makers. The behaviour of the front-line leaders was crucial in building this. All leaders from the most senior manager at the venue to the volunteer team leader were briefed on the style of leadership that was based on recognition. Tasks had to be completed but part of the leader's day job was to make sure they knew their teams by name, regularly stopped and thanked them for their contribution and asked them for their observations on what could be

Image 7.1 The London 2012 closing ceremony

done better. This is what games makers still talk about today, how they felt a valued part of the team.

At the closing ceremony when Seb Coe thanked the games makers the audience spontaneously stood and cheered non-stop for over 10 minutes – the ultimate emotional recognition.

How did they know what to do?

I am often asked how we got the games makers to behave in a way that outperformed everyone's expectations, probably including their own. The answer again is simple: we gave the volunteers as much confidence as possible by training them in the tasks they would be asked to perform, then described a vision of 'hosting' our games in a way that gave them huge scope to bring their personalities to work and have fun with our 9 million spectators. By defining the 'why' and the 'what' but not the 'how', each games maker brought their own ideas to the games as to how to create memories for visitors from around the world. Spontaneous actions such as singing songs, making up rap rhymes, high-fiving the kids, creating finish lines with toilet paper for children's running races – none of these were in any training manual. This came from a truly engaged team who just knew what was the right thing to do to make sure everyone had a fun and memorable day.

Too often service organizations try to control every aspect of the relationship with customers by over-scripting every detailed interaction. This takes *all spontaneity and humanity away from the people who are delivering the experience, as well as delivering a robotic experience for customers.*

I am enormously proud of the London games makers who smashed the belief that British people can't deliver brilliant and memorable customer service.

It is evident from Linda's example that autonomy, mastery and purpose were front and centre in the philosophy used to manage the games makers. She also used the principle of 'loose/tight' to allow the games makers the freedom to behave in a way that allowed their personalities to communicate to the spectators. The result was an unprecedented standing ovation lasting over 10 minutes. Not all customer experiences are quite as emotional or measured in such a dramatic way. But measured they must be.

Autonomy, mastery and purpose are also very evident in our next example. Timpson is a family-owned business that was founded in Manchester, England in 1865 to make and repair boots. It is now run by the fifth generation of the family. It is not high-tech like Zappos; in fact it is so anti-tech that the chairman dumped all of their expensive electronic point of sale (EPOS) systems in a skip ('*dumpster*' to American readers). Nor is it glamorous like the Olympics with the focus on celebrity athletes. It has a policy of recruiting from prisons, but it exhibits many of the same characteristics we have observed in our purposeful brands. Yet whereas Zappos starts with the customer and works back, Timpson starts with the employee.

Timpson

Timpson is a family-owned, fiercely independent and proudly maverick high-street retailer. For over 100 years, the company has made, sold or repaired shoes. In the mid-1980s, as trainers started coming onto the market, the shoe-repair business declined by 25 per cent because people don't repair trainers. That was having a big hit on its profitability so it undertook a strategic review and asked how it could use its small but conveniently located shops with their skilled employees to meet an unmet customer need. The answer was cutting keys. In 1986 that service was worth about £500,000; it is now worth about £40 million. Today, Timpson offers shoe repair, key cutting, engraving, photo processing and watch repairs through its 1,350 stores. All of these are convenience-based services that are low cost but high value for customers and performed by well-trained, customer-focused people.

Timpson's purpose is to provide 'great service by great people' and it is renowned for its 'upside-down management' philosophy that pushes as much control as possible to the people running the shops. It champions a culture in which store managers set prices, order the stock and have huge scope to provide excellent customer service. They have created a level of employee engagement that has made Timpson one of the best companies to work for again and again – placed in the Top 10 of the *Sunday Times* 100 Best Companies to Work For awards every year they have entered.

Timpson is also renowned for its philanthropy and has aligned the business's drive for profitability and excellence with its social mission. It is the UK's most active recruiter of people from prison. At first sight this seems a strange policy for a customer-centric organization that places as much power as possible in the hands of its people. But as we shall see, this is all part of the DNA.

Given that Timpson is about upside-down management, we decided we would start the case study with one of the most important people in the business: one of the branch managers, and leave the chairman until last, which is exactly the way he would wish it.

Michael Carter – Timpson shop manager, Barnes High Street

I've worked in total around 25 years for Timpson. It's a very special company. Everything is done in front of the customer. I say that this shop is my theatre, I am the actor and my customers are the audience. The shoe repairs, the watch repairs, key cutting are all done in the front of my store – there's no back space out of sight of the customers where things get done.

The emphasis at Timpson is doing a proper job for the customer. We work very quickly but there's no rush to get it out. We don't churn out stuff. It has to be perfect for the customer. That's how you're taught at Timpson. We get excellent training and it's ongoing. We have to reach certain levels of expertise in all the core services we offer (shoe repairs, watch repairs, key cutting, engraving etc). It's very demanding as far as quality is concerned. Everyone who is a manager is good but of course there are some superstars and they eventually become area managers. My area manager is Sid Hubbard. He is amazing. He's not just good at the job; he's great with people. That is the most important thing about Timpson. The way they treat people – customers and Timpson people. In some companies, if you got something wrong you would be told off or worse. That does not happen at Timpson. If you have got something wrong, if there is a problem, they teach you how to fix it. They'll sit down and say 'Okay, how did this problem happen, how can we fix it?'

I look after the running of the shop, like any shop owner. I have a set wage and then, depending on how much business I am doing that week, there is a weekly bonus, It's based on a simple formula that you can calculate yourself:

it's around 15 per cent of the value of transactions over a certain limit. Almost every week I get a bonus, and in busy times such as the run-up to Christmas it can be quite substantial.

And as I say, this is my store; they leave me to get on with it. I love the interaction with customers. Of course you can get difficult customers from time to time but it's my challenge to turn them round and we never quibble – if I've not fixed something properly, I fix it again for free; or if something is going to take me no time to fix, I might not charge at all. It's my decision. That's what I mean by having fun here. You are taught to do a good job, have fun and help people.

Lee Nicholls, regional manager

Rain is good for us, because that means the holes in the shoes will be found! I think most of our purchasers that come into our branches are grudge purchasers, you know, it's not something you want to spend your money on, getting your shoes repaired, or getting a spare key. You don't actually get anything new for your money that you look forward to. It's always something that you've got to do, because you've got a hole in your shoe.

As a result, the customer tends to come in not overly happy, so if you can put a bit of personality into the transaction, and make the customer think what a nice person, then I think that's half the battle won. There are so many different personalities in the business, and they all attack it from a different point of view. Some are big and bold and bouncy, some are very professional, it's just down to the individual, but they've got to have a bit of personality. I think that's what makes it work.

We drum home the personality bit for the area managers and the area teams. You know, it's about that person. If someone turns up for an interview in jeans and a T-shirt, that doesn't matter. It depends how that person is. If that person seems to have a personality, seems bright and bubbly, and basically their answers to questions are a default 'yes', then that's the person we want. There isn't a mandate that it has to be a certain type of person, or a certain type of service, but it's got to be great service.

I spend a lot of time out in the field, watching the customers as they come in and go out. We use mystery shoppers, with a little hidden camera. Then we see how the colleagues are serving, which is great, because nine times out of ten, if you get feedback that's not good, the area manager will sit down with that particular colleague and show them the video footage, and 99.9 per cent of the time the colleague will say 'I can't believe I've just been like that.' Then the area manager will go and see the individual colleague and they have a discussion about what went wrong and what we can do better.

We're quite old-fashioned, in a way. We don't advertise, it's just word of mouth and repeat business. Our market is the people who actually come in the door. And that person has got a husband or wife, son, daughter, cousin. So if we make that one customer happy, then word spreads...

The turnover at the branches reflects the way the customers are being treated, because a lot of the big-turnover shops are getting repeat business all the time. If we've got a shop that has poor performance, the chances are that the customer service is probably not right. The loyalty comes down to the individual in the branch. When I started with Timpson I went in at branch level, and I built my branch through repeat business. So it is all about that particular colleague, and their attitude towards customers.

Unfortunately, you can't please all the people all the time: I accept that. I say to the guys in the shops that if a certain customer is having a bad day, it doesn't matter what happens to that customer, they are still going to have a bad day. We can do nothing to change their personal life. So the only thing you can do is be nice to that customer for that five-minute transaction.

We do a Friday ring around: the area manager will contact each branch on their area to discuss turnover for the week, what's up, what's down, any problems for the week. They then fill in a figure sheet, it's like a Friday flash figure, if you like. They then send their complete sheet to me, and then I will just ring back the area managers if there's one that's particularly down. We'll have a discussion on what's gone wrong. And then that sheet, in turn, goes to Timpson House. If we've got a shop at the end of the year that's in a minus from the previous year, we need to go and investigate and see what the problem is.

It's an old-fashioned bit of paper that gets sent out, and then it gets sent back. We like paper. If I had my way I think we'd have an abacus, to be honest.

We encourage the branches to do what they want. If they want to have a special key-cutting deal this week, fine, go for it. If they want to do a special window display, or they want to contact the local council, or the local cub group, fine. They can do whatever they want to do, whenever they want to do it. Then their area manager will evaluate with them how well it's working or not. If it works, tell us. If it doesn't, let's put it back as it was.

I think the success of the company is because we let people get on with their business. They know best. The guy who runs things in Bournemouth will know the town far better than I ever will, so we have to empower that colleague to make the decision for his branch.

It's the nearest that you are going to get to having your own business without having your own business. And when they are successful, you feel that you are visiting their very own shop. They make it their own, they've got their own little quirky ways.

That same philosophy reflects all the way through the company. I run a region that consists of eight areas, and just over 300 shops. And I get the same freedom as a colleague would in a branch. James Timpson, the managing director, will ask me to go and do a job, and he'll trust me to do it my way.

If James, or John Timpson, the chairman, see an idea, they will then encourage that colleague to have a go. John spends most of his time visiting shops doing exactly that. He'll go in and ask the colleague 'How are you? Is there anything we need to do for you? Can we help you?'

It's just a common-sense approach. It's not complicated. The two major things we focus on are: you need to look the part, and put the money in the till. So, look the part – and everything else is up to you. Our brand promise is all to do with service. Just, as it says on the sign, it's great service by great people. We don't get it right all the time, but we try.

Gouy Hamilton Fisher, director of colleagues and support

My sole purpose is to support those great people giving great service. To do that, you have to strip away all pretence of authority and power that, often, is embedded in head-office types and in head-office culture. We remind all the people here that they are here to support. If they don't like it, there's the door.

We don't do questionnaires, except one, the 'Happy Index', which is one question. The question is simply: on a scale of 1 to 10, 'how do you rate the support you get from colleagues?' So for the branches, that's 'how do you rate the support you get from your area managers?' And these are the people who are the first line of support to the branches. They do all the recruitment and the day-to-day disciplines, and ensure standards are maintained.

Then for the area managers, the question is; 'how do you rate the support you get from Timpson House and all its constituent departments?' Of which, mine is one of those departments. That is the one that we're measured by here. We pride ourselves on having such an aggressive tool, because what it means is that the colleagues can speak and be heard. We have demoted area managers as a consequence of the Happy Index. We have more area managers in branch than we have as existing area managers. It's used as a measure as to their compliance and demonstration of upside-down management. It's a very blunt tool and it has a very basic message, that if you can't support the guys giving great service and you lose their support, you're out. It has been so effective in forcing through upside-down management.

We have one main mechanism for internal communication, which is a weekly newsletter. We have a couple of rules for the newsletter and that is: 1) there's no bad news; 2) it's to be full of colleagues and their news. So that goes to every branch. If there are two things to happen throughout a Timpson week, one is that the newsletter must go out, even if there is no news. The second thing is that colleagues must have access to whomever they wish. So, often, my day starts with receiving e-mails from John or James, saying; 'this colleague's contacted me, can you make sure this is dealt with, please?' – showing that colleagues don't need to go by their line manager, they don't need to go by colleague support here. They can go straight to the owners of the business and say they are either unhappy, or they have thought of some-thing great that would improve the business, or it's something that we ought to know about.

That open-door policy is supported further by little notepads. One notepad had a cartoon picture of James on with the words: 'Dear James, I have some news to tell you'. That goes straight to James's hard-copy mailbox. They have access to his Twitter and they have access to his e-mail, obviously, and his mobile phone. Occasionally, colleagues will just turn up at Timpson House, and that can be quite exciting So somebody has driven all the way from Lincoln, Arbroath or Exeter, and wants to see someone, but we don't mind.

There is very little in Timpson that is measured, because the sheer act of measurement is often merely to justify someone's position. And so our view is: go and ask; the job is not about preparing statistical information, but about realizing relationships.

A great example, and one I love to repeat, is with EPOS. We acquired our biggest competitor on 8 April 2003. And all of their branches were linked up electronically through their cash tills, and that told them what to order in terms of stock, that told them what the sales were. So there was no verbal communication between management and branches. Well, that business was going so poorly because of the way it was managed that we ended up acquiring it, despite it being twice the size of us.

The first thing James did, just to prove the point, was to get a skip, and to put all these very expensive EPOS terminals into that skip. The branches were stripped of EPOS. It was suggested that we would be shot at dawn, despite our service, if we ever, ever took any of that EPOS equipment out of that skip.

That sort of action puts a very severe filter on recruitment to certain types of positions and individuals. So your head of IT, for example, might feel quite offended by this attitude. The head of finance, head of property, and those roles that tend to rely on information, find this policy a challenge. I despise HR practices, which are stupidly trapped in providing more and more stats, when no one really does much with them or their relationships.

We don't call our colleagues employees, because that tends to suggest that they're not as equal as management. Timpson House is always Timpson

House. It is never, never, ever our head office. My badge says, Gouy, and it just says I'm a fountain pen geek because I hand write my letters of condolences, and congratulations, and birthdays, and the like.

We deliberately recruit in our own image. I remember the TV broadcaster Esther Rantzen telling me that that was risking discrimination, and we said; 'Yes, it does.' It doesn't actually risk it; it promotes it. We would discriminate against poor performers, people who are not going to give us their best, or who we don't believe will give us their best. There is no scientific method to the way we recruit. What we simply say is that interviews must be one-on-one. So we don't carry out panel interviews to scare the candidate to death. And we don't look to use any particular software tool to help filter. It is simply that if I'm interviewing you and we get on, then it's 99.9 per cent certain that I'll employ you. There is no way that we define, measure or try to track personality. It is simply that our passionate belief is that we can train all the rest. What you can't train is if somebody has to look somebody in the eye and smile and talk at the same time. There are very few barriers to employment with us.

Training is on the job. We don't tend to do much by stats, but the geek in me has identified that about 47 per cent of the people that come to us, come by way of a friend. So that fast tracks the learning curve and the training, the induction, because the colleague will have talked to their friend and said, hopefully, what a good place Timpson is to work, sufficient for that person to want to apply. We pay the colleague for the referral to that person. If they stay with us 16 weeks we pay the colleague again, and again if they're still with us a year afterwards. Most colleagues would not besmirch their name by introducing somebody that wouldn't fit well with the business, and our success rate with the stickability of those that have remained with us, after being introduced by a friend, is far higher than any other group of colleagues that come to us.

It is exactly the same process we use for recruiting from prison. There are 86,000 prisoners in this country of which one-third are wholly employable, and we have a couple of hundred of those, and some of those are our best managers. And the other one-third, we're working on. So they all come under the Timpson Foundation umbrella, and that's my responsibility.

The route is that somebody leaving prison will go to an agency, which will put him or her on to us. We always guarantee prisoners and also ex-military people an interview. They are guaranteed an interview above everybody else. The second route is where we have academies in prisons. It's almost like a Timpson shop, so we're giving them the skills to be able to work in our business, should they wish to do so. If they don't, then fine, you know, at least, that they will have skills that can enable them to work elsewhere.

When they come to be released from prison, we give them another pledge, that they can come to us and we'll guarantee them a 16-week trial. If we've got a vacancy and they are good enough, we'll take them on, and if we haven't, we'll put them on a waiting list. If someone is not up to the job we tell them why and refer them to a buddy organization.

We have a culture committee to try to protect the culture. It is formed from the people who were mentioned in the Happy Index results. So the Happy Index, as well as being a means by which to correct failures in the culture, also identifies the cultural champions. I collate those names, and make sure that the organization is aware of who the heroes are, the cultural superstars, the cultural ambassadors. The beauty of it is that it is future proofed because it refreshes itself each year, because we've run the Happy Index every year. It keeps it culturally aligned, it keeps it culturally relative, and it redefines what culture actually is, because these are the people who are determined by the colleagues themselves as practising it.

I think everybody struggles with the definition of leadership. We have a very crude one, and it's the amount of people that will follow an individual, rather than be told by them what to do. And we try to breed leaders, rather than managers. Managers are two a penny; you can train anyone to manage. That's not what we want.

You know, when I did my MBA, I came away thinking, great, I shall now show Timpson how a business should be run. And what an idiot I was not to recognize that the family has been doing this so long, they do their MBA over the breakfast table, you know, day in, day out. It is so inspiring to have such leadership. It is the actions of the individuals that give value and credibility to what it is that we do.

John Timpson, chairman

What drives me is the fun of getting ideas to work. The whole of this upside-down management approach we have is very satisfying. I just love doing new things and coming up with new ideas, so that's what we keep doing.

Profit is important – that's the measure of how good we are, but I'm not interested in financial exits; the business is not for sale. I want to make sure that it's a business that my son James can run, and his eldest son is already starting to show an interest, so it is about keeping a family business together. We happily chat four or five times a day; we don't have any secrets, we pretty much see it the same way. If we have the odd disagreement and if it isn't terribly important it doesn't matter, it's upside-down management – he does what he wants. And it's great – it works.

My job is strategy and culture but culture is the most important thing because you have to have the right culture; a business is more about people than anything else – it's certainly not about processes. Then if you can make the right strategic decisions, it makes it a lot easier for them to be successful.

You can't delegate forward thinking because it's quite difficult to get people who can look ahead. I've got to do the risk management and try to work out where the business is going to be in 20 years' time. For example, how will technology affect our business in the future, things like 3D printing, smartphones that become keys etc? Funnily enough – the older you get, and I'm probably older than just about anyone here, the better you are at looking at the future.

I learned a lot by our boardroom rout. I was 27 and I'd just been made a director and all the other directors came to me and said 'We've decided your father should retire and that your uncle should take over.' Then they went ahead and did it – six votes to two – and my father was out and that taught me an awful lot. A bit later on I had the chance to do a management buy-out; I made sure I got more than 50 per cent and then when I got the chance to get the full 100 per cent I grabbed the opportunity even though I had to mortgage my house to do so – it made my wife very unhappy for a bit! We don't have to worry about shareholders, we don't actually have any borrowings from the bank – actually we're not indebted to anybody – and that takes away a lot of the pressure – we can do what we want.

When we introduced upside-down management, we had a real problem with middle management, particularly the area managers. They were pretty resistant – and I can understand why, because they'd all come up from the shop floor themselves – we don't recruit into our field staff from outside, everyone starts as an apprentice. So they'd been told what to do by their bosses and they've now got what they thought was going to be the suit and the briefcase and they were going to go round and tell everyone else what to do. I turn up and say 'No, it's not like that any more, you're not allowed to issue orders – your job is to look after your people and be nice to the ones who are great and so on.'

And so you could understand why they were a bit resistant. I was asking them to still be responsible but to give the authority to their people. But managers feel more comfortable doing it the other way round – let employees have the responsibility of getting on with it and I'll have the authority to tell them what to do. So this is exactly what they said – 'How can I be responsible for the results of my area when the people working for me can do whatever they want? I've got to tell them what to do, I've got to watch, I've got to make sure they're doing it my way.' So that was the first problem.

The other thing I couldn't get them to do was let their assistants do a real job. They had assistants running shops and being relief managers and I wanted them to do the training and do real management jobs, but they were resistant to handing authority out like that to other people because they thought if I give assistants those jobs, what would be left for the area managers to do? And so they had to learn a new job, which is finding the people who are 'nines and tens', and looking after the atmosphere, making the whole culture work; looking after people who had personal problems – that's what their job is, and they've now learned that.

One of the tests that we use for our area managers is that I ask them to give the name of the dog, or whatever, of one of their people to see how much they know about their people. It's a 'how well do you know your people?' test – literally it is those sorts of questions. What car do they drive? Where was their last holiday? What is their partner's name? What are their children's names? Because we reckon that to be a good boss you've got to know your people very well. How can you reward them with the present that they want if you don't know what presents they like to receive? You've got to know which football team they support – you've got to know that. We regard that as being an important part of being their boss.

Our people feel they share in the business – they don't technically have shares, but the bonus scheme makes them feel it's their shop. Loads of our customers think that the shops are franchised – which they're not – it's only Snappy Snaps that is franchised. As far as the people who work in the support side of things, who aren't involved in the weekly bonus scheme, we have a very generous profit-share that is based on a formula. I make sure that they feel they are very much part of the success of the company. The better we do, the more they are going to get.

We have a department that we call 'People Support', we chose not to call it HR and I approve of that because they are there to help our people – not to tell people what to do. We don't get tribunals – and that's not because we settle before we go in there, we just tend not to get those problems.

It's not for me to tell other businesses how to do it but there must be ways in which they can trust their people more. There must be ways they can look after their people more. It must be a jolly good idea for them to give everyone their birthday off, I would have thought, just try it once – just as a way of celebrating some good year, or an anniversary of some kind. That's how I started it, because I invented a centenary. If you look at our shops, up on the fascia, on the Timpson line, it says established 1903 – I started that when we refitted the shop in Fleet Street in 1996, and I picked 1903 because I thought 2003 would be a great year to have a centenary. And when we had the centenary we gave everyone their birthday off and it was so successful we've done it ever since. But it all depends on the chief executive – none of this works unless the chief executive is committed to it.

In my book, I say, 'The world has forgotten that management is an art, not a science. If you run a business by the book you will create a healthy, safe, and diverse workplace at the expense of the profit-making flair that you really need to succeed.'

Let's take how we got into watch repairs. I called at a shop we had in West Bromwich – actually it was then a little kiosk in West Bromwich – and Glen was running the shop; I hadn't met Glen before, he'd just joined us because it was part of an acquisition, and Glen apologized to me because he was actually doing a few watch straps and batteries on the sly. The money was going in the till – no problem – but he was not doing as he was being told, because he used to work for a watch repairer. Glen has made the company a fortune – within a year he was running the first workshop, he's done all the training, and he's helped us to develop a service from nothing to being a £20 million business – and that started by spotting someone doing something that was out of the ordinary. Lots of other things – we have a lifetime guarantee that we offer, started by a guy in Beverly. You find someone doing something that seems to work, have a go at it – if it works, try it in 10 more shops – if it works, put it in every area – and away we go.

I also said in my book: 'Obeying the rules creates extra costs and guarantees nothing but a mediocre performance. Companies are throwing money down the drain in a national campaign for a corporate conformity – I prefer to challenge every regulation in the cause of common sense.'

Our main company charity is a programme called 'After Adoption' – for obvious reasons. We have adopted two children ourselves as well as fostering a lot – and so we collect money in our shops. We used to do a lot of jobs for free, such as putting a little hole in a belt or a little sticky job, that sort of stuff – and I changed tack about 12 years ago and said instead of saying 'No charge' we say 'No, don't pay me – just put a pound in the box for charity.' And we collect about £5,500 a week that way. Customers like it – and it goes to a good cause. But I must finish with this one point – I think some people miss this – that before looking after charitable things, people outside the company, the number one cause that we look after is the people who work for us.

Chapter Eight
Experience measurement

Every organization needs a way to 'keep score'. In the case of the London 2012 games it was the number of satisfied spectators who returned home with fond memories of the games and the games makers. All too often, organizations keep score by measuring what is easy rather than what is important. Step forward the usual suspects: sales, costs, churn, average call-handling time, shrinkage, earnings per share (EPS). The list goes on. But how many of these can the average manager, let alone employee, really influence?

We advocate building a scorecard of linked measures combining employee engagement, customer experience, customer advocacy, brand reputation and business results (Figure 8.1). The employee and customer experience measures are the leading indicators that managers can directly influence. The brand reputation and business results are more lagging indicators that are a result of many variables, most of which are beyond the control of the individual.

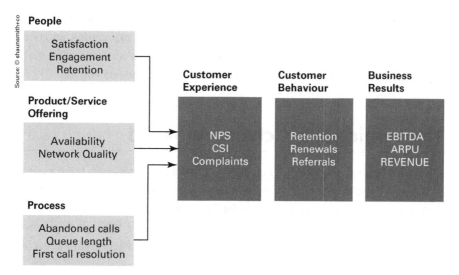

Figure 8.1 Example Telecom score card
Note: CSI = Customer Satisfaction Index, ARPU = Average Revenue Per User,
EBITDA = Earnings Before Interest Tax Depreciation Amortization

CitizenM is a good example of an organization that uses this approach by linking customer satisfaction, which managers can influence, to brand reputation. Michael Levie explains:

'We use a programme called Review Pro that screens some 250 third-party common sites, whether this is TripAdvisor or online travel agents, and they score the sites to create what they call the global index; so a guest satisfaction index.

> 'We can measure the hotel against itself and against the other hotels
> within the chain; but we can also measure against others in the local area.
> I think third-party social media sites are where you get the broadest finger
> on the pulse, because it has become common practice for people to use
> them for reviews. We solicit directly and use a net promoter score for
> that. We ask if you would recommend us and, if you would, then we drill
> down into five key areas. Every Monday morning I get all those reports
> from the hotels.
>
> 'The hotels only deal with anything and everything guest-satisfaction
> related. They are rewarded on a monthly basis with incentives that only
> relate to guest satisfaction; they do not have any sales targets or anything
> financial, purely 100 per cent guest satisfaction.'

The concept of managing leading and lagging indicators, and the relationship between the employee experience, the customer experience and business results, are well known. Joe Wheeler, Shaun's co-author of *Managing the Customer Experience: People who deliver a great brand experience*, and our US partner, runs the Service Profit Chain Institute (SPCI), a consulting firm that specializes in this concept. Joe shares his best practice advice with us.

The service profit chain: reloaded

Just over 20 years since its first publication, the service profit chain still appears in the presentations of leading companies at conferences around the world.[1] Perhaps no other management model has survived the test of time and scrutiny by both business and academic leaders. Why? Well, perhaps the premise is difficult to argue with. The chain describes how you create a 'cycle of capability' that:

> *ensures high levels of employee satisfaction, which*
>
> *generate greater retention and productivity, which*
>
> *create more value for customers, which*
>
> *significantly improves satisfaction, loyalty and financial results.*

A mouthful to be sure, but for organizations described as 'service profit-chain leaders' the results speak for themselves. The service profit chain enables an organization to take a holistic view of their business, make cause-and-effect relationships explicit and keep score of things that matter to all three stakeholders: employees, customers and shareholders. Our research with service profit-chain leaders reveals three major reasons why it has stood firm over time:

- It explains how the business actually works: companies that take the time to identify and measure the unique elements in their operating model that connect the links in the chain simply have a better understanding of what creates superior value for all stakeholders. They have more than a theory of the business; they have an adaptable management system that facilitates 'double-loop' (a form of iterative feedback) learning. In fact, at their best, service profit-chain leaders are able to predict future performance based on leading indicators defined by the service profit chain, and take corrective action before they miss critical indicators of deteriorating performance.

- Culture as competitive advantage: James Heskett, co-founder of SPCI, in his recent book The Culture Cycle (2011), presents evidence of the degree to which a superior culture influences the profitability of one marketing services organization. It is worth reading, but visit any service profit-chain leader to see how the power of a culture focused on the company's common purpose and core values definitely confers a competitive advantage. This is at the core of service profit-chain thinking. As Lanham Napier, the former CEO of Rackpace Hosting, one of the world's leading cloud providers, told us: 'Our culture and the awesome people we have are the things I am most proud of... I would say it's impossible for our competitors to copy. They'd have to start over and build it from scratch.'

- Leadership's change model: running an organization is hard work. Technology has helped to reduce barriers to entry across most industries. Finding and retaining top talent is as competitive as finding and retaining target customers. The service profit chain provides leadership with a clear road map to strategic success. Harvard Business School Professor Michael Beer's formula for effective change tells us:

Successful change = D (dissatisfaction with the status quo) × M (model) × P (process) > C (cost).

What this means is that change is successful when dissatisfaction with the status quo (D) is enabled by an operating model that works (M) and a process for facilitating change that is effective (P) and, finally, the benefits are greater *than the cost (C) of the effort. For countless organizations around the world, the service profit chain has been the 'M' in Professor Beer's insightful equation.*

In 2008, we wrote The Ownership Quotient, *as a follow-up to the original* Service Profit Chain *book. We were struck by the degree to which service profit-chain leaders such as Wegmans Food Markets, SAS and others had created even higher levels of advocacy and ownership with both employees and customers. From co-creating new product and service ideas with customers, to applying digital and data science technologies to anticipate and predict customer needs, these companies had pushed the boundaries of what we could only imagine back in the mid-1990s. Today, these insights have helped us to accelerate the results achieved when our clients were determined to stand firm.*

Based on our experience, we recommend that readers charged with leading their company's efforts to enhance customer or employee experience take three recommendations to heart:

1 *Make sure you understand the 'defining element' of your customer experience: we learned this lesson back in 2002 when Shaun Smith and I wrote* Managing the Customer Experience, *but it is just as relevant today. A company that really understands this is IKEA, the Swedish furniture manufacturer. Although their products can be purchased through different channels, they have apparently figured out that if you are going to choose furniture that is going to be just right for the look of your home this is most effective while in the store, standing in front of that particular item. They understand the 'defining element' of the IKEA experience and don't dilute it with distractions that move them away from something they are not.*

2 *Apply technology that adds value – not just cost: building on the first recommendation, be careful not to be seduced by all that glitters. For example, one retail customer in the technology business removed touchscreen panels piloted in several stores and replaced them with simple round tables with bar stools. Another, a toy retailer, redesigned their customer experience with touchscreen technology that interconnected the whole shopping experience. Both realized substantial increases in average ticket and transaction volumes. There is no one right answer, there is just the brand promise you have committed to deliver and the most consistent, intentional and differentiated way you have designed for your customers to experience it.*

3 *Be in the 'relationship' rather than the 'transaction' business: I'll admit, it is tempting when you see the cost-effectiveness of introducing more*

digital transactions in your business. For large organizations managing millions of transactions, even a few basic points of channel migration can represent significant cost savings. Service profit-chain leaders understand, however, that they are not in the transaction business – they are in the relationship business. Their goal is to build lifetime value for their target customers and earn their loyalty by delivering an experience that creates significant advocacy. As a result, they drive down the cost of marketing and put those dollars to better use for real value creation. As Robert Stephens, the founder of Geek Squad, has said: 'Marketing is the tax you pay for being unremarkable.'

Don't be unremarkable. Leave that to your competitors. Stand up, stand out and most of all – stand firm.

Joe's third point 'be in the relationship rather than the transaction business' is exactly right, but it requires organizations to value, measure and reward different things. O2 is looking at how it moves from being a transaction business to one that values relationships by reducing extrinsic rewards and increasing intrinsic ones.

We have had some great advice on how to hire people, train them, motivate them and finally measure the results. What does all of this look like when it comes together? We asked Francisco Sordo who manages the citizenM properties in Amsterdam to tell us.

Putting it together

Francisco Sordo, citizenM

CitizenM stands for creating a great environment for the staff and then from there you bring it out from within to the guest. It treats every single individual that is working for the company as an individual, and respects them for who they are and how they do things. I say many times that whenever I'm looking for a new ambassador, as we call them, I'm not looking for an employee. I'm looking for an individual who is going to enrich our team. And by encouraging people to be themselves you automatically bring out the best in them.

Many times people are put in little boxes and many times society doesn't allow them to do things. You're not allowed to do this or you are just allowed to do that. Here, as long as we explain to our people where we want to go, how they get there is actually part of the journey and is up to them. We have created a micro-society and we know what the values are, and we know that we need to be respectful and playful.

The words we use, the way we use them, when we use them, how we use them, and the joke that you can make with one person that is absolutely not the same joke that you can use with another – it's about values and common sense.

It helps that our team are part of the generation that we target. They like travelling. They are young, or of the younger generation, so they are really into media. They like nice, expensive things and luxury items, but they don't earn that much in comparison with others to be able to afford it, so they all believe in the affordable luxury concept... you need to believe in what you sell.

We're looking for somebody who is outgoing, somebody who is not shy, somebody who wants to engage with others, who likes people, who likes to help people, from the heart.

I am not that interested in previous hotel experience. I think that if I were to hire somebody who has been in the hotel industry for 10 years he or she would not be as productive, because this person would have to erase everything they had learned. Sometimes to change behaviour is more difficult than to learn behaviour in the first place.

Our ratio of ambassadors to guests is about 1 to 10. A typical luxury hotel is 1 to 3 or even lower. For example, a formal restaurant within a hotel needs to have waiters, busboys; you need to have the chef, the assistant chef, the dishwashers, so you've got already a minimum of 10 people, easily. At the front desk you have the front desk manager, the front desk assistant manager. You have too many chiefs and to run it you have metres of front desk that requires four people to man at the same time. We don't. We just do it with one or two ambassadors, because the guest is the one who checks themselves in. We assist them, and that is where we connect because by taking away the desk we take away the distance between us.

Our people stay with us because of the culture of the company and because of the way we treat them, because of the way we allow them to be themselves. For example, we don't mind if they have a tattoo as long as it's not offensive to anybody. And I think that my biggest role is encouraging them to flourish and open themselves. There is a girl who works at citizenM who, when I was interviewing her, was terrified. But I said, just let go and she became a bit more relaxed and started to come out of herself. And I thought to myself, she is going to be great because of her kindness, because of her smile, because of her friendliness. Everything else we can teach her. So we hired her and she opened up like a blossom, like a beautiful flower. Months later

I came in and she was literally dancing along helping somebody to check-in; it was a beautiful thing to see.

One thing we do not tolerate is when somebody is not respectful. We were training one of the assistant managers, a young guy, who was a bit naive. One of our best ambassadors didn't agree with the decision that this young guy took. He pointed at him with his finger and told him to learn. That ambassador was really one of the best people I had, but he crossed a line. So we sat down and I said, you don't need to agree, but he is the assistant manager. He is running it. And if he says green, it's green. You may see it blue, but it is green. And at the end of the shift, if you don't agree you can sit down and say, 'Can we talk about it?' I finished by saying 'Now we're cool, but if it happens again we're not going to be cool.' And then he said, 'Well, if you want to fire me, just fire me.' And I said, 'Okay, the conversation ends right now.' He was one of the pillars of my team but I let him go because he was disrespectful. He crossed that line.

We're here for a purpose and that purpose is the guest. We are very impor- tant but there is somebody else who is even more important: the guest. We focus on the guest's satisfaction. We are measured on guest satisfaction. The financial numbers at the end are, of course, important. However, you can have fantastic numbers but if the guests are not pleased that is not going to be a sustainable model.

The difference between us and the Holiday Inn across the street is not the building, it's not the technology – it's the citizenM culture. And if we keep that in mind then whatever we do is going to be the right thing. I always say there's no wrongdoing when you're doing the right thing.

We interviewed Francisco and heard his comments. But to what extent are they accurate? To find out we stayed in the citizenM at Schiphol Airport and had a chat over a beer with one of their most regular customers to find out.

Michael ten Hove, mobile citizen

I first experienced citizenM in autumn 2010. I was coming to Amsterdam for one or two nights a week and was recommended by colleagues of mine who were commuting like myself, and spoke very favourably about the brand.

I describe citizenM as 'affordable chic', because they are trying to have more of a vibe, a groove to their place than just a standard hotel and they do it all in an affordable way. So you feel like you're in a boutiquey kind of place without them having made a great investment in ridiculously expensive furniture. But it still achieves the vibe that they are going for. And they are consistent. In the three years I've been experiencing the brand they have always been very consistent with that.

It really comes down to two things: the first thing that comes to mind is the people. The people here are really extraordinary. I've rarely experienced this level of service-mindedness and attention to detail in any category. The second thing is the concept of the rooms themselves. Either you love it or you hate it. I think there are very few people who are in the middle ground. I hear people at the bar or at the restaurant who say 'Gee, I just checked into my room, can you imagine how small it is?' There's no closet as such, there's no real private space to go to the bathroom. For myself, I find it a lot more comfortable than many hotels.

I like the public area very much. I like the fact that it's cozy, in a homely way, because when you look across there are books that you can just grab and read. There are interesting artefacts. So it's got a funky, interesting, attitude and vibe to it. If you go to the airport Sheraton it's just boring; the rooms are kind of, beige. The beds are great, I'll give you that, but everything else is boring and sterile.

Turning to the people, I'm a special case because I've been here for so long, but even early on the staff call you by your first name. Other hotels don't even know my last name let alone my first name. I call the staff by their first name as well. They're very friendly. I don't know how much of it's in their training. I certainly think it's in the recruitment because there's a certain kind of DNA in people that tend to work here. It starts with the management, I think. Take Francisco, he's somebody who really cares about his clients. He'll go out of his way to stop and say 'Hi, how's things?' Just last week, in fact, I was walking to my office, and he was walking to his office and he asked me 'So how are they treating you?' You don't feel a sense of hierarchy here. It's about rolling up your sleeves. It feels to me that that's part of the internal culture.

The thing that impressed me the most of all my experiences was a couple of months ago I was speaking with one of the ambassadors, Georgia, and I was telling her that my wife was going to come up for one evening and would she be around, so that she could meet her.

I checked in that next week. I walked into the room. There was a beautiful bouquet of flowers for my wife and there was a message for me. I like to write music and songs, which I record, and post on the internet. They had taken the trouble to listen to the lyrics of my songs and find a song – I have this one song called 'Home' – and relate it to the fact that I was coming back to citizenM.

Image 8.1 citizenM at Schiphol Airport

All this goodwill has translated into additional business for them because there have been people who I've recommended who have stayed here. Whenever I've organized things in Schiphol I've said we're putting everybody in the citizenM. Forget about the Sheraton, put them in citizenM.

Note

1 The service profit chain was conceived by James L Heskett, Thomas O Jones, Gary W Loveman, W Earl Sasser and Leonard A Schlesinger.

Chapter Nine
Never stand still

*'In this very real world, the good does not drive out the bad,
the energetic displace the lazy.'*

BILL BERNBACH

*'The common question that gets asked in business is, "why?"
That's a good question, but an equally valid question is, "why not?"'*

JEFF BEZOS

That Berber moment...

The year is 1885 and the British and Egyptian governments are facing a major uprising in the Sudan. The revolt, a bloody and sustained onslaught, has been raging for a number of years, led by the fearless al-Mahdi and his followers, the Mahdists.

General Gordon, one of Britain's top military commanders, having been sent to evacuate the region, has been under siege in Khartoum for over a year. Despite being cut off from supplies, surrounded and outnumbered by a hostile force, he has managed to keep the Mahdists at bay.

Sensing the urgency of the situation, a British relief force, led by General Wolseley, has been despatched to Khartoum. Having swiftly made its way to Africa, defeating rebellious forces along the way, and making such good progress down the Nile, Wolseley decides to rest his men at a place called Berber, rather than continuing at the pace already set. They stop for a day before carrying on to Khartoum. Their purpose can wait.

Alas, they arrive too late. One day too late.

Less than 24 hours beforehand, Gordon has been killed and Khartoum has fallen, along with all of its 4,000 inhabitants.

The subsequent inquest into the debacle of Khartoum concluded that Wolseley had 'inexplicably delayed at Berber on the Nile'.

Businesses cannot afford to have their 'Berber' moment

In business, stopping is not an option; consolidation is no longer a sensible policy. Businesses of all shapes and sizes that are performing well are possessed with a sense of urgency, a desire and the capacity to keep the momentum going. Innovation is part of this, of course. But it is only part. Momentum is about constantly delivering value to your customers and clients, about moving swiftly to execute plans, about being possessed with a sense of urgency. Joseph Cyril Bamford, who lent his initials to the manufacturing company he founded, JCB, believes that it was this impatience for action that was the hallmark of success. As he put it:

'The world is full of very competent people who honestly intend to do things tomorrow or as soon as they can get around to it. Their accomplishments, however, seldom match those of the less talented who are blessed with a sense of the importance of getting started now.'

Get started and keep going

Getting started is only the start – obviously – you then have to keep going. This restlessness is so important that we feel it deserves a chapter to itself. It embodies some of the principles of innovation discussed in Chapter 5 but it goes way beyond that. Nokia was innovative, so was Pan Am, so was Blockbuster but it wasn't enough to stop them disappearing. True innovation is not just the ability to come up with new ideas; it is the restlessness that means you can never sit still.

Over the many years that we have worked with and talked with business leaders, consultants and academics all over the world, we have identified three reasons why businesses stop moving forward:

1 Complacency: the business settles into a comfort zone; it loses its entrepreneurial culture and becomes managerialist. It attempts to turn the dynamic but risk-led growth that led to its success into predictive, risk-free growth. People come in expecting an infrastructure to support them in doing what has always been done before.

2 Capital (lack of it!): the business reaches a certain size at which it needs access to capital to fund new growth, it can't fund it from its profits; unfortunately these businesses either cannot or will not seek and make the case for the capital they need to grow.

3 Customer indifference: they take their customers for granted, paying only the least possible attention to them and not sticking as close to them as possible so that they can anticipate and respond to their changing needs and trends.

Each of these is fundamentally caused by a lack of a sense of purpose driving people on. If you believe in your purpose and feel it is your duty to deliver it to the world, then your hunger will drive you to listen to customers, seek capital, and never, ever be complacent. Think about Amazon: they get criticized for the odd mis-step (such as Fire phone) and for burning through investors' money, but that is exactly what has fuelled their extraordinary growth and why investors are happy to continue to invest in the brand. They have a purpose to be the 'most customer-centric company on earth' and to become the world's largest online store – when you have a vision as grand as this, complacency is out of the question.

Many of the businesses that we have talked about in this book are succeeding because they refuse to stand still and wait. Metro Bank, which we discussed in Chapter 4, is not only the fastest growing bank in the UK in terms of customer acquisition, they are also the fastest growing in terms of branches. They are not complacent, they have access to capital and they are as far from indifferent to customers as you can get. Their strategy is based on bringing banks physically closer to customers, to get people back into branches. It is a capital-intensive strategy and one that is funded by deep-pocketed investors, and they are showing no signs of slowing down. Momentum and critical mass are vital. As of February 2015, they are opening almost one new branch per month, while the other high-street banks have been closing theirs rapidly. Barclays, HSBC, Lloyds and others closed 470 branches in 2014, a 140 per cent increase on closures in the previous year. Apologists point to the fact that people's habits are changing and we are moving to online and mobile banking apps rather than a desire to go to a physical branch. There is truth in that. However, Metro also offers online and mobile banking apps but they are opening branches at a rate of around 25 per cent a year. More importantly, in terms of the sense of customer-led purpose, which this book trumpets, the banks who are closing branches are reneging on a promise. Lloyds Bank is only one of many who have gone back on a promise that they would not close a bank branch in a community if that were the last branch in town. So outraged were consumers by this breaking of a promise, that the UK government had to write to the bank demanding an explanation. Metro realize that a physical bank branch remains a potent symbol of and focus for a community. Being local helps in being loved – and being the bank people love is core to Metro's purpose.

Metro's financial figures are impressive too: in 2014, deposits climbed from £1.3 billion to £2.9 billion; new customer accounts were up a staggering 63 per cent; new jobs in those branches were up 50 per cent and the free food, balloons, face painting and music that accompany every branch launch increased as well! Moreover, in terms of the momentum of the business, Metro has opened business banking and within one year 64 per cent of total deposits in the bank came from business accounts. Metro's chief executive Craig Donaldson said: 'We're excited to continue innovating and providing a real banking choice to the British people, as well as maintaining our commitment to deliver the best in service and convenience.' They keep on going.

It's not just new and challenger brands such as Metro that have this sense of urgency and momentum. No one could say that IKEA, LEGO or Apple are challenger brands, nor Coca-Cola, JCB or Procter & Gamble. They are all large, long standing and yet share a restlessness in their pursuit not just of product innovations but also of ways of staying relevant to their customers and consumers. For a company like Coca-Cola, for example, seasonality and occasion to purchase are vital to understand. When and why are people's behavioural habits likely to change or to be heightened? For Coca-Cola, a year of momentum will involve planning for everything from religious festivals, holidays, big sporting events and movie launches. It will also include anticipating regulatory changes, social trends, environmental or sustainability concerns. They need to be constantly engaged and engaging with customers, consumers and opinion formers to plan and execute, at speed, campaigns that make people (consumers and shareholders) happy.

One of the biggest trends that companies like Coca-Cola are responding to and beginning to drive is the increased importance of impulse and activation in store, in street, at home and online. In the past, there was a formula of brand building that involved big, expensive TV advertising campaigns, which take time to research, plan, shoot, produce and sign off. Then they require a lot of spend on media spots over time in order to sustain and create a brand image that pulls people into shops. These are becoming less important to brand owners such as Coca-Cola than agile shopper experience campaigns that drive purchase, create buzz and can then be turned into an advertising campaign that amplifies consumer behaviour. This is not innovation; this is about momentum, about responding swiftly to trends.

Brands that are stuck in the habit of spending big on campaigns are being out-thought and out-fought by brands that are creating moments of truth in the customer or consumer's experience. Many of the successful campaigns that Coca-Cola has run in the past few years have not been big advertising campaigns, they have been packaging and point-of-sale driven: Coca-Cola cans and bottles with yours or a friend's name on them; a campaign in Germany where Fanta bottles had white space left on the packaging label to encourage consumers to draw their own pictures. Both were driven by insights into consumer behaviour at the point of sale, which then became campaigns that both drove sales and an emotional relationship with the brand. There is no doubt that Coca-Cola will continue to change these campaigns regularly while still staying true to its purpose:

- to refresh the world in mind, body and spirit;
- to inspire moments of optimism and happiness through our brands and actions;
- to create value and make a difference.

IKEA

IKEA is a great example of a business that never stands still. Possessed of a purpose, which is the democratization of design, it constantly develops and extends itself. In 2015, IKEA was voted by Fast Company to be one of the most innovative companies. But it is not so much innovative as relentless. The design ranges that they produce are not so distinctively different every year – they look like what they are: affordable Swedish design. Their business model is essentially 'volume selling'. They make huge quantities of the same stuff, which means they can achieve good prices from suppliers. And then they sell huge quantities of the same stuff at low prices. One of their most iconic products, the Billy bookcase, is sold every 10 seconds! And they sell it in the same way everywhere. Their retail stores don't change noticeably from year to year or from market to market; they remain largely unattractive big blue warehouses where customers are route-marched through IKEA's chosen path. But they are relentless in rolling them out because more stores mean more volume, which means they can continue to keep prices low; in 2014, IKEA cut prices for its products around the world by an average of 1 per cent. What really marks them out is the commitment not so much to innovation as to growth of a consistent format globally and the continuous updating and reinvention of parts of the experience in order to keep the brand relevant.

In 2014, 821 million customers visited IKEA's 361 stores worldwide. Conscious of and responsive to customers' changing habits and, especially, what customers are and are not prepared to tolerate, IKEA has addressed those parts of the customer experience that customers find to be a 'pain'. One of the pleasure points of the IKEA experience is the way they beautifully lay out showcase rooms in the store. Conversely, the 'pain' is the worry of what the furniture will actually look like when you get it home. So they have invested in a 'catalogue app' through which you can choose a piece of furniture, point your smartphone at the area of your home that it is intended for and get a 3-D image of it in that space. Since families often have to traipse around the IKEA stores together, as they are often warehouses that you need to drive to, IKEA have introduced a family card, which as well as offering discounts also entitles you to an extra 30 minutes of complimentary babysitting at the supervised play centre. Fast Company reported that IKEA's family memberships had jumped from 4.3 million to 6.9 million within one year.

Of course they continue to invest in product developments (with some products now assembled with just four screws) and keeping up with trends by offering affordable Swedish-designed standing tables. But, as we say, none of these are 'innovations'; they are rather a manifestation of the relentless desire to improve the complete customer experience in line with IKEA's purpose.

That sense of purpose and the values associated with it are reflected in the way they treat their employees. As Fast Company reported:

'In 2014, IKEA's US arm invested in another part of the in-store experience – its people. It now uses the MIT living wage calculator, not local requirements, to determine the hourly rate for each particular market. As a result, 33 of the 40 US stores increased their wages on 1 January (five stores already offered pay above the living wage) and 50 per cent of its US retail workforce will see a pay bump in 2015.

'Happier employees mean happier customers.'

IKEA's growth plan is for €50 billion in sales by 2020 in 500 stores worldwide. They will grow because their core target audience, middle-class consumers with 'thin wallets' (a company expression), will grow worldwide. IKEA cannot afford to stop growing.

This need for growth is echoed in the words of Ove Arup, the founder of the global architectural and engineering firm that bears his name. Speaking in 1970 to a conference of the firm's senior managers, Arup explained the importance to the business of its sense of purpose. He talked of 'total architecture', in which all elements of design and environment must be considered, in the pursuit of quality. Arup's speech is still used today in the company to induct all employees into an understanding of the *raison d'être* and values of the business:

'We are then led to the ideal of "total architecture", in collaboration with other like-minded firms or, better still, on our own. This means expanding our field of activity into adjoining fields: architecture, planning, ground engineering, environmental engineering, computer programming etc, and the planning and organization of the work on site.'

It is a sentiment shared by another Swede, IKEA Group CEO Peter Agnefjäl: 'We're guided by a vision to create a better everyday life for many people. That is what steers us, motivates us – that is our role,' he says. 'We feel almost obliged to grow.'

Being committed to your purpose obliges you to grow because growth is in pursuit of that purpose. As Robert Stephens pointed out, purpose does not have to be altruistic. Growth and profit are laudable aims, providing that organizations are authentic in their ambitions and don't say one thing and then do another. Growth can only ever be on the back of creating value for customers and if providing it is not at the expense of your people, suppliers or society at large.

One brand that has been relentless in pursuing purpose and in driving itself to new levels is Nissan.

Nissan

Lucas Ordóñez loves racing cars. He loves the excitement, the thrills – that adrenaline rush as his car screeches past the next by a hair's breadth. For Lucas, however, the action all happened on screen. Lucas was an online gamer – and a very talented one, but his only experience of racing had been restricted to his Sony PlayStation. That is, until Nissan stepped in with the GT Academy.

The GT Academy (a partnership with Nissan Nismo and Sony PlayStation) took gamers who liked playing racing-car games on their consoles through a series of competitions. For the winners, it gave them the opportunity first to drive a real racing car and ultimately to compete in a real race. Lucas Ordóñez was one of them and went on to become a highly successful racing driver.

From sitting on his sofa with his PlayStation to standing on a podium at Le Mans: it is a story that dramatizes the very essence of Nissan's purpose – making innovation and excitement accessible to everyone.

From bland to extraordinary...

In 1999, the Nissan company was on its knees and the brand was little loved. Carlos Ghosn transformed the fortunes of the business with a number of bold moves, including a life-saving alliance with Renault. Such was his trans-formation of the business that his heroics were captured in the Japanese Manga comic book *Big Comic Superior*, a seven-part series featuring Carlos Ghosn as the true superhero of his time. He even has the honour of having a Japanese Bento Box named after him.

Having saved the company and returned it to financial health, Ghosn's next priority has been to build Nissan into a brand that is globally recognized for innovation and excitement. Saving a company is one thing, building a global brand is quite another. One requires urgent action and a sense of survival; the other requires long-term sustainability and a sense of purpose.

Nissan's purpose is probably best seen in two bold moves. The first was the invention in 2007 of the 'crossover', a car that combined the best of two types of vehicles. The first 'crossover' was the Nissan Qashqai, which combined the roominess of a SUV with the compactness of a hatchback. The Nissan Qashqai won numerous awards but above all won the hearts and minds of a whole new group of customers. As of 2015 more than 2 million Nissan Qashqais have been sold across Europe and the latest version launched in 2014 was voted Car of the Year.

Image 9.1 Nissan's crossover range

The second bold move was to pin its future to electric vehicles (EV). Its major investment in and long-term commitment to the technology and the infrastructure required to make EV the future of automotive driving will take many years to yield a financial return. It is, however, already yielding significant returns in the perception of Nissan as a brand; its first EV, the Leaf, won the coveted International Car of the Year award and Nissan already is the leader in EV sales.

Europe has been one of the most important markets for Nissan. Steve McLennan, who is the general manager of Brand Power at Nissan Europe, explains how the importance of a bold purpose drives a relentlessness to deliver for consumers and customers.

We were struggling as a brand and a business, because we didn't own a clear sense of a purpose towards the customer. In the late 1990s, we were providing cars that were by and large 'me-too', into quite traditional and highly competitive segments of the market. They were worthy products, but didn't really bring anything new to the consumer.

Then Carlos Ghosn arrived as CEO. He recognized that if he was to turn the business around, we couldn't take a me-too approach. His real challenge was how to appeal to mainstream segments by doing something different. That challenge was answered through customer insight, which led to a new product concept. The insight was this: the attractiveness of SUVs for customers was at a tipping point. Consumers loved sports utility vehicles for the practicality and the size that these vehicles offered, but mainstream customers didn't like the running costs, the high fuel inefficiency, and the high levels of CO_2.

So the crossover was born out of a very simple equation, which was to offer the strength, the imagery and the practicality of a sports utility vehicle but, through clever engineering and design, to combine that with the agility and the running costs of a traditional hatchback. That should excite consumers to step outside their traditional choices and take on board a new concept.

The crossover concept really transformed Nissan in Europe, and beyond as well. What we learned from that was the value of confidence within an organization. From that moment, Nissan started to develop a clearer sense of purpose in making innovation and excitement accessible to everyone. We became more adventurous. We started looking at some of the bigger societal trends, longer-term trends, and answering those with different concepts as well.

A great example, of course, is fossil fuels. It didn't take a rocket scientist to work out that fossil fuels were not the future for the automotive industry.

Carlos Ghosn committed and challenged the organization to substantial investment in developing battery technology, and Nissan was first to market with a mainstream EV car for the road, the Nissan Leaf. But without that original sense of purpose with crossover, I don't know if we would have had the boldness for EVs. So I think it's really, really important that once you gain that sense of purpose, once you develop confidence within the organization, the organization becomes braver, more challenging and stretches its thinking. It needs to look further into the future, and really drill down as to what the main societal issues are going to be, and try to respond.

The impact of cars in mature societies is quite obvious. First, there is congestion. And, then there's safety. We are developing technologies that can answer that societal benefit of minimizing accidents, and zero fatalities.

These are what we call autonomous driving technologies. These are technologies that proactively inform, warn and protect the driver from any imminent dangers that he or she might not have noticed. There are some standard technologies that are already going onto cars, such as blind-spot warning, lane departure warning and reversing cameras. Nissan have been first to market those for the mainstream. But we have even bigger plans, cars that can park themselves, drive themselves and interact with other cars – and, indeed, infrastructure to improve the whole driving experience. In the UK alone, five cities have been designated as autonomous driving pilots. Nissan will continue to drive that forward.

The other societal trend that autonomous drive can answer is the ageing population. We think the autonomous drive technology, when it is fully delivered, will mean that consumers will be able to drive into their later years. And that has to be a benefit for society.

Nissan are relentless in their approach to the market, bringing to the mainstream driver ideas that will excite and enhance the driving experience; thinking of the future and turning that into solutions for now. However, to have the confidence of a sense of purpose, as Steve McLennan discusses, you also need to have the organization fully aligned behind the brand. Of the many things that Nissan has done to deliver its purpose, perhaps the most important has been to put the brand at the centre of its business.

Paul Willcox is the chairman of Nissan Europe. He is ultimately responsible for everything that affects the customer's experience of Nissan; from the research and development (R&D) centres and the manufacturing plants to the sales and marketing businesses in each country. He explains the bold moves he oversaw at Nissan to put the brand and its customer-driven purpose at the heart of the organization.

Nissan is a great company that has built first-class products, but in the past we didn't have a clear enough focus on what our brand should stand for. So for me the most important thing to do was to get the organization aligned to a common purpose, a common understanding of what Nissan stands for, and to put the customer first and foremost at the front of our decision making.

That means having much more precision in everything we do, in terms of the product, the services that we provide with the product, or through our dealer network, and the way we communicate and consistently deliver through the organization.

With a global company like Nissan that's not easy. Even within the region I'm responsible for, we operate through 35 different countries, offering more than 20 products, and if you take the broader organization beyond just our direct employees and include the dealer networks, you're probably talking 40,000 people. So to get that kind of direction is difficult but it's critical in terms of driving commercial performance. When we have a common direction then we're much more efficient and effective in driving demand. It's actually as simple as that.

So, I took the decision to take the brand out of marketing, and made it a cross-functional responsibility of the senior vice presidents, vice presidents and general managers of each of our different entities. So people in different parts of the organization couldn't think that it was not their responsibility, that it was someone else's responsibility. Because whether you work in Finance, Customer Support, Sales, Marketing or in Engineering, everyone has a role to play. The easy route is to say, 'Oh, let's put the responsibility into a very narrow focus of marketing,' but I think that is completely wrong. For sustainable overall performance, everyone has to align to a common brand purpose, and as I said before, it doesn't matter where you work. Everyone needs to understand their role and their responsibility in delivering that.

I think many companies make the mistake of assuming brand development is purely a function of marketing communications, that good advertising is the way to build up a brand. From my perspective, that's nonsense. Obviously it's very important that you get the communication correct, but without content, without consistency, without consistent delivery to the customer in everything you do, then the promise is fake. It's a vacuous promise.

We are building our brand on the key drivers that influence purchase decisions, and we took a very clear view, based on customer feedback, that there are basically two things we need to achieve. One is to build trust. It's very clear, through any consumer research, that if you don't build trust then no matter what else you do it's of limited value.

The other is that I want all functions within the European organization to align to deliver the highest levels of quality – not aiming for top quartile, aiming for number one – and the measure there is the consumer perception of quality: do consumers perceive that Nissan is a quality brand? So we set that as a foundation. Of course, all our competitors will want to have very strong quality, so we also need to differentiate ourselves. Differentiation for us means delivering accessible innovation through technology leadership. And we have three very clear dimensions as far as technology goes: EV leadership, crossover leadership (which we have in Europe) and autonomous driving.

I have two main responsibilities to help deliver alignment to the brand. The first is to support the central Brand Power team; this is outside any function. It effectively sits at the centre reporting through a function directly to me.

It is a small, dedicated group whose sole task is to ensure that throughout the business we have the understanding and the traction to drive the actions that are required in the business.

The second is to be conscious as the chair of the management team in Europe, always to think about first and foremost the customer. So to make sure that all of our executives understand our products, how they compare in the competitive sense, and how they stand against the brand filter.

What I have found interesting is that not everybody finds it easy to align to this because this is very difficult. It's so easy when you have a task-orientated role where someone says, 'You go and do these three things; come back tomorrow and tell me how you've done and I'll give you the next three tasks.' When you start talking about 'How do you shape the attitudes of customers towards your brand? How do you go away and shape people?'– then that is much more challenging for people and some people struggle with it. Manufacturing is a control process; you put control measures in, and you get an output that is expected. Brand is not as simple as that, because you've got an unknown quantity, which is called a consumer.

What Paul Willcox is essentially explaining is how he is dealing with two of those three Cs that stop growth, which we mentioned at the start of this chapter: complacency and customer indifference. Nissan doesn't have a big problem with getting access to capital. The key challenges for a business that is so big, so capital intensive and so diverse as Nissan is to stay agile, hungry and forward thinking. Transforming the way the business operates so that the customer-focused purpose (brand) is at the centre of everyone's thinking is a major task. However, the approach taken by Nissan both guards against complacency and ensures that the customer is integrated into every decision, short and midterm.

Nissan Nismo

One powerful way in which Nissan keeps the sense of innovation and excitement alive and tests ideas that will be eventually brought to the mainstream market is through the Nissan Nismo sub-brand. Nismo is technically Nissan's Motor Sport Division (hence the Nismo name). But in reality it is much more than that. Most major motor manufacturers have a motor-sports arm. Traditionally, they were used as a way of providing credentials for their ability to deliver high-performance engineering. Many manufacturers even have teams that compete in Formula 1 such as Mercedes, Toyota and Renault. Rarely, though, are the 'on-track' technologies, which 'petrol heads' know about, integrated in any meaningful way into the road cars that most people drive. But Nissan takes a very different approach. For Nissan, the purpose of its performance division is not to win a Grand Prix, though it is extremely serious about competing in races; its purpose is to be a laboratory in which maverick engineers can create exciting ideas that will find their way into mainstream road cars eventually. Moreover, it transfers the excitement and the maverick edge of innovation that it builds into the Nismo sub-brand directly into on-road vehicles. The Nissan Juke, for example, which is another highly successful crossover vehicle, has a Nismo grade – as does Nissan's sports car, the GT-R.

Image 9.2 The Nismo DNA

But Nissan Nismo is more than product. It is an attitude that affects everything, including marketing and consumer experience. Darren Cox is the head of Nissan Nismo globally and he explains why and how it helps to fulfil the purpose of Nissan's brand, making innovation accessible and useful to the many, not just the few. He also conveys the sense of urgency, of restlessness that brands who refuse to stand still display.

Brands have written down on pieces of paper bullsh*t that no one believes in, unless you are living that brand. In our case it is innovation and excitement for everyone – and Nissan NISMO is the maverick edge of the brand statement. We are pushing the envelope, doing exciting stuff like garage 56 at Le Mans, ZEOD RC, GT Academy, Juke R and LMP1, which will show that we live the brand.

The best example is GT Academy. There is an established way of doing things in motor sport; the whole business model is built on it but it's not fair and it's not for everyone. Nissan's brand is about including people, so we set up GT Academy as a way of doing that. We get the widest selection of people to do their dream job, which is to become a racing driver. It's completely different to anything that anyone has ever done. Innovation is uncomfortable when you start doing it and lots of people didn't want to do it, but now everyone looks back and says that, of course, it was a brilliant idea! I keep saying that GT Academy was 2 per cent inspiration, 98 per cent perspiration. It was all down to the bloody-mindedness of knowing this was a good idea and not giving up. And that's what you have to have – single-mindedness. However painful it is.

We use Nismo as the test bed, trying things out that others wouldn't; not just in product and technology but also in approach, in marketing. We can do stuff and it can fail but it won't hurt the mother brand because we are a bunch of mavericks in an innovation hub and we are prepared to fail. Accepting that every now and then you will fail is something that no one ever talks about, which is amazing. I remember we spent quite a lot of money on something called Free Race. We had success with GT Academy and thought 'Okay, where else can we take this?' We thought we could do a mixture between Fight Club and Fast and Furious using social media. We wouldn't even talk about the fact that we were Nissan, we would just talk to drivers and get them along to an event, such as an underground rave at night. We had cars burnt out upside down, we had oil drums with fire coming out and people were filmed racing around those in disused car parks and airfields. The idea was great. You were the best driver, in a raw way – you just turned up to this underground society and the best driver would win a race, a proper race. But it didn't work. Because social media wasn't as advanced as it is today. We wanted it to create a natural buzz that built momentum, but in the end we needed a push behind it, we couldn't do it just on social media. And it ran out of steam.

But that helped us with what to do next with GT Academy. There, we had a ready-made audience base in gamers – we were not trying to create a new base of fans, because there was already something that existed. So we concentrated on them and made them feel special by using gaming in a way that no one else does. We believed, like them, that gaming is a very rich experience and not just child's play. The guys that were playing on Gran Turismo One are now buying Porsche 911s, GT-Rs and Aston Martins. Those 18-year-olds are now 40 and 45. So we don't underestimate who is using these tools now – whether it be social media or gaming or Twitter, or even that some sites we work in partnership with look very childish – because the way they promote themselves means they have a huge following of the right kind of people who will be driving our cars in the future.

Image 9.3 Nissan's global advertising features Usain Bolt as Director of Excitement

We have a strategy that we call 'the regular and the spectacular'. You have to put something up every three or four days that will drive people to Nismo TV, so they subscribe to the channel. We build it organically, we don't buy views, we don't buy followers because in the end that's just numbers, and it isn't authentic. But our average view time on Nismo TV, for example on the LMP1 video, is 180 per cent. In other words, people are watching the video twice! They are not robots just starting the video then stopping again. In the end the engagement matrix will be the one that everyone will talk about, not the number of followers you've got or subscribers or whatever. That's why I say that it is our job to be storytellers. We have to find and tell the best stories that already exist in the company and we have to go out and create new stories – the regular and the remarkable.

www.youtube.com/nismotv

We have more YouTube subscribers than any other motor-sport brand. From a minimal budget. We're bigger than Renault who has got a Formula 1 engine, we're bigger than Honda, and we've got more subscribers as a motor-sport brand than anyone else. Why? Because we've got good guys who just love what we're doing. And because we never stop. We never give up.

Some readers of our previous books have told us they enjoy the stories but wonder if they can be applied to their own situation. Despite the fact that we have written about almost any type or size of business, for some people the impression remains that only brands that are consumer focused or that have big budgets can be bold, can stay true to their purpose.

So we finish the chapter with a case study that is about as far removed from a consumer brand as we can think. It's a B2B, it's a manufacturing company, it's based in an unprepossessing business park in Letchworth, England, and what it does is ubiquitous and unglamorous. At least, that's what some people might think. But this business is possessed of a great sense of purpose, has a bold vision and is focused on growth that is driven by integrating customers deeply into its plans and processes. The company is called Altro.

Image 9.4 Nissan's GT Academy

Altro

Altro is one of the most successful specialist manufacturing brands in the world. You might not have heard of it but you will have walked all over it. In 1947, Altro pioneered the concept of safety flooring – making floors that were inexpensive, hygienic and stable to walk on for large surfaces in big public areas such as factories, hospitals, schools and on public transport. It replaced the expensive and hard-to-clean ceramic tiles that had previously been used. They remain proudly independent, committed to manufacturing and innovation. A multiple-award-winning company with a turnover of £120 million per year, it has offices around the world, including in the United States and Asia. It is passionate about its people, having been voted one of the *Sunday Times* 100 Best Companies to Work For for eight consecutive years (as of 2015). And it is driven by a commitment to customer insight. Its pioneering 'Voice of the Customer' programme integrates the views of its customers directly into the processes of the business. Its values are succinctly expressed as 'valuing our customers, valuing each other'. If Timpson champions upside-down management, Altro is an advocate of and evangelizes outside-in thinking.

The company is always in pursuit of the new. It understands that it cannot stand still and it has a bold vision of its future, which will deliver its purpose of 'safety, hygiene and sustainability' to people's homes throughout the world.

Richard Kahn, CEO

'Am I good enough to run this place?'

That was my first thought when I took over the organization.

Managers had come through the business and reached a senior level, but then came the question 'Okay, so what are we going to do with these people...? We'll put them on the board.' So we had a UK sales director and overseas director, we had a manufacturing director, a technical director. In fact, we had almost double of everything and it was more difficult to make those harder decisions. Also, everybody was sitting there waiting to be told what to do at every level.

I was sitting there thinking, 'I can't bloody do all this.' And so I had to turn it upside down.

Turning the organization upside down

We reduced the board (it is now five people); we gave a clear direction and we empowered more people in the business to take the initiative, to have ideas. It's all about leadership and not management.

My main observation, however, when I took over as CEO was that we had a five-year plan but we weren't all pointing in the same direction. So I introduced my first attempt at a new style of five-year plan. However, if I'm being completely honest, when I look back to our 2008 goal, which was our first five-year plan goal – it was so catchy in terms of the financial bit, that's what everyone latched on to. It was financially driven.

However, now we have inverted that. Now at board meetings we put purpose at the top of the agenda – and then our core values and our vision. Purpose is everywhere. It is driving everything we do. We said 'If we get this right, the finances should sort themselves out.'

So whereas we used to have a financial goal right at the top of our strategy, we've now got one that is sitting at the bottom. If we get this right, we should have growth in the business of 6.5 times, taking us to $1 billion.

So we have our purpose to take responsibility for safety, hygiene and sustainability at the top. Then we have our core values of valuing the customers and valuing each other. Finally, we have our vision for the business. We have put in place measures so that the board is monitoring on a quarterly basis how we are getting on, ensuring that the purpose, the core values and the vision are all aligned.

Vision

Our long-term vision is completely in line with our purpose and our core values. For me, it is absolutely critical that you have all three completely aligned. You need everybody to understand – from the very top through the organization, through to the customers – that it is all completely aligned.

The vision is to operate on a truly global stage; at the moment 50 per cent of our sales are outside the UK. It is a vision of Altro as a household name everywhere.

Our products are going to be smart. They are going to be interactive; they are going to be sensory. They are going to provide a service for the customer that is more than just a floor and a wall. They are going to be something beyond what we understand at the moment.

One of the products we are looking at in terms of smarter products is a floor that when you walk on it would generate energy – energy harvesting. Imagine a hospital corridor with all the lights being powered by all the people walking down the corridor, that's a very different proposition to just providing a roll of flooring.

The interactive part is important as well. The wall panel in an operating theatre or on a train or plane won't just be observed; people will be able to do their work on our surfaces; there will be temperature control or technology that identifies germs etc.

We also can't really achieve our purpose without digital. Digital could revolutionize our product range. Think about areas in hospitals, big walls and all the rest of it with people waiting, people working. Imagine if you could interact with the floor or the wall and you use it as your computer – or if the kids could draw on the wall.

Product development has always been very important within the company but only now – due to our purpose and vision – have we decided to resource the more creative innovation. We have increased the headcount of R&D by 50 per cent, including a dedicated team of five people working purely on innovation for the long term. Our purpose is to take responsibility for safety, hygiene and sustainability. So our products will also have to be 100 per cent recyclable in order to drive towards sustainability.

We need our products to be sustainable both in the sourcing of raw materials and in their recyclability after use. We haven't sent any products out of this factory for landfill for six or seven years so we have sorted out the factory waste and we have one of the leading schemes in the world in terms of return material from installation. So we have sorted out the installation waste. Now we are sorting out the post-consumer waste. When flooring is ripped up it brings half of the subfloor with it and is very, very difficult to recycle. So we invented a floor, XpressLay, which can be loose-laid so it doesn't bring up half of the subfloor with it, which means it can be recycled.

XpressLay was used in huge quantities for the Olympic Games in London because they wanted a product that they could recycle. After the Olympic Games it was reinstalled in local schools. That for me is leading the industry: to have a product that in terms of both content and post-use is completely recyclable.

Image 9.5 Altro XpressLay flooring for the London Olympics, reused at a school in Kent

Core values: customers

One of our core values is valuing our customers. We want our 'Voice of the Customer' programme to be the benchmark around the world. When people are looking at this type of programme anywhere in the world, they will be coming to Altro saying, 'Wow, how the hell did they do that?' To take that beyond where we currently are, we have to understand not only the voice of the customer but also the behaviour of the customer. And those behaviours will lead us to develop new concepts and products.

Valuing customers is not just providing world-class customer service, because lots of people are doing that; it's getting your customers integrated into your business. So we've got a measure that, by 2016, 50 key business decisions across the global business will be taken each year following customer feedback. This should cover products, place, promotion, price and people. In fact, we are already ahead of the target. More than 50 key business decisions were taken last year as a result of customers saying, 'We think you should do this.' It is about getting those customers really feeling like they are part of the business and using them to help drive the business.

We are taking a leadership position and working very closely with customers on their bigger issues in order to understand how to solve the long-term problems. We are focused on transport, health care and education, which are big infrastructure areas so it is worthwhile investing the time to understand our customers' needs at this level.

With an ageing demographic, there will not be such a clear split between public services in terms of health, education and your private life. More and more people will be looked after in their home. We're going to have to manage society's needs right across the community and, obviously, building design is a real key part of that. People's home environments will need to be more flexible.

As we listened to customers, one of the things that became clear was that we needed to sharpen our purpose so that we had a consistent language throughout the organization and a common focus through which to make decisions. For example, people would ask, 'Why aren't you selling really cheap vinyl tiles that are £3 a square metre? I could sell loads of that for you in the United States.' I would say, 'Well, that's not really what we are about. Other people do that, other people compete on volume and price but we don't.' So I felt we needed a clearer way to articulate what we are about and why we are making certain decisions. The customer feedback within our industry was that we were the only ones that even had some level of specialty. So I said,

'Well, let's not dilute that, let's not just be stuck in the middle and let's remain true to our roots.' It was a combination of our history, strategy and standing out in the marketplace.

Core values: valuing our people

It's not just about valuing our customers, it's about valuing each other, communicating well with each other, people understanding a sense of direction, about the teamwork, about taking responsibility, about people having autonomy, people being recognized, people being rewarded. It just so happens that the Sunday Times 100 Best Companies to Work For survey is one measure of that. We are more or less the only manufacturer in the top 100 for eight years in a row.

I think we were always great at valuing each other and working together but was it always for the ultimate good of the customer? Probably not, which is why we gave equal emphasis to valuing customers.

Recruitment is really important. We have run an exercise a number of times, where we said to people, 'If you were to leave tomorrow, what are the qualities we should be looking for in replacing you?' And we ran this exercise, I don't know how many times, and we've got one flip chart with hard skills, and one flip chart with soft skills. And of course it ends up almost 80 per cent soft skills. So we are now recruiting pretty much on soft skills.

I'm looking for very open-minded, collaborative people who have the ability to challenge, and want to help us make the future. Sometimes you get very challenging individuals and then often the feedback is that they might offend too many people, but I'm not too worried by that. Let them offend a little bit, they are good for the process. The recruitment company tells us, 'You are too hard, you are too picky.' We think it makes all the difference. There is a huge difference between a person who is average on those points and a person who is really good.

Tonia Millson, HR director

Our purpose is not profit

Our purpose is not about being profitable; it is something that is much deeper into the psyche of the organization. It facilitates and informs decision making. If we're sitting in a product development meeting, if we decide to prioritize, then we will ask ourselves the question: does that fit with our purpose? Is that taking responsibility for safety, hygiene and sustainability?

It permeates throughout the organization, because it empowers indi-viduals, it helps them make decisions, because they have a reference point. It also helps us when we're talking to customers. We're able to say how we differentiate ourselves because we have this purpose. And also with our suppliers, as it also helps us to understand whether they are also aligned. So we have been communicating that to all the stakeholders.

We want to integrate our customers into the company. We bring them into our sales conferences. We bring them into our training workshops that we run with our staff. We bring them into interviews, when we interview staff. We listen to them and then we give them the examples of where we have made key business decisions, based on their feedback.

The feedback we've had has been tremendous, absolutely tremendous. It's getting us closer and closer to the customers. Similarly, with the suppliers, we have been bringing them into our internal meetings; they have been coming to a number of our training workshops that we run. We've presented our pur-pose and core values to 150 suppliers. They've been telling us, 'We've never had that from any other customers, we understand more about what you're about.' So, when we're sitting down with them to have our annual meetings or our quarterly meetings, we're able to understand each other better.

We've now identified 10 key drivers that we believe, as an organization, we will need to focus on in order for us to achieve our vision. We've shared those with the senior- and middle-management teams so they are involved right from the beginning, because obviously it is going to be a long journey and we want to make sure we keep the momentum going. Each director will then work with their own functional team to come up with their supporting functional objectives, which in turn will become individual objectives. Everyone in the business is involved and engaged in the process. It informs perfor-mance management and the competency framework that we have in the business. This is how it is brought to life, through ensuring that it is lived every day, through the operational plans across every department. Otherwise, they are just words, aren't they?

It means that we are thinking about the kinds of individuals that we need to bring into the business, or how to train our own staff, to bring up the skill-set level that we need. As a result of the core values work that we did, for example, we have a tailor-made personality test that we use for all candidates who come for interview, in order to ensure that they are aligned to our culture and core values.

It is a huge amount of work. But it's worth it because we are getting feed-back from our staff on a regular basis. They also feel proud that we are not just about profit, that there is a much bigger purpose.

It never stops

I don't think it ever stops – because things move on, don't they? I've been in the business 15 years and I have been involved in about four cultural change programmes in that time. It's not about revolutionary changes; 15 years ago, our purpose was actually much the same, but we didn't pay as much attention to it as we should have done. We didn't get it as embedded in the organization as we should have done.

So, every opportunity we have, we put it all together, so that people can remember our core values, our purpose.

Image 9.6 Altro Design Centre, London

Terry Oakley, 'Voice of the Customer' programme

The 'Voice of the Customer' programme started in March 2008 as a project about acquiring and retaining customers. We decided to launch 'Voice of the Customer' because it was felt that we could do a much better job if we obtained customers' feedback.

We started in the strongest possible way by bringing in one of our flooring contractors who was a clear advocate of our main competitor. He then proceeded in a four-hour interview to absolutely tell me how it was with Altro, and how he perceived Altro, and how we were not in the same ballpark as the competitor.

The feedback I was taking was quite severe. The main themes were: 'You're arrogant, you're aloof, you don't listen and you're corporate, and what that means is that you treat all customers the same and you don't treat them as individuals.' So that was quite a lot of difficult feedback that we took in the early stages.

If I take the first, say, 12 customers that we invited into the plant here, it was a very similar story. Richard Kahn, our chief executive, called me and he said, 'Look, Terry, I want you to invite one of the directors to be with you at all times when we've got customers in. I want them to hear this first-hand.' He thought it was very important for them to hear it, so that's what we did. So it then changed from not just myself talking, having a business discussion with a customer. Instead I had a fellow director with me.

The initial feedback was difficult, but with each year that feedback has changed, it's become more of a partnership with our customers. If you look at the feedback that we've had over the last couple of years it's been more along the lines of 'We love that product that you've developed, could you do this with it?' So it's been more of a partnership about how we can improve, how we can deliver exactly what they are looking for. It's been a difficult journey in some respects, but it's been very valuable.

There are two reasons the programme has succeeded. One is that my sponsor on the board of directors is Richard Kahn, who is saying that this is critical for the future of the company – that I think is a must. I have a regular one-to-one with Richard every month. We talk about the feedback, we look at what trends are showing, and we look at what we need to decide to work on to improve.

The second reason it has been a success is I decided that people in the business heard exactly what the customer had to say. It wasn't a salesperson moaning about the figures not being good and saying, 'You need to fix this, you need to do that, and you need to change that.' And it wasn't me because I made sure that I remained unbiased. I had no allegiance to any department in the company, so I was delivering exactly what the customer was saying to me and then I was sharing that throughout the organization globally. I think that is a key part because it is not what Terry Oakley is saying, it's not what the sales manager is saying, it's not what the finance director is saying: this is what our customers are saying and this is what they think. Whether we like it or not, this is the perception they have. I did that by actually feeding back into the business in report format – after every customer visit – exactly what the customer said. Even to the point where we had a customer that was criticizing Richard's behaviour in a particular project and I went to him before I issued the report. I said, 'Richard, this is what the customer said. What would you like me to do?' He said, 'I want you to publish it. I know what he's had to say, he's right, it's what the customer said and that is the key point for me. I want you to publish it as it is.'

The information passes throughout the company, and where people have shared with us their frustrations or what we call 'pain points' of dealing with Altro, we've got clear examples of where we've fixed it and we've communicated back that we've fixed it to the customer, so we've closed the loop.

I ask Richard if he'll write back to that customer that gave us the initial feedback to let him know that actually we've taken the feedback on board and we've fixed it and this is what we've done.

The other thing we do is take net promoter scores from customers and we find that to be a good measure of how customers perceive Altro. We're getting some world-class scores now.

I also take a snapshot measurement of sales, so I look at the sales performance for the customer six months before they come in to see us and then I go back six months after they visit us, take again a snapshot of their sales, and then I compare the two and you can tell from the figures that they clearly gained confidence from the visit. I know that the relationship is certainly different as a result. The sales representative has been very clear that when they go back in to see that customer after they visited, the relationship is different. It's closer. They're prepared to share with us their information on the projects they're working on. They share competitive information with us that is very useful for us to hear.

We ask for customers' feedback on everything we do. Why give customers something they don't want or value? It's pointless. If you go back and think about that arrogance, that aloofness, I can remember in January 2005 we launched 10 products in one go that was unheard of for Altro – it was a real challenge for the whole organization. But within two years of launching those 10 products we had to withdraw five of them because they just were not required by the industry.

And that is because we had an inward focus where we assumed we knew what the market wanted, that we knew what our customers wanted, and we went ahead and developed those products at high cost and then in a very short period of time we had to withdraw them. That no longer happens, and I can honestly say now that since those horrible days, since we have started to incorporate customers into the whole process, we've had none of those issues. In fact, we have gone the other way. We developed our Aquarius product based on a lot of feedback from customers. That product is now the fastest-selling product ever in the Altro range.

As time has gone by people have seen the power of the programme. They know that the feedback is accurate. They know that it's not filtered. Our sales managers contact me to get condensed customer feedback about a particular subject that they will then build into their business case that they will put before the board. It becomes part of business planning, and when you've got customer feedback in your business plan for which you're hoping you can get some release of resource, it becomes very powerful.

I do a 'Voice of the Customer' induction presentation to every new employee, including our manufacturing staff. Whenever we have customers in, everyone sees them. I think that is important because there is analysis that says 65 per cent of the employees in every company never see or speak to a customer. Here that is not the case, because even when they are walking through the plant, they get the opportunity to ask to say hello to the customer and to acknowledge that the customer is there.

All of this feedback goes globally. It is not unique to just this country because we're a company of 650 employees with subsidiary offices in Canada, America, Germany, Sweden, Spain and Australia.

I always acknowledge the customer after the visit and they always give me the same feedback, 'I can tell by walking, meeting your people, looking around the plant that they take a pride in what they do and they all seem to have a smile on their face.' You cannot beat that. You cannot bottle that. You cannot force people to do that, but that's what people do here.

It's our people that are our strength in this company.

Image 9.7 Altro flooring in Nestlé HQ, Spain

John Patsavellas, technical director

We've been manufacturing in the UK for a very long time. We export half of what we make in this factory in Letchworth across 30 countries. There are not many British manufacturers who export 50 per cent of what they make to all corners of the earth. Manufacturing is in our DNA. The success of the business is based on innovation. The Altro Safety Floor was a unique product. Now other people have copied it successfully, but still we are the original and we keep innovating on the same platform and introducing products, which still resonate with the marketplace.

For example, one of our best recent products that we launched in 2012 is now a key part of our sales. It's called Aquarius. It has been invented here and it has being manufactured here, so the technical and the manufacturing power of the business is very important.

We have a culture of openness and engagement with people. We're not a command-and-control military kind of company. Our purpose is not to make money. Our purpose is to make the world a better place, and if we do that well we will also make some money. Now that might be the romantic view of the world but I believe it. It enables people like me and people in my team to have the freedom to think about what could be. To open up our minds to what can be done, to possibilities, to options. And to face down any fears that perhaps we cannot do something.

I'm a big believer in getting universities involved with the manufacturing business. I have a very strong manufacturing background, also a business background with pharma, fashion, food and print. I have built plants around the world, closed plants in Europe, moved them to China. I've seen the good, the bad and the ugly.

We also sit on an advisory body to government about manufacturing policy. This is because we're an award-winning company. Last year we won our fourth manufacturing excellence award run by the Institution of Mechanical Engineers. We spoke in the House of Commons a number of times on automation and supply chain initiatives. People want to hear what we have to say – and we want to share our experiences.

Last year we implemented a lean manufacturing programme, which saved our business a substantial amount of money. I asked my boss to use some of that money to create an innovation team looking at what we call disruptive innovation. We pretty much understand how to innovate as a manufacturer, we have the incremental innovation. We've got the radical innovation, which is new products and services within the same theme and platform. And we have disruptive innovation, which is things that don't exist.

So we have a team, soon to be a team of five people, who have some really interesting projects, one of which I can tell you a little about because we're doing it in collaboration with the government and a university locally. It's a project that involves us bringing onto the market an energy-harvesting floor. It takes your kinetic energy and turns it into micro-electricity. That micro-electricity will be created from a normal vinyl floor in a roll. You can't tell it's something special; it's something ordinary from which we form something special. It's not mega-expensive and it's not impractical. A hospital can think, 'Well, for a normal price, I can have something that generates negative carbon footprint.' But this isn't just a floor; we're selling a system. We can say to the facilities manager or the architect or the consultant or the investor, 'We can help you choose your system, choose the colour, choose what properties you want. We will install it, we will maintain it. At the end of its life we will take it away and we will deal with the end of its life through reuse or recycling.'

The 'Voice of the Customer' programme gives us a lot of snippets from the customers, which we collect and these are reviewed by all of us. We then gauge how important some of the snippets are and we take different decisions in our incremental innovation. The problem with radical and with disruptive innovation is that you can't ask people about things they don't really know. That's where we go away and observe people. Rather than have the voice of the customer, we'll look at the behaviour of the customer. When you ask people logical questions, they'll give you logical answers because it actually makes sense. That's not necessarily what happens in reality. We understand that. That's why we're able to invest in disruptive innovation and especially on our radical innovation. Incremental innovation is somewhat easier because it can come just from the voice of the customer.

Our purpose and values manifest themselves on a day-to-day basis, habitually – because we value feedback and we talk to everyone and they feel happy to talk to us. There is a lot of engagement. For example, we have what I call an agile meeting at 12 noon every day. We have a stand-up meeting, we talk only about three things; every area and department – technical and manufacturing, logistics and planning – and they can say, 'Here's our priority for the day,' 'Here's our sticking point for the day,' 'Here's one of our successes from yesterday.'

We have that at 12 noon because people have had a chance to catch up with their day, it's only 20 minutes and if we haven't finished in 20 minutes, we get out. It's not mandatory attendance. It is whoever wants to show up. It enables us to understand the priorities in a big factory like this. We often circle back after the meeting and say, 'Okay, let's talk about your sticking point.'

The ways of working here are progressive. We're not using any unique technologies that someone else doesn't have in our industry, but we're very close to the leading-edge world of technology. What is unique here is the ownership of the business; we have a very enlightened owner. He is a unique individual, he's engaging and he loves to do things right with people. That makes a huge difference and encourages all of us to do the same. In the next five years we will be bringing out some products that will blow minds.

Chapter Ten
On Purpose profile

The *On Purpose* research findings

In this book we talk about numerous brands (the good and the bad). You've read the stories, felt the passion and hopefully been inspired to think about applying some of the principles to your own organization. At times you probably nodded your head in agreement, shook it in violent disagreement at our choice of some of the featured brands, and protested loudly about the omission of some much-loved purposeful brands that you thought should have been included, but weren't. (Perhaps even one that you own?) Whatever your thoughts, the most important question is... what does this all mean for you?

How does your company compare? How do you measure up against those principles and practices that mark the difference between the brands that simply *talk* about their purpose, and those that actually *act* on purpose? And what are the tools you can use to help you become one of them? Start by taking a quick look at the eight questions below. Think carefully about your brand and your organization as you go through them:

1 Are you purpose driven?

2 How purposeful is your leadership?

3 How infectious is your communication?

4 Is your customer experience distinctive enough?

5 Do you continuously innovate?

6 How strong is your culture?

7 Is your employee experience as distinctive as your customer experience?

8 Do you place as much emphasis on measuring the experience as you do on measuring results?

You will get the chance to think about these in a little more detail at the end of this chapter.

Eight practices common to all purpose-led brands

The eight questions listed above are important because these are the very factors we identified as being common to all purpose-led brands. They are strongly rooted in the research we did for our last book *Bold: How to be brave in business and win*, in which we created a survey that measured the eight practices that described these organizations. As has been said, one of the things that emerged strongly from that book and that research was the sense of purpose that drives bold organizations. It was that insight that led to this book.

We have now evolved the *Bold* survey to reflect the latest thinking and findings from our research with the 'on purpose' brands. As you would expect, given that one was evolved from the other, there is a great deal of similarity, yet the importance of purpose shines through.

Each of the eight dimensions is supported by five attributes that describe what purposeful brands actually *do*. These were derived from the analysis of the many interviews we have conducted for this book as well as *Bold*. As we have told the stories throughout this book we have attempted to illustrate these practices in action. There was one final check we wanted to make before reaching definite conclusions about what makes a purposeful brand purposeful, and that was to conduct a survey with some of the executives featured, as well as executives from random brands.

We asked some of the brands we use as case studies in this book to complete the survey and we show the results over the page along with the comparison profile. This comparison was derived from asking readers of **http://www.mycustomer.com** (the leading customer experience portal in the UK), **http://customerthink.com** (the leading portal in the United States) and **http://gccrm.com** (one of the best customer experience sites in Asia) to complete the survey. These respondents were self-selected from random organizations in the UK, the United States and Asia to provide our 'average company' profile.

The sample of data is not large, but the results are statistically significant – we are happy to provide the T-Test results for the statisticians among you, but you only need look at the profiles over the next pages to see that there is a large difference between the way the executives of the on purpose brands responded to the way that the executives of the random brands responded.

Our conclusion is that the quantitative research supports what we found in the interviews, namely the executives of the on purpose brands place emphasis on quite different things to many executives in typical companies. In particular you can see that being 'purpose driven' and having a 'cult-like culture' are high points for the brands we feature.

In answer to the survey question *'Overall, I would describe my organization as having a clear sense of purpose'* the brands we studied and who participated in the survey scored an average of 4.7 versus the 3.5 of the comparison brands, so the perceptions of the people in these organizations support the findings from the individual dimensions.

In answer to the question *'Overall, we deliver a distinctive customer experience across multiple channels'*, which of course is a measure of intentionality – our other use of 'on purpose' – the brands we studied scored an average of 4.4 versus the 3.1 for comparison brands. Once again, there is a clear difference in the way that the respondents from the on purpose brands perceive the experience their organizations deliver from the respondents in the comparison organizations, and the gap is even higher than for being purposeful.

As we said, the numbers are not high at the moment but we are confident about our conclusions and, as we continue to collect data, we can add to the findings. How does your organization compare? You can complete our online survey and by doing so contribute to our continuing research. Complete the On Purpose survey here:

http://on-purpose.questionpro.com

Or you can complete the survey over the page and plot your scores for each section to find out how you compare to the on purpose brands and average company profiles as they stand at the time of going to print.

Please use this survey to assess your own organization. Rate each individual statement as accurately as you can, awarding a 4 or 5 if you feel that your organization is distinctly different or market leading, 3 if it is average or you don't know, and 1 or 2 if there is considerable room for improvement or this is an area where your organization does not currently focus.

1 – Strongly Disagree, 2 – Disagree, 3 – Neutral, 4 – Agree, 5 – Strongly Agree

1) PURPOSE DRIVEN	STAND UP
We have a clear purpose that drives activity in the company	1 2 3 4 5
We are willing to trade short-term profit to achieve our long-term vision	1 2 3 4 5
We have a clearly defined brand/customer promise	1 2 3 4 5
Our purpose, the customer promise and our customer experience are closely aligned	1 2 3 4 5
We are boldly changing/challenging the traditional thinking in our industry	1 2 3 4 5
2) PURPOSEFUL LEADERSHIP	**STAND UP**
There is a unique leadership style in this organization	1 2 3 4 5
Leaders communicate our purpose consistently and clearly	1 2 3 4 5
Our leaders stick to our purpose and demonstrate it through their actions	1 2 3 4 5
Our leaders spend time with customers and employees talking about our purpose	1 2 3 4 5
We tend to be guided by instinct and intuition rather than data and analysis	1 2 3 4 5

Image 10.1 On Purpose Survey

1 – Strongly Disagree, 2 – Disagree, 3 – Neutral, 4 – Agree, 5 – Strongly Agree

3) INFECTIOUS COMMUNICATION	STAND OUT
We clearly and honestly communicate our brand promise to customers	1 2 3 4 5
Our customers are actively involved in helping to improve our brand/products	1 2 3 4 5
We use innovative digital marketing and social media to communicate with our customers	1 2 3 4 5
We foster active customer communities that support our brand	1 2 3 4 5
We aim to achieve high levels of customer advocacy that drive referral business	1 2 3 4 5
4) DISTINCTIVE CUSTOMER EXPERIENCE	**STAND OUT**
We deliver the customer experience across each of our channels in a way that is consistent, intentional, differentiated and valuable to target customers	1 2 3 4 5
Our customer experience clearly demonstrates our brand promise and values	1 2 3 4 5
We seek to bring alive our brand promise for customers in distinctive ways	1 2 3 4 5
Our entire company is focused on delivering a distinctive customer experience	1 2 3 4 5
We have a strong alignment between marketing, operations and HR around the experience	1 2 3 4 5
5) CONTINUOUS INNOVATION	**STAND OUT**
We constantly innovate in this organization	1 2 3 4 5
Innovation is driven by a deep understanding of what our target customers value	1 2 3 4 5
Our products, services and people are constantly evolving to meet customer needs	1 2 3 4 5
We apply innovative technology and processes to support the delivery of a competitively superior customer experience	1 2 3 4 5
We demonstrate market-leading customer service skills and capabilities across channels	1 2 3 4 5
6) CULT-LIKE CULTURE	**STAND FIRM**
Our people believe in, and are committed to, a 'higher purpose'	1 2 3 4 5
Our internal values are closely aligned with our brand values	1 2 3 4 5
We have a distinctive culture and a brand 'DNA' that permeates our company	1 2 3 4 5
We reward our people and share their stories about delivering our promise to customers	1 2 3 4 5
We have our own unique phrases or language in this organization	1 2 3 4 5
7) DISTINCTIVE EMPLOYEE EXPERIENCE	**STAND FIRM**
Our employee experience is as distinctive as our customer experience	1 2 3 4 5
We hire first and foremost for attitude and fit with our culture	1 2 3 4 5
Our reward system reinforces our values and desired behaviours	1 2 3 4 5
Our people are trained in innovative ways to help them deliver our brand promise	1 2 3 4 5
We do not tolerate people for long who fail to demonstrate our values	1 2 3 4 5
8) EXPERIENCE MEASUREMENT	**STAND FIRM**
We have a clear focus on target customers and what they value	1 2 3 4 5
Our customer measurement systems provide performance data on the complete customer experience, not just satisfaction	1 2 3 4 5
We regularly gather feedback from the front line about the experience we provide	1 2 3 4 5
Our executive team focus on the employee and customer experience, not just the bottom line	1 2 3 4 5
We understand and measure the upstream indicators that drive economic results	1 2 3 4 5
9) SUMMARY STATEMENTS	
Overall, I would describe my organization as having a clear sense of purpose	1 2 3 4 5
Overall, we deliver a distinctive customer experience across multiple channels	1 2 3 4 5

Now calculate the average scores for each of the eight practice sections. Plot the average scores for each of the eight practices on Figure 10.1 and 'join up the dots'.

– *Overall, I would describe my organization as having a clear sense of purpose*

On purpose brands = 4.7. Comparison brands = 3.5. My brand =

– *Overall, we deliver a distinctive customer experience across multiple channels*

On purpose brands = 4.4. Comparison brands = 3.1. My brand =

Which are our strongest practices?

1
2
3

Which practices do we need to focus on?

1
2
3

So how do you compare to the on purpose brands or the comparison companies in our survey? Compare your profile with Figures 10.2, 10.3 and 10.4 and the results for your summary questions.

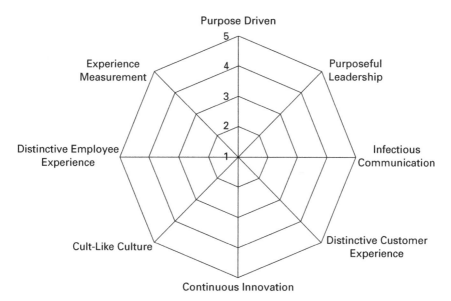

Figure 10.1 My company profile

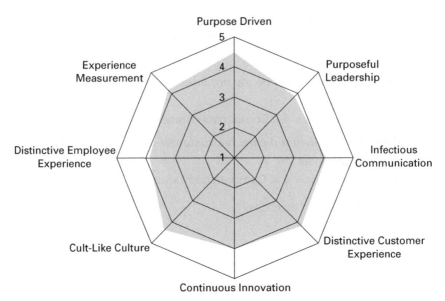

Figure 10.2 On purpose brands (n = 72)

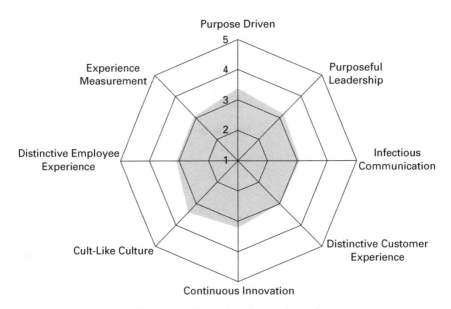

Figure 10.3 Comparison brands (n = 86)

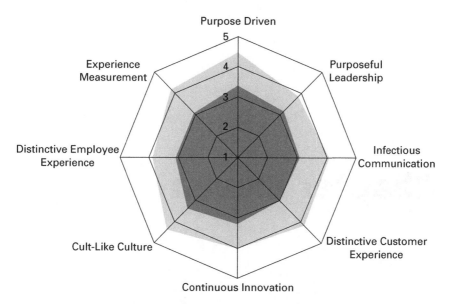

Figure 10.4 The profiles compared

The most significant difference is that the on purpose companies pay much more attention to being purpose driven. The comparison companies are significantly less focused on creating a distinctive customer experience across channels – the intentionality part of our on purpose concept. These findings, as we expected, endorse the findings in our book *Bold*, but lend greater clarity to the notion of purpose.

You may find it useful to plot your profile to overlay Figure 10.4 so that you can see precisely where your opportunity areas lie. We hope this is helpful for you, but if you would like a more in-depth insight please see details of our Masterclass in Chapter 12.

Chapter Eleven
How to implement – successfully

We hope that at this point in the book you will agree that the 'stand up, stand out, stand firm' framework is a simple yet powerful way to describe what purposeful brands do and why they do it. It is not, however, a model that describes *how* they do it.

Just as a travel guide is a vital source of information for describing what a place might be like and some of its most notable features, it does not actually tell you how to get there. For that you need a satnav or map that provides the direction and key steps on the journey.

The map that we use to help organizations become purposeful brands and differentiate themselves through the customer experience (CX) is what we call our 'CX Seven Step Guide'. There is nothing magical about it except that it works and manages to avoid the pitfalls that many organizations fall into. It provides a simple strategy for implementation. And that is sorely needed. As we said in the Introduction, 'on purpose' refers to being focused on something other than profits but it also refers to creating a customer experience that is intentional.

Our own experience has taught us that there are seven deadly sins to implementing customer experience successfully and they relate to a number of the Forrester findings. (Forrester, State of Customer Experience Report, 2013)

The seven deadly sins of customer experience (CX)

1 *Lip-service leadership*

Leadership is vital for any significant organizational change yet all too often leaders fail to commit. Senior executives, having concluded that the brand is underperforming, decide that it is the result of customer-facing staff behaving in ways that are 'off-brand'. They then issue a directive exhorting employees to 'put customers first' or something similar. Executives then return to the important business of focusing on the financials.

Our own work and research have shown time and time again that the most significant factor in creating strong companies is having leaders who take personal responsibility for communicating, demonstrating and rewarding brand or company values.

2 *Silo thinking*

In many organizations the customer experience is fragmented. For example, one function owns the contact centre; another runs the retail operation; whilst

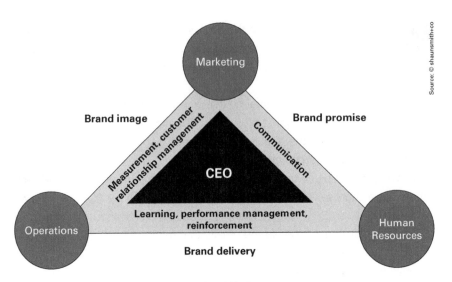

Figure 11.1   Triad power

marketing communicates new propositions, forgetting to first ensure that the front line can deliver them. Worse still, the board announces a new customer experience initiative only to backtrack at the first sign of pressure on the share price.

To be successful the senior management team must own the customer experience. Each function has its particular part to play but the functions must operate in what we call a 'triad' to optimize resources, efforts and budgets to create an organization-wide strategy for delivering the brand (see Figure 11.1). Aligning marketing, operations and HR is critical to getting the internal commitment needed to deliver your experience.

3 *Assuming all customers are equal*

The starting point for our work is collecting customer data to inform the definition of a promise and to design the new experience. The most frequent client response to this suggestion is: '*We already have lots of customer data and research so you don't need to bother*'. In reality, whilst organizations undertake customer research and collect mountains of data, relatively few know who are their most valuable (not largest) customers. The fact is that a few customers will typically represent the significant proportion of your profit and these are the ones to focus improvement efforts on.

It is all very well knowing who are your most profitable customers, but you also need to know what these customers value and the three or four most important attributes that drive their intention to repurchase. Without the answers to these questions you may have data, but you do not have insight.

4 Assuming all touchpoints are equal

Whether you are bidding for new business, selling a product, delivering a service, dealing with complaints, submitting proposals, operating your call centre or negotiating contract renewals – each touchpoint will create an experience that either builds value for your brand or destroys it. Increasingly, brands are realizing that the entire customer journey must be seamless across different channels. But seamless does not mean that it should be the same across all touchpoints.

Where many organizations go wrong is to assume that all touchpoints are equally important and therefore they should try to excel in all of them. In fact, some are more important than others, either because they represent greater value to customers or because they provide the opportunity for you to differentiate your brand or dramatize your brand promise. Trying to excel at every touchpoint will either drive you out of business on cost grounds or create confusion about what is really important.

5 Thinking training is the answer

So many organizations 'do' customer service training. Yet so few deliver a great experience. Most often, it is because organizations rely on undifferentiated training to deliver a differentiated experience. If you cannot bring your brand alive during training for your people, then you cannot expect your people to bring it alive for your customers.

The other issue is that all too often training is done 'to' your people rather that done 'with' them. Bringing in external consultants to conduct a two-day workshop (the classic 'sheep dip') may have a short-term effect but the benefit is rarely sustained. But the greatest sin is to think that training is all you need to do. We have seen many companies invest a lot of money and time in training their people, but fail to change any of their other HR processes. The ways you recruit, motivate, measure and reward people all need to be aligned. Most importantly, the employee experience has to mirror the experience you wish to deliver to your customers. That is why starting with your leaders is vital.

6 *Putting technology in charge*

One Bearing Point report (Insight Executive Report) estimated that 55 per cent of CRM systems drive customers away and dilute earnings. This is because most CRM systems are installed before organizations are clear about the customer experience they are supposed to enable, and without any thought about how they might add value for the customer.

Letting technology dictate your customer experience is a bad idea. You end up with customers feeling hunted rather than wooed. Our definition of CRM is 'Constantly Receiving Mailshots', because so often the systems are used as a blunt instrument to sell rather than create value for the customer.

7 *Measuring satisfaction rather than experience*

Peter Drucker's famous maxim that *'what gets measured gets managed'* is still true today. Yet many organizations focus exclusively on end-result measures. Market share, profitability and earnings per share (EPS) growth are all vital measures of business performance but they are all lagging indicators; they are a result of differentiation, customer loyalty and brand preference.

Nor is measuring customer satisfaction enough. Smith+co research found that 80 per cent of customers who switch suppliers express satisfaction with their previous supplier. Satisfaction has become the price of entry not the way to win. The only true customer measure that correlates with improved business results is advocacy. We define this as those customers who give top-box ratings for their experience. Nothing else counts – yet we see many organizations adding up the percentage of customers who give 'somewhat satisfied', 'satisfied' and 'very satisfied' ratings and then congratulating themselves that '87 per cent of our customers are satisfied' or, even worse, 'delighted'.

Summary

The good news is that these seven sins can be avoided by using our CX Seven Step Guide (see next page). The CX Seven Step Guide is a quick, simple introduction to managing some of the tricky stuff around customer experience. It also shows links to a set of nine simple but useful online tools and templates that you can access for free (**www.smithcoconsultancy.com/cem-toolkit**).

It is not a prescriptive set of rules, it's not big on theory and it is in no way intended as a replacement for the many excellent books out there on customer experience management (including our own!). It is simply a few suggestions and reminders of things to think about – and some of the other pitfalls to watch out for. Some of the pointers may seem incredibly obvious and some may seem quite basic. But, as we've come to realize from our many years of helping organizations with their customer experience journey, there is a tendency to overcomplicate the process and forget the simple things that actually make the difference between success and failure.

The CX Seven Step Guide ENGAGE

What is the number one priority for customer experience management (CEM) success? Engaging your team with a compelling reason to proceed. This ensures an aligned and committed team behind your implementation plan.

Here are a few things you can do

Quantify the benefit in a simple way. The 'power of one' is a good starting point. For example, what would be the financial impact for the year if each of your customers bought one more item, stayed one more day or referred one other person?

Define the type of customer experience needed to achieve this change in behaviour. At this stage, it is not about thinking about the detailed design – it is about stimulating your team to envision something bolder, better and more differentiated than the experience you currently provide. Outline a practical road map to show the steps needed to implement the experience and how this could be achieved within the organization's existing resources. Keep it simple at this stage and break it into phases with clear deliverables and benefits outlined for each.

We generally prefer a more qualitative approach. Don't build it around figures that the accountants may dispute, but create a compelling vision and narrative of what the brand could be like from a customer and employee perspective. This helps to create emotional buy-in and pride in the brand rather than bogging it down in debate about the numbers.

However, if yours is a financially driven organization, you may have to build the business case for the long term, highlighting the potential return on investment (ROI) over three to five years, and the potential negative impact of doing nothing on your market share or customer base.

For more on determining the ROI of your programme, take a look at our CEM calculator tool (see the *On Purpose* toolkit, **www.smithcoconsultancy.com/ cem-toolkit**).

> ### Watch out for...   Fear of the big leap
>
> CEM implementation can seem daunting. So dip your toe in the water with a small, relatively low-risk pilot to help demonstrate the benefits, learn what works and what doesn't, and create a strong case for company-wide roll-out.

The CX Seven Step Guide INSIGHT

What drives loyalty in your business?

Defining the top three or four values that drive customer loyalty is key to defining your promise and designing your experience. Here are a few guidelines to help you:

- Start with your most profitable customers. These are the ones you want more of because they represent the biggest returns.

- Identify the key customer touchpoints. You will want to use these as a framework for your research.

- Start with qualitative research. Focus first on a small group of representative target customers. Use focus groups or interviews to probe for likes, dislikes and loyalty behaviours. The main question to ask, however, is: 'What do you value most from a supplier offering our type of service/product?' Ask them to prioritize and rate your brand against these expectations. Now you are ready to move to the quantitative stage.

- Focus on the top 20–25 expectations and use these to build a survey to validate with a larger group of target customers. Correlate the results with *intention to return* or *recommend*. This forms a core set of value drivers that will become the basis of your brand promise.

- Create an expectation map to identify what customers expect at each key touchpoint with your brand. This will help with your experience design.

- Hone your own instinct to help interpret the data. Step into your customers' shoes and try to experience the same type of journey as your customers. A good way of doing this is to select a similar brand of which you yourself may be a customer, and then identify the different elements of the experience as you interact with that brand. This gives you understanding not only of a customer's practical needs, but the emotional needs and the factors that influence them. For more on this, see our CEM guide on customer loyalty in the online toolkit.

Watch out for...

Slicing and dicing by every single customer segment. Focusing on multiple market segments is good for communicating your promise but useless for defining it. You will end up trying to be all things to all people. Focus on your primary target customers, what you stand for as a brand and the value you bring. You can always fine-tune the experience to suit other segments later, in the form of specific propositions.

The CX Seven Step Guide DEFINE

How do you ensure that your customer experience really differentiates your brand?

By starting off with a really clear brand promise, which defines the differentiated value that you deliver to your target customers.

A brand promise is an articulation of what target customers can expect from their experience with your brand. It reinforces your purpose; it replaces or aligns the numerous disconnected missions, visions, company values and customer charters evident in so many organizations that are often contradictory, confusing and of little practical value in running a business. And, as we said in Part Two of the book, it is the heart line that runs throughout your customer experience.

So how do you create it?

Here are a few guidelines

1 Bring together HR, Marketing and Operations. A brand promise is usually seen as being the Marketing Department's baby. But if HR and other operating functions don't buy into it, it becomes little more than an advertising slogan. All key functions need to own the promise and commit to doing whatever is needed for delivering it.

2 Start with your brand positioning. Be absolutely clear what your brand stands for and the value this represents for your target customers. Your brand positioning provides the context for your brand promise.

3 Next, go back to the value drivers you identified in your research. Define a brand promise that will deliver those values, differentiate you and align with your brand positioning.

4 Create a set of clear concise statements that underpin this promise. These must be actionable, ie able to be understood by employees and translatable into behaviours that deliver your promise. (See our CEM tool for more on how to define your brand promise. Go to **www.smithcoconsultancy.com/cem-toolkit**)

Watch out for... Copywriter seduction

It's all too easy to focus more on the sizzle than the substance. Don't let the effort default to creative copywriting rather than nailing the fundamental commitments you will make. Focus on content first, creativity second.

The CX Seven Step Guide DESIGN

How do you manage a seamless branded experience across an ever-increasing number of multiple channels?

You can't.

Here's what you can do

Experience is whatever the customer perceives it to be – and you cannot micro-manage it completely. But what you can do is influence that experience by being very intentional about where and how you deliver your brand promise – in a way that is absolutely consistent at every touchpoint. This is what we call *designing the experience*. Here is a simple summary of steps to take:

- Map the experience from beginning to end, including social media. Use the customer's perspective, not the organization's. You could map one touchline covering the entire experience but if this is too complex, map a touchline for each key customer interaction.

- Identify the pain points, inefficiencies, redundancies or inconsistencies in how customers experience your brand.

- Consider your brand promise and how well you deliver it at each point in the touchline.

- Ensure you think about your most valuable customers and their top expectations.

- Identify opportunities to streamline and improve the experience. Look also for opportunities between existing touchpoints, such as the space between making a purchase online and actual delivery of the goods.

- Identify hallmark touchpoints that will really differentiate your brand and emotionally engage your customers. These are the touchpoints that you need to over-index.

- Create a blueprint for approval and identify implications for people, process and product/service and then move to implementation planning. For more on designing your customer experience, take a look at our CEM+ Survey tool in the online toolkit.

Watch out for... Design by committee

You need cross-functional input, but if you present a blank sheet to the team you will get bogged down in arguments and paralysed by too many voices wanting to go in too many different directions. So begin by creating a strawman design and then set aside a day with the cross-functional team to debate it, evolve it and plan to implement it.

The CX Seven Step Guide ALIGN

How do you prevent silos and politics from pulling in different directions?

Get cross-functional ownership, get board-level sponsorship and create an alignment framework.

Here are a few things to think about

Create work-streams led by members of the CX steering group, responsible for progressing the implementation. These work-streams should focus on the following:

- *People*: recruitment, training, performance measurement and rewards are essential elements in ensuring you have the right people to deliver the experience, that they have the know-how and skills to do it and that they are incentivized and rewarded against customer experience key performance indicators (KPIs). You will also need to prepare managers to lead the implementation. It seems obvious, but all too often these elements are not aligned.

- *Process*: people need the tools and supporting processes and technology to help them deliver the experience, so get your team thinking about the internal changes needed to support them.

- *Products and service*: think about how you will dramatize your brand promise, and what new propositions and service changes are needed to enable this.

- *Internal communication*: many people resist change, so good and constant communication is vital – what is happening, when, how, who, why and the potential benefits to employees, not just the organization. Brand the communication. It should be engaging, both visually and in its content. Too often we see messages lost in corporate PR speak and dull uninspiring materials.

- *Measurement*: design a customer experience scorecard so that you can measure pre- and post-implementation to demonstrate the results. For more on this, take a look at our CEM+ Alignment tool in the online toolkit at **www.smithcoconsultancy.com/cem-toolkit**.

Watch out for...   Wimping out

It is at this point that many people focus on the easy things rather than deal with the 'elephant in the room'. These are the big issues that will hold you back.

Here are a couple of things you can do to avoid backtracking on commitments. First, get the initiative on executive meeting agendas right at the beginning of the project, so that issues get addressed right from the start. Second, get your CEO to announce his or her commitment at the beginning, and use every opportunity to reinforce this to employees.

The CX Seven Step Guide MEASURE

How do you ensure that you demonstrate real results so that effort is sustained?

By focusing on the leading rather than the lagging indicators that drive your financial results.

Here are a few things you can do

- Measure leading indicators. Profitability and EPS growth are vital measures of business performance but they are lagging indicators – the result of differentiation, and customer loyalty. You need to measure the leading indicators of customer experience and your performance on the key drivers of customer loyalty and advocacy.

- Build an integrated scorecard to align your financial reporting, customer experience and other operational measures. Link KPIs to this to ensure you can measure and reward people for the right behaviours so that effort is sustained.

- To do this, you will need to identify the critical measures for each part of the scorecard and identify the goal, metric and target for each. Test it. Validate the scorecard, with your executive team and stakeholders involved. Review often and test the relationship between metrics to identify the key leading indicators.

- Continuously communicate results to embed the measures and hard wire this as the way you do business. For more on this, see our CEM+ Scorecard tool in the online toolkit at **www.smithcoconsultancy.com/ cem-toolkit**.

Watch out for... Measuritis

The debilitating condition in which everyone is obsessed with capturing data on everything that can possibly be measured. Only focus on the few key metrics critical to success. Measure what matters and ignore anything that doesn't – otherwise it will scramble your brains.

The CX Seven Step Guide INNOVATE

How do you keep innovating your experience to stay ahead?

'If you want to remain number one, you have to think like number two.'
(Tom Fishburne, *Where Complacent Brands Go*, marketoonist.com)

Here are a few things you can do

- Start with your vision or purpose and work back rather than starting from industry practice and working forwards. This helps you to challenge many of the beliefs and conventions that underpin your market.

- Stand *for* something and be brave enough to *stand up* for it. That way, you'll *stand out*.

- Dramatize your customer experience. Dramatically over-index the key touchpoints where you want to really bring your brand promise to life. Forget timid tinkering. Make it memorable.

- Make customers part of your brand. Use customer co-creation and social media tools to listen and engage. Marketing is no longer something you do to customers. Make them part of it. Make employees part of your brand.

- Create social networks internally so that your employees can be part of your R&D effort. They are closer to your customers and therefore often better informed about the opportunities to innovate.

- Look beyond your industry. Study comparators rather than competitors. Brands can often learn more from brands outside their sectors than within.

- Continuously communicate results to embed the measures, and hard wire this as the way you do business. For more on this, see our CEM+ Innovation tool in the online toolkit at **www.smithcoconsultancy.com/cem-toolkit**.

Watch out for...   Job done

There is a natural reaction to take it easy once the implementation phase has been completed. But customers are changing so fast, you can't just stand still. So change your mindset now from *managing* the experience to *innovating* the experience. Take a look at how other brands are leading the way.

So, enough of the theory. How do these steps work in practice? Well, we thought the best way to show you would be to share a couple of case studies of clients that have followed these steps, or something close to them, and let them tell you in their own words what they did, how they did it and the results they achieved. They finish by sharing some of the things they learned along the way.

Throughout the case studies we have highlighted the key steps from the CX Seven Step Guide as a route map for the reader. We have also shown some real examples of the tools being used. Of course, projects are rarely quite as straightforward and linear as this, but in order to make the learning easy to assimilate we have written them to follow the steps we have outlined.

Chapter Twelve
Putting the principles into practice

Liberty Global Business Services – case study

As we go around the world speaking about customer experience we are challenged with objections or questions along the lines of, 'Well, that is okay if you are in B2C but it doesn't work in B2B,' or 'Well, that may work if you are part of a small company but not if you are in a large plc that is financially driven,' or 'You can do it if you are working for an entrepreneur like Sir Richard Branson but you try implementing it in a corporation.' So, our first case study is the Business Services division of the huge Liberty Global group. Liberty Global is the largest international cable company with operations in 14 countries and nearly 28 million customers. You many not have heard of Liberty Global but you may be familiar with their operating brands. Business Services focuses on the B2B market across Europe, operating through local brands such as UPC Business, Telenet for Business, Virgin Media and Unitymedia. We had the opportunity to work with UPC Business on their customer experience journey, along with our Netherlands-based partner TOTE-M (**http://www.tote-m.com**). UPC based their initiative around the principles we have described in this book.

Let's hear from Frans-Willem de Kloet, at that time the managing director of Liberty Global Business Services Europe, about why they embarked on their journey:

> 'There are a couple of reasons why I started the customer experience initiative across our markets in Europe; one is because I strongly believe that this is the way to differentiate ourselves. If you look at our competition in the B2B market, and especially in small business, then there are two types of competitors. The first are the Telco incumbents and the second are what we call price fighters. In most countries the incumbents choose to compete through product innovation, that's where they are most strong and where for us it would be very hard to compete or differentiate. The price fighters compete through operational excellence. So that leaves a space for us to fill in the area of differentiating through customer intimacy. Our markets have, by tradition, been very local and close to our customers and they are often a result of acquisitions of smaller cable operators in local communities. For this reason it feels very natural for us, both from an internal culture perspective but also how customers define us already. They say we offer a very good service for a reasonable price; we're not the cheapest, but we provide great value for money – and a lot of them mention that we

*offer a more personal approach. That is why we believe that our purpose
is one that is authentic and rooted in who we truly are.'*

Engage

Frans-Willem knew that he would need to have the expertise and resources
to implement the strategy and so he appointed Soraya Loerts as Director of
Customer Excellence and Operations.

Soraya knew that one of her biggest challenges would be to engage the
leadership team to build a consensus and commitment. So Frans-Willem and
Soraya decided to launch the initiative at their 2012 annual leadership conference. Having recently read *Bold: How to be brave in business and win*, they
asked us to run a *Bold* masterclass focusing on the 'stand up' phase.

This was an important first step for Soraya, and she realized that answering
the question 'Why?' was going to be a key success factor for this senior group
of peers:

> *'It became very clear that I needed to start on the 'Why' first, building and
> creating the belief that customer intimacy would be crucial in sustainable
> differentiation and therefore the way forward, which of course was a
> challenge in itself. Our superior network is very much a differentiator, and
> will be over the coming years, but B2B customers in the end are seeking
> a partnership – and customer intimacy is the only way to sustain that
> relationship.*
>
> *'So, I started with why do we actually need to do this at all? Why
> do we need to create a new differentiator if we already have a superior
> network? Second, why this particular strategy? Here, we touched on
> practices we have used with our bigger customers and were able to
> say that that relationship building has proven to be successful. Well, of
> course, the network is the first entry point but keeping your customers
> for years is more about the relationship.*
>
> *The leadership conference was key in bringing it together and for the
> executives to work together and try to find common ground in this belief
> about customer-centricity. We successfully did that with the help of the
> 'Stand Up' Workshop along with some strong ambassadors among the
> senior management team. By the time we got to the end of the session
> everyone was very enthusiastic and saw the benefit of proceeding on this
> path. So much so, that after that moment no one asked me for a business
> case again and everyone started embracing customer intimacy thinking,*

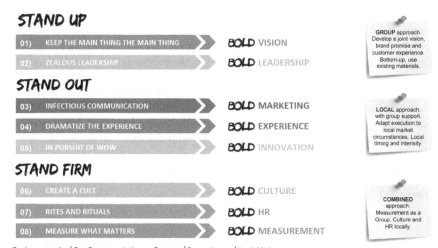

It all began in Scheveningen last year…

LIBERTY GLOBAL

Image 12.1 Stand Up Workshop agenda

which I think was an interesting shift from short term to long term. We really needed to build upon belief, and that proved very successful for us.'

But Soraya also realized that belief only takes you so far and then you have to show results. She thought the time was now right to pilot in a couple of the operating units:

'When I realized that okay, the belief is there, we're talking about the things that really matter – customer loyalty, but now is the moment to show some success, because if you wait too long that belief slips – I started to implement very small programmes in different countries, just taking the most enthusiastic operations, such as Poland for example. Poland is a market that is very traditional and very transactional as well. So if you wanted to take a first step in a market and build upon that belief that customer experience brings benefits, Poland for me was the right market to start with. They are not the smallest, they are not the biggest, they are not seen as Central Europe but not seen as Western either, so an easy country to copy things from. So I started a small programme where we said, "Okay, since we're so transactional and so traditional, from now on we are going to empower the employees that have contact on a daily

LIBERTY GLOBAL

We at B2B firmly believe that telecommunications is a people business. That it is about building relationships over time. Customers personally interact with us, while buying and experiencing our products and services. And where the way we deliver our products and services is just as important as the quality and reliability of those products and services.

This is why we have the customer at heart in everything we do. And why our employees will do everything in their power to make sure that the customer gets exactly what we promise. We truly believe that the success of our business hinges upon providing superior service, every chance we get. Day in, day out.

Business service | Our Customer intimacy Strategy | Soraya Loerts | April 2014

Image 12.2 Liberty Global brand beliefs

basis with our customers to follow their nature, to interact and build relationships, because that's what they want to do but we're preventing them because of our processes." We said to the team, "Just do what you think is good for this customer and fix it." So eventually they were able to work outside the processes and we saw their NPS go from –33 all the way up to +26.

'We did some testing with them and we measured their employee satisfaction and compared that to the control group and found this was also 26 NPS points higher than for the control group. We asked the pilot group what we needed to do to improve our customer experience. We asked it of the control group too and there were two completely different answers. The pilot said much more about building relationships, like take time to listen to the customer and respond and act on that, whereas the control group said, "We need more tooling, we need a better system." So small programmes but really tangible results. Coincidentally, at this time, there was a regulatory change happening in Poland: customers had a chance to get out of their contract. We lost some customers in this process but it gave us the means to actually measure what happened to the customers that went through this pilot group versus the control group and we found that the customer churn was 50 per cent lower in the pilot group.'

Insight

The next step is customer insight because the danger is in making assumptions about what customers value or trying to improve everything, which is often the default in these initiatives. The outcome is a shopping list of improvements that might never be achieved. The alternative is to be really focused on what customers value and then to design an experience to deliver it. We carried out a customer experience survey for our Liberty Global local companies to determine the value drivers and the touchpoints that offered the greatest opportunity for differentiation and driving NPS scores. We created experience curves, what we call our 'ECG' curves, to show what the current experience was like as well as the desired experience that would differentiate the brand.

Soraya offers a good example of how this insight guided the thinking:

'The key is to understand the difference between doing those things that generate loyalty and just doing the job customers expect from you. One good example of that was installation. Our company has been talking about installing equipment such as modems for years; that we needed to do it quicker, cleaner, better etc, which all comes with a high cost, of course, because a technician has to do all of those things. We stopped that. We said, the satisfaction level that we're at is already good enough for our customers and all of the initiatives we're building to be quicker, faster etc are wasted because they are not going to drive loyalty. We could see from the experience curves ("ECG" graphs) and data correlating relational NPS to touchpoint satisfaction what it is that really drives loyalty and that was more about the ongoing customer relationship. We realized that success would come not from striving to do everything perfectly, but from really excelling where it matters to our customers. That was the way to create a memorable experience.

'Some of our operational people had difficulty grasping that concept so we used an example to help them understand; if you go to the baker and ask for bread you don't necessarily become very loyal if you get that bread in three seconds instead of waiting 10 seconds. However, you might become more loyal if you were to get warm bread or a smiling face from the person you engage with. These are benefits other than the bread itself. We had a lot of conversations saying that our installation process is just what customers expect from us and was not the way we were going to differentiate. So we made a clear decision that despite the fact it has been the focus for years we were not going to excel there. Yes, it needs

to be on par, we need to do it well, we cannot have the customer wait for six weeks to get an installation, but the place to over-index is customer care and therefore we are building our programmes to deliver simplicity, the personal approach and top-class service.'

Define

Conducting customer experience research of this kind leads to insight and the identification of the value drivers. These then provide a firm foundation to define the brand promise, a more detailed articulation of the brand positioning and purpose. The brand promise is used primarily as an anchor for experience design and to communicate the 'what' to employees. Some organizations are brave enough to communicate this to customers as well in the form of a guarantee. Our next example, Premier Inn, did just this but for UPC the brand promise was defined to articulate what the group meant by 'customer intimacy':

'One of the things we asked ourselves was, "Who do we want to be in the market? What do we want to deliver?" We tried to encapsulate this in three simple principles: "simplicity, personal approach and top-class service". We then defined what we meant by these principles because they are still very broad. We did this with all of our executives in Europe, the owners responsible for B2B customers in 12 countries together with our MD of Liberty Global Business Services in Europe. We had a long discussion around the questions: "What do we stand for?" "What do we want to be for our customers and how do we operationalize that?" We then started to look at what does the journey look like today and is that journey the same across Europe? We found out that 26 of the 35 touchpoints are exactly the same across Europe so we started to frame them and standardize.

Next, we did research with our customer base in different countries to find out if there are cultural differences when we ask about satisfaction, and what customers think are the most important touchpoints. We found that there were no significant differences, so we could proceed with our European framework. So we worked together with the executive team to frame our customer strategies and principles, and to agree what is the current customer journey, what is our ideal customer journey, where do we need to improve and build loyalty.'

Overall, our principles entail the following

LIBERTY GLOBAL

Simplicity	Personal	Top-class Service
We deliver easy to understand solutions in a clear and transparent way. We take care of things, so you don't have to worry about them	We give individual attention, and provide proactive advice. Our passionate and knowledgeable employees are dedicated to supporting your business needs	We provide consistent, timely and smooth service. We go the extra mile

- ✓ Simple and clear all-in-one bundles
- ✓ No thresholds
- ✓ No small print
- ✓ Extensive support

- ✓ Consultative selling
- ✓ Easy access to a person
- ✓ Problem owner
- ✓ Knowledge sharing

- ✓ Highly professional staff
- ✓ Excellent availability
- ✓ Treat customers and prospects equally

DEVELOP FRAMEWORK

Business service | Our Customer intimacy Strategy | Soraya Loerts | April 2014

Image 12.3 Liberty Global scorecard

Frans-Willem de Kloet, at that time managing director of Liberty Global Business services, also made the point that the process of defining the principles was a valuable way to bring people together in consensus:

'We spent quite some time with the teams in the countries defining customer intimacy. What does it mean and what does it mean for our customers? And defining our three key brand principles of "simplicity, personal approach and top-class service". We took quite a while to agree on them, but once we did we realized that we can actually get to a much deeper level of emotional engagement with the customer. Through simplicity, personal approach and top-class service, you ultimately touch the emotions of the customer. So then we went to our customers and our employees and we said "Okay, what does simplicity mean to you? What would it look like?" We applied that approach to all three principles and that gave us an overview. Then we said, "What are the underlying principles to create proof points?" And that resulted in a brand promise and a customer commitments document and presentation that communicated this direction to all of our people.'

Design

The value of defining the brand promise is that it clearly indicates the way that you wish to differentiate. That is a crucial decision, and one that many organizations fudge. Being in the mass market does not mean that you have to be all things to all people. Strategy is about choosing how to be different in a way that represents value for your chosen target audience.

Erik Wiechers, general manager of UPC Netherlands, expresses this very clearly:

> 'When I joined the company we had fast-declining revenues and EBITDA [earnings before interest, taxes, depreciation and amortization], so we needed to make a shift in strategy. I worked for GE for about four years at the time when the CEO was Jack Welch and his saying, "control your own destiny or someone else will", really applied here. I also worked with Michael Treacey and Fred Wiersema, who wrote the book, The Discipline of Market Leaders, and one of the things I learned from them is you need to make a choice as to where you want to excel. For me, the only sustainable competitive advantage in the long term is customer intimacy.
>
> What we have defined at UPC is a unique customer journey, because the only things that people remember in life are the highs and the lows from an emotional point of view, so that's what we really tried to achieve.'

How do you design an experience that differentiates? We usually run a two-day customer experience workshop that refines the brand promise and then designs the experience to deliver it. In the case of UPC, the first workshop was just one day and focused on the 'stand up' piece. This led to the research and piloting that we have already discussed. In 2013 Soraya decided to conduct a 'stand out' workshop at the annual leadership conference. The purpose was to design the new experience based on the research that had been conducted, and to share the results of the pilot activity in Poland that she saw as being so important to cementing commitment to the broader roll-out:

> 'We have 12 different markets across Europe and of course some perceive themselves as more mature than, for instance, Poland. We hear local company executives say, "We are different, we are special", but, you know, often it turns out that the similarities are bigger than initially thought.
>
> So we ran the 'Stand Out' Workshop and the Polish team presented their programme but they focused mainly on the emotional change. Figures are important – show them by all means but try to build upon the belief and emotion. So we did some rehearsing to get that right and

it was just spot on. Everyone was applauding at the end because they could feel the team leader's passion. During that day everyone said "I want to copy that programme and, by the way, can I hire this manager?" So tapping into that belief and enthusiasm and trying to get the people in the audience involved was the right thread throughout the whole journey.

'All the countries actually took on a challenge: to come up with something to stand out in their market. It needed to be new for their market, but they could copy something from another country.'

The Stand Out Workshop was an opportunity to really make some strategic choices about which touchpoints to over-index. It led to some fierce debate but the outcome was a clarity that had not existed before. That clarity then led to identifying the innovations and technology that would deliver the experience. The sad fact in many organizations is that it tends to work the other way round: the technology dictates the customer experience. Erik Wiechers summed this up in his usual forthright style:

'What most telcos do is to try to improve everything, but improving everything makes sure you remain a "flat liner," and a flat liner is a "dead liner" in our industry because it means that you have no differentiation at all. Everything we do adds to the brand; the brand is a huge asset for us if we build it well. So, the real question is "How will this initiative add value to our brand?" – and to the customer, of course. So we only do those things that add value at the touchpoints that differentiate the brand and add value for the customer. Sometimes people think it strange that we don't invest in everything, but doing so doesn't make you a unique organization, it makes you look rather like everyone else in the industry.

'Increasingly, of course, we have to consider digital as well as the human interface. We've got eight channels that can be used by customers and they are all aligned with the customer journey; it's one experience, there can only be one experience otherwise it's too expensive to build because we have an industrial environment here. I've got thousands of customers, and they all will have the same overall journey, but the thing we will do is to make the online experience personal. So the customer calls, has a question, and we make personalized video in real time to help them. How that works in practice is that we will have video of all 27 steps in the customer journey, and the computer will select from those 27 steps, based on the customer question. Of those steps six, say, will be selected and edited and made available as a video, depending on the need of the customer – so it will feel very personal.'

Align

One of the 'seven sins' is silo thinking. The antidote to this is to ensure that the initiative is cross-functional. Soraya, as the director of customer excellence, was clearly in the frame to deliver the experience strategy but she knew that she couldn't do it alone so she looked at forming natural alliances across the business such as marketing, operations and segments both within corporate and our local companies to help her. One such relationship was with Michel Pilet, the marketing and communications manager of Liberty Global Business Services:

> *'Up until now my role was to translate the customer intimacy strategy into our communication, where Soraya really drives the strategy and the implementation in the carrier organizations because that's where the main opportunity for improvement lies at this stage, really fixing the basics.*
> *I will be moving more into the proposition part – how we want to stand out as a brand, and how to make that more tangible.'*

Alignment is also about creating a common approach across different operating units. This is particularly difficult when those units are acquisitions and have their own legacy systems and cultures. It is even more difficult when one of those acquisitions happens to be called Virgin Media, a brand that knows a thing or two about customer experience. So how do you align people behind a common goal?

Soraya took a very pragmatic approach:

> *'The interesting thing was that we had just acquired Virgin Media in the UK. At first I held off that they needed to restructure etc, but they were present at the workshop and as they became part of the family they became more interested in this journey. Virgin Media have this image of being an entrepreneurial organization – and they are. If you go into their building you can see that they are. They are also very good at drilling down to the lowest level of detail and quantifying it, but in that process of quantifying everything they lost track of the emotional element, according to their operational people. Having customer journeys that show the emotions, and explaining how we can build upon that emotion in the contact that we have with our customers, triggered them to get an in-depth understanding of the path that we were on. So they came over to Amsterdam for a full day to learn about our approach – and they were mostly interested in the emotional part.*

'The main thing for me was not to try to standardize everything to the lowest level because we have very successful teams running our country operations, let's not forget that. So what I wanted to create and deliver to them was more of a framework to win – so this is the playing field and we have some rules; everything you do needs to build upon simplicity, personal approach and top-class service. Within that framework to win we have clear loyalty drivers and you can decide how to apply them to your business. You can decide where you put the emphasis and how to do that. That means in reality that we have different programmes running in different countries. However, they are more similar than you might expect, probably because they are all building to the same means of simplicity and seeking to achieve the same metrics. For example, the Netherlands has been very successful in looking at where to over-index the experience; Telenet for Business, our Belgium affiliate, are really putting the customer at the heart of everything they do; Germany have fully embraced the strategy and have restructured their front line to be the customer experience centre; UPC Business Austria has developed a complete end-to-end service road map; UPC Business Poland is accelerating their cultural change programme on a daily basis; UPC's cablecom business in Switzerland is becoming a very relationship-driven company; and Virgin Media business is driving the business through NPS. Finally, Czech Republic, Hungary and Romania are running welcome programmes and really looking for improvements based on data from customer feedback. So you can see how each market has developed its own approach, but they all relate to the loyalty drivers.

'The Customer Experience Workshop helped us to create alignment around the direction. That was, I think, the start of it all. Obviously we did some thinking before that, but the first thing we wanted to do was to wake people up a bit; to show them a mirror, and say, "If you were a customer why would you choose UPC or any other Liberty Global brand?" We showed the executives that we didn't have a clear differentiation; we didn't have a clear vision. So we created the need, and they asked us to help them.

We mentioned the concept of 'loose/tight'. Most organizations are very 'tight' when it comes to telling operating units and their people what to do and how to do it but very 'loose' when it comes to 'What do we stand for? What kind of experience do we wish to provide? What do we promise?' Our philosophy is to reverse these two so that *what* you stand for as a brand

and *why* it is important are clearly spelled out – as is the kind of experience you wish your customer to have, but *how* it is implemented is left to the front line to figure out. This avoids the robotic 'Have a nice day' behaviour that you see in so many organizations. Michel Pilet used this very approach when thinking about marketing campaigns:

> 'We really had to think from a country perspective because we know our businesses are the ones executing marketing and operations locally and our business model was decentralized. For me, it was more about supporting them. For instance, we created a booklet that was based on our research in several markets. Luckily the research showed that there were not big differences between markets, so we could follow a common approach to our brand promise and experience. We can't standardize delivery and we don't need each country to do exactly what other markets do.
>
> 'The nice thing about it is we can see if a programme has success in one market, and if it does we can try to leverage that into other markets to move more towards a consistent approach where possible. For example, I think it is inevitable that we need to include all channels to deliver the full experience and that experience needs to be aligned across all channels. We hardly do any social media, for instance, but it is on the list this year. It may be part of a bigger plan, to see how we need to operate as a business brand. I think, as we become more and more differentiated, and bigger, we have an opportunity to differentiate from the other parts of the business also. When something fails in the B2B market the customer wants immediate help because their business is their lifeline. Their broadband is not just for a television programme they are watching, they need it in order to do business, and so the impact of service disruptions is way bigger in business than in consumer. And then, obviously, the more diverse the clients and their needs, the more dedicated and tailored solutions they require.

Writers such as Larry Bossidy and Ram Charan have argued that the hardest part of strategy is the execution.[1] We agree. Getting your people to behave differently is vital, but how can you do that? We advocate what we call 'Branded Customer Experience Training' – that is, training that brings alive the brand promise and experience for your people. As Vanessa Hamilton described it in Chapter 7, it is more holistic, experiential and leader-led. Erik Wiechers realized that this would be key and so took an innovative approach to communicating the desired experience and new behaviours to his people:

'The most difficult part for me personally and for my staff is how to you make sure the strategy is delivered. My guys and I are all academically trained, we can grasp the idea, but how do you make sure your strategy lands with the front line? How do you change their behaviour for good, so they understand this is the best thing for them and the customer, and the shareholder?

'We've got 27 moments in the SOHO (Small Office Home Office) customer journey, and at a certain point in time you need to dramatize this for all your staff so they understand it. So, we had 27 people lined up on stage, each responsible for one touchpoint. So, for example, the first person said, "I'm Sarah, I'm responsible for orientation in the SOHO journey, and especially on the landing page; my responsibility is this, and this is how I will make a difference to our customers", and so on for each touchpoint along the journey. It was very visual, very committing; it created one group feeling, working for one customer. There were 27 people lined up on that stage, each committed to make the UPC customer journey unique, and that is what we are all about.

'The nice thing about this company is that we have white-collar and blue-collar workers and they all participated in suggesting ideas as to how to make a difference for the customer. It's their customer journey and they really feel personally committed to improving it. We gave dinner vouchers for people contributing great ideas. We also have a 10-day call, so one of our call-centre agents will give you a call, and ask, "How did the installation go? Is there anything we can learn? How was your experience?" And that really works well. As a result, our NPS has really gone through the roof.'

Measure

There has been much debate over recent years with a number of different metrics and methods vying for dominance: NPS, Customer Effort, CSAT (Customer Satisfaction) and many others. Our view is that there is no one metric that works for everyone – so we prefer to build a scorecard that draws on both lagging and leading, soft and hard, customer and employee measures. However, at the end of the day it is what is most important for the organization that determines the measure of success, and we try to identify this early on and focus our efforts on moving the needle on it. We try to identify the key metric(s) as part of the customer experience workshop but then build a scorecard of all of the primary business, experience and employee indicators prior to implementation so that there is a solid benchmark to evaluate success against. For UPC this was very clear. NPS and the number of contacts were the most important as early indicators that the customer intimacy strategy was working:

> 'The main metrics are transactional and relational NPS along with contacts per year per customer; together they measure the amount of effort put in by our customers.
>
> 'Obviously we want to relate those to churn and customer lifetime value and we are starting to see the first sign of improvements there, being able to correlate data in some markets now.
>
> 'At the moment we are still very transactional, moving from –33 in NPS to now being a positive NPS figure. Now that we are at an acceptable level we can really impact churn and loyalty. We started this journey two years ago and it takes at least two years to really start tracking churn, because customers are in contracts. As I said, results are becoming visible, detractors are dropping and promoters increasing, and we are starting to see a correlation with churn. The plan over the next six months is to really see the impact of churn as compared to two years ago.'

Erik Wiechers was clear that a leading indicator of NPS was employee satisfaction. We agree with him. Those of you familiar with the 'service profit chain' will know that there is a strong cause-and-effect relationship between employee satisfaction, customer satisfaction and business results (for more on this see Joe Wheeler's piece on the service profit chain in Chapter 8):

> 'If you want to have loyal customers you first need to make sure your employees are happy. Five years ago we had an employee satisfaction level below 6; we're roughly at 7.6 now and we have an employee loyalty score of 8.6, which is unique in our industry. My thesis is that only with loyal employees can you make loyal customers; that's the basis of everything. So, that was what we did. And through that and through the customer journey, our NPS really went up, and then our operational cash flow increased, and then I had even more money to invest in the programme. So, I learned, improve your employee satisfaction and increase customer satisfaction, which lead to higher operational cash flow. The reason for this is less churn and, second, more up-sell moments. Those are the financial whys; and the third one, for me personally, is that it feels a lot better, having fun in your job, and really making customers happy. It shouldn't be only financially driven. Your employees are happy if they can make happy customers.'

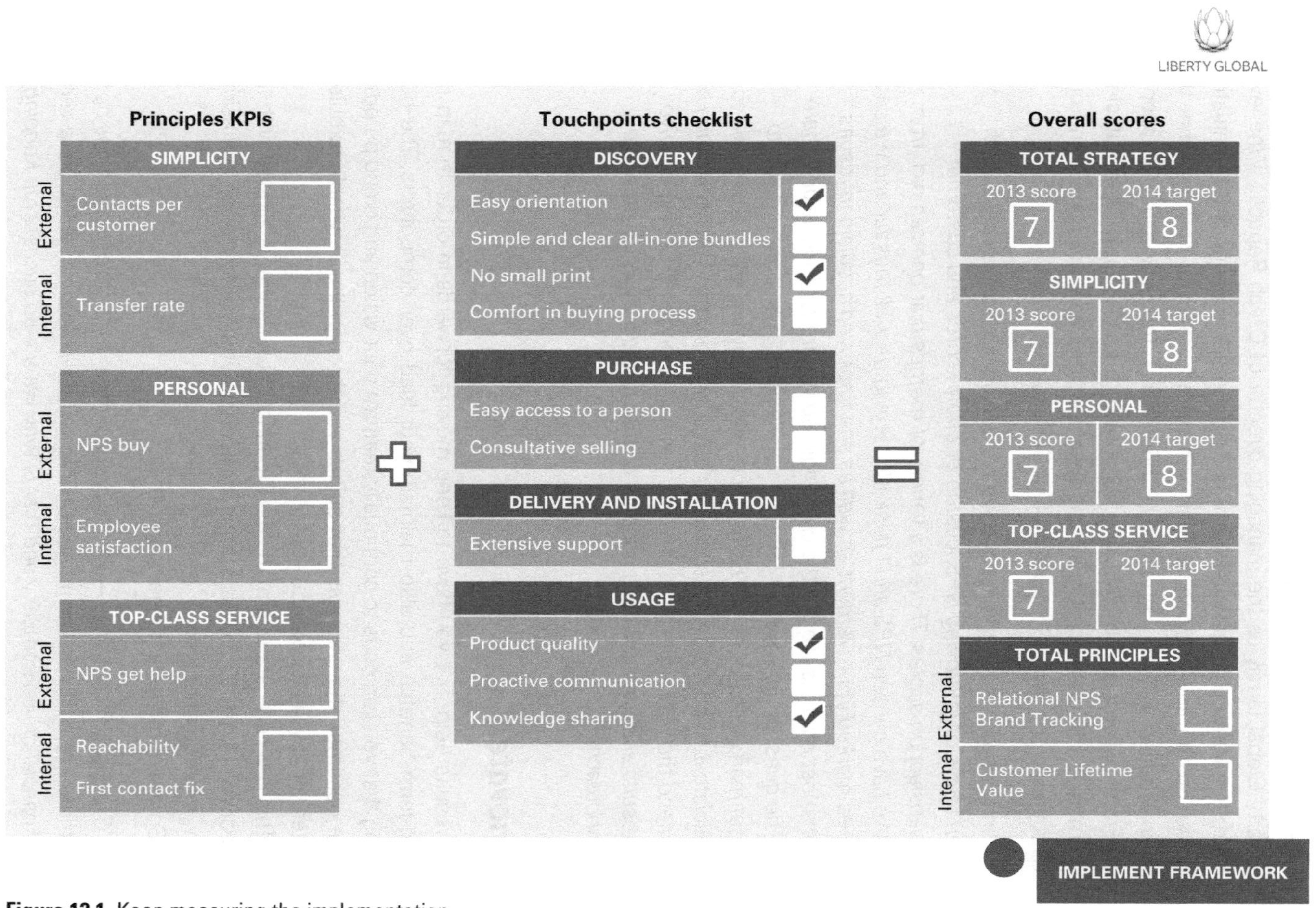

Principles KPIs

SIMPLICITY

| External | Contacts per customer |
| Internal | Transfer rate |

PERSONAL

| External | NPS buy |
| Internal | Employee satisfaction |

TOP-CLASS SERVICE

| External | NPS get help |
| Internal | Reachability |
| First contact fix |

Touchpoints checklist

DISCOVERY

- Easy orientation
- Simple and clear all-in-one bundles
- No small print
- Comfort in buying process

PURCHASE

- Easy access to a person
- Consultative selling

DELIVERY AND INSTALLATION

- Extensive support

USAGE

- Product quality
- Proactive communication
- Knowledge sharing

Overall scores

TOTAL STRATEGY

| 2013 score | 2014 target |
| 7 | 8 |

SIMPLICITY

| 2013 score | 2014 target |
| 7 | 8 |

PERSONAL

| 2013 score | 2014 target |
| 7 | 8 |

TOP-CLASS SERVICE

| 2013 score | 2014 target |
| 7 | 8 |

TOTAL PRINCIPLES

| External | Relational NPS Brand Tracking |
| Internal | Customer Lifetime Value |

IMPLEMENT FRAMEWORK

Figure 12.1 Keep measuring the implementation

Ultimately, of course, any business that is responsible to shareholders has to show business results. Chris Coles joined in 2014 as managing director to replace Frans-Willem de Kloet, who has continued his career within the Liberty Global family as the managing director of Czech Republic. Whenever there is a leadership transition of this type there is a danger of the initiative going 'off the rails' as people wait with baited breath to find out what the new direction will be. Fortunately, Chris shares the very same philosophy as Frans-Willem, and by focusing on showing results Soraya had sufficient ammunition to convince Chris right away that this was the correct and only direction to continue. So much so that Chris told us:

> 'In the business-market space we are seeing signs of success, both in terms of improving NPS, customer effort scores and customer satisfaction scores. There is a variety of metrics that one can pick from. We have chosen NPS and I think it's serving us well thus far and we can see marked improvement as well as see improved acquisition results. In most markets we are the challenger so we are typically taking share. The question is: have we bent the acquisition curve more in order to get market share faster? Early results would say we are. Are we able to isolate it to one or two discrete variables or economic? We're working on it and the first signs are there and, yes, we're certainly seeing positive results and we attribute a good bit of that to the way in which we're approaching the market.'

Innovate

So results help, but you have to keep moving forwards in order to reap the long-term benefits and also maintain your lead over competitors. The best thing that you can do is to continually reaffirm your vision and brand purpose. That becomes the compass that guides you through the inevitable turbulent waters of any large corporate organization.

This is where 'stand firm' helps. Creating a culture that is aligned with the direction is vital, as are constantly challenging your performance and asking how it can be improved.

Soraya sums up this need very well:

> 'Our biggest challenge – and it's probably true for a lot of companies out there – is our short-term financially driven financial culture. We are a very financial-driven company and that is why we are so successful. Keeping in mind this longer-term strategy and making sure that you keep everyone

on board, although you cannot show the financial impact immediately, is the biggest challenge. I think we are very successful in doing that but we need to stay focused, repeating the message every time, everywhere. It goes back to our purpose and our belief. Building on belief and evangelizing are key, I think, and a very bold move in a corporate organization. Now that we are seeing clear results to back that belief obviously helps in focus and investments.

'The plan going forward is to build out more programmes, copy more proven results from one market to the other, but mainly track results, tracking churn and showing that it helps our long-term success. Finally, going back to where we started this conversation, we are a people business, so sustaining success by hiring the right people. By that I mean people with the right attitude towards customers.'

Innovation is not always about being better; it is sometimes about being different. Doing more of the same may prove to be an unworthy investment, so as your customer experience initiative matures, it is worth revisiting your 'ECG' and questioning where you should invest in innovating the experience. Erik Wiechers puts the case for this very clearly:

'We were at minus 40 NPS when we started the project, and we're now at zero. The question, though, is do we want to go for plus 20? If our competitors are still at minus 20 do we invest in improving to plus 20 or might it be better, perhaps, to invest in a new customer gateway? So, that is the balance we need to strike between sustaining competitive advantage and levels of investment.'

The other critical point in a customer experience journey is knowing when to hand-off the initiative from the corporate functions to the operating units. Too early and you lose some of the synergy and best-practice thinking, too late and you risk it becoming wholly owned by a corporate function and failing to gain traction at the local level. Erik summed it up by saying:

'Our customer journey is a programme, but at a certain point you need to hand it over to the operation; when exactly should the cut-over moment happen? We had a long-lasting discussion about it and agreed that, for us, the cut-over moment is as soon as the programme manager has operationalized it in such a way that it is measurable, then he or she will hand it over to the director of that specific department. And then the second challenge is, "Whose responsibility is it to come up with new innovations?" Is that the programme director, or is it the operational unit?

As with most answers in life, it is a hybrid, so it needs to be stimulated by what we see in the field, but at the same time the programme manager needs to be a thought leader and provide stimulus to the operating units.'

But what role should corporate functions play in this case? The answer is to take a broader perspective on the business, to observe the latest trends and what customers are seeking, to innovate new approaches and technology and then to facilitate the conversation with the operating units to introduce it. Chris Coles sees the task this way:

'Our purpose should be to both solve the current needs of our local markets and customers and introduce them to new solutions that are coming down the pipe that are probably going to solve some of their developing needs. A lot of it comes just by watching industry trends and buying behaviour, and how technology and solutions become adopted. Having a customer representative in our corporate environment is a crucial role to us, we are not in contact with customers every day, someone needs to keep us honest and thinking about the customer. Our job is to make sure that we're there as a quiet partner in the process.

'What we try to do is to get folks to step back from the day-to-day and to think about it in that context, because it goes a lot better if you wake up in the morning energized by what you're doing. If you have a line of sight to how the customer is going to experience what you have done that day, or what you are contributing to the process – and keep that paramount – it should help to simplify some of the other dynamics in your day: the frustrations, the politics, the interpersonal challenges that are there in any business, big or small, start-up or large corporate.'

Results

At the time of writing, Liberty Global Business Services have seen significant improvements in their customer experience and year-on-year NPS. Looking at the three 'hallmark' touchpoints, we see NPS has increased +5 points for 'buy', +17 points for 'get help' and +8 points for 'relational' and, from Liberty Global's own research, improving NPS has a clear impact on reducing churn.

Our monetization of the strategy
Improving our Get help NPS will reduce churn

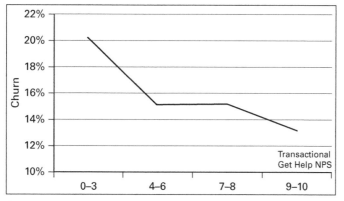

Churn percentage drops when transactional Get help NPS improves*
- When able to shift 0–3 NPS scores to 4–8, churn drops by 28% (from 21% to 15%)
- When able to shift 4–8 NPS scores to 9–10, churn drops again to 13%

*Based on 3 year NPS and Disconnect data from UPCNL

Figure 12.2 Liberty Global monetization strategy

Advice for other leaders

We asked the Liberty Global Business Services team to share their insights and advice to others embarking on a similar journey. We thought that it would be interesting to conclude their story with their top tips:

'Keeping a clear vision is really key and our role in leadership is both to keep in touch with market sentiment, as well as to help play it back into the business, because most people are not on the front line and yet their roles impact the front line and may not be appreciated. We want to make sure they understand that what they do does, in fact, matter.'

(Chris Coles)

'What I really learned in the past two years was to broaden my perspective a bit. You need to understand where other people are coming from. People may be more financially driven, or have a different background or different targets, so you need to convince them in a different way. You need to show results. The boldest thing we have done is going ahead with this strategy, this direction, while the parent company

had a different philosophy. Liberty Global is a very financially driven organization, and we decided to say, we need to achieve results, however, we want to achieve them differently. To stand up and say, "This is who we want to be." I think that took some guts.'

(Michel Pilet)

'My tip for the future of customer experience is this: it's the "super promoter". We spend a lot of time getting all the customers scoring 5, 6, 7, 8, 9 and 10. I think it's easier, cheaper and more effective to make the 'super promoters' – the nines and tens – really work for you, because they are your brand advocates and, at the end of the day, that is what we all want.'

(Erik Wiechers)

'My advice to companies choosing this strategy is to really spend time on the "why". What is the purpose of your organization? I believe that whether you talk about individuals or you talk about organizations you have to be authentic, otherwise it is not going to be believed. You really need to think about the culture of the organization, to ask "Where are we coming from? What are our values?" From that, create a message that resonates because it is authentic. So first of all you need to create the "why" – and it's something you need to spend a lot of time on, to think it through and chew on it almost. And then you have to be bold and stand up for what you believe in and not get deviated from your original thinking.'

(Frans-Willem de Kloet)

'Start with building the belief. The road is so clear now, no one is asking questions, we are operating as one team and that is a big plus. Follow up with a clear strategy and execution plan that is understandable for everyone in the organization and track results. That is really what has made us successful. And it's working. Based on the voice of our customers, they can feel the difference! Looking back I will never change the approach again.'

(Soraya Loerts)

So, some great advice from the Liberty Global Business services team. You may wonder about why they have been so generous and open in sharing this level of detail with readers, some of whom will be competitors. The answer is that the value comes from the journey, not the destination. Remember, you can't 'force it, fake it or fudge it'. Attempting to copy some of Liberty

Global's output without going through the same process is a recipe for mediocrity.

Now let's take a very different kind of organization from a completely different sector, but one that shares a similarly competitive environment and is part of a group that is equally results driven but also one that challenges another objection we often hear:

'Customer experience is all very well if you are a Ritz-Carlton, Burberry or Singapore Airlines, but if you are a budget brand in a highly price-driven market you can't afford to worry about delighting customers.'

Premier Inn proves them wrong.

Premier Inn – case study

Premier Inn is part of Whitbread PLC and is the UK's leading hotel brand in the value segment as rated by YouGov, with nearly 700 hotels in the UK and forecast to grow by 45 per cent to 75,000 rooms in the UK by 2018. Whilst it has grown rapidly it has gained a reputation for providing a consistently good customer experience. But how do you take the experience to the next level and sustain it when you are adding a new hotel every 10 days? That was the question that occupied the then Managing Director, Patrick Dempsey, in 2012:

'We have something in Premier Inn, which I call our "pixie dust". I've been running the business now for eight years, and it has always been there – but I wanted to see how we could really galvanize it. How could we get that pixie dust to be a bit more formal? Half our estate used to be run by the restaurant business and now we have put it all together under Premier Inn and I wanted to get that one business behind one objective. That is why purpose becomes important. Why do people come to work? Why do they do what they do? So that was part of the motivation for starting this work.

'The other is that John Forrest was new to Premier Inn in his role as Chief Operating Officer. I really wanted John to have something that he could lead, and people could see that he was driving. We talked about the idea together and agreed that I should sponsor it, but I wanted John to shape it, because it was his team that it was going to have the impact on. I wanted John to have something that would be his legacy as such, that people will always remember John for – our purpose and the campaign to deliver it, "Bigger, Bolder, Better".'

Patrick could not have chosen a better person to lead 'Bigger, Bolder, Better'. We have worked with many organizations over the years and hundreds of executives, but few come close to John Forrest in their ability to lead a customer experience initiative of this kind. The reason is that John is a passionate believer in the power of purpose:

'My personal journey started when I was Operations Director of Whitbread's Table Table restaurant brand. The brand was broken and we couldn't fix everything, so the question was what were we going to do to win because we needed to turn it around. So that started me thinking about how to do that and I read your book Uncommon Practice: People who deliver a great brand experience – and that sowed a seed in my mind. I also came across some work by Simon Sinek about putting "why" at the centre of an organization. I recognized that we were phenomenal at the "what, when, how" but we weren't very good at "why". And then I took over the operations role in Premier Inn and found the same.

'We are brilliant at looking after our guests because we've got these phenomenal team members, but no one knew why. No one could work out how come, despite the fact that we had grown from being a very small business to being quite a big business, we still had that same feeling. We had been through recessions and restructures that split up the business. We put it back together again, but one thing never changed, which is the consistency of the warmth of welcome, the wow of the team, and the lengths that they would go to for our guests.

'So Patrick and I felt that this was really important to understand, because as we grow, as we expand internationally, as we have a more distant business model, we cannot rely on the personalities of the senior leadership alone to make it happen, so let's try to work out why we are as good as we are and how phenomenal we could be if we grabbed hold of it and then took it to another level.'

It was clear that Patrick and John shared a common cause. There was a clear business need, strong sponsorship and a leader in place charged with implementation – but how to start?

Engage

Patrick had previously been involved in an organization-wide customer experience initiative when he was with TrustHouse Forte Hotels, and had seen the power of engaging people behind a common purpose. He decided to take a similar approach with Premier Inn, so Amanda Brady, director of HR for Whitbread Hotels and Restaurants, was made co-leader with particular responsibility for the employee elements. John and Amanda realized they could not do it alone – they needed the active support of the leadership team. So they decided to start with answering the question 'Why?' with the help of the Premier Inn leaders.

The first thing John Forrest did was to start introducing his own senior team to the notion of organizational purpose and the need to 'stand up' for something. He wanted them to get there 'under their own steam' rather than him launching a campaign and asking them to implement it. He did this through talking about his own beliefs, teaching them about Simon Sinek and exposing them to other people's thinking:

'I brought my operations team to hear you speak at the London Business Forum about being bold and on purpose.

http://www.londonbusinessforum.com/events/ customer_experience_3

'And at least two-thirds of them got it on the spot, and got really excited about it. And then we started engaging the executive group, step by step. Most of the executive team were behind it but one person said that if it wasn't broken why were we going to spend money on trying to make it better? There were no numbers to support why we had to do it but there was a belief that we needed to have something to galvanize everybody, and to protect the difference we had achieved.

'When I think about how we developed our purpose, with hindsight, the most interesting part of it was the fact that it was an iterative process. At the time that felt really frustrating. Not because we weren't doing what we needed to do, but because I couldn't get all the executives to agree. At the same time, Patrick was making some changes at the executive level and so we had to keep taking a step back to align people. As a result, we ended up moving the launch back nearly six months in the end. But in hindsight that made it stronger.'

Patrick also believed that engaging the executive team in defining the purpose was a vital step in the journey, because whilst he could sponsor it, he could not implement it without the active support of his executive team:

'Our purpose is to "Make our guests feel brilliant, through a great night's sleep." When people stay in a Premier Inn, or a budget hotel, they don't stay there for a luxury stay, or a spa experience. They are staying there because they are there to do something else. And therefore our job is to give them a great night's sleep so that they can be brilliant the next day. Getting to that purpose was the most difficult part but we did so by really talking it through as an executive team.

'I wanted to get everybody in the organization to think about our purpose, because if they are not doing that, what are they doing? That meant we had to drive it through the organization. Having someone like John leading that, and really getting behind it, was important. I don't think I could have driven the purpose through the organization on my own. I very much sponsor it, and I'll talk about it. But, actually, in terms of implementation, we are very lucky to have John and the team who worked on the implementation, what we call our "Bigger, Bolder, Better" campaign. They all pulled together.'

Many organizations define a purpose or vision statement, but as soon as they hit the first poor quarter or are faced with making difficult decisions that impact short-term results they cave in and business-as-usual trumps the longer-term strategy. The Premier Inn purpose was tested earlier than Patrick expected but became all the stronger for it. We facilitated a workshop with the executive team and the regional operations managers to prepare them for launch of the 'Bigger, Bolder, Better' campaign that was to launch the purpose and training to support it. That workshop became a watershed in the commitment to the purpose, because Patrick Dempsey and the executive team took a multimillion pound investment decision in the moment to act in faith with the purpose:

'One of the things that you warned us about was that our purpose would be tested at some point and the way we dealt with that as a leadership team was crucial. I remember we had quite a difficult meeting when one of our regional operational managers raised the issue of poor air conditioning in some of our hotels. It was clearly a "sticky moment" because the credibility of our purpose rested on the decision we took. We had been putting that decision off because it represented a huge capital investment for the business but as a result of that meeting and that moment we committed to a refurbishment programme across our estate. We invested in a five-year programme to upgrade all of our hotels. Our purpose of "Making our guests feel brilliant, through a good night's sleep" has made us focus more on the fundamentals we need to fix to deliver on it.'

This was a real 'Road to Damascus' moment for Premier Inn and the executive group, and from the moment the decision to refurbish the rooms was announced the cynics faded away. Clearly, Patrick's decision was hugely influential in aligning his leadership team, because Simon Jones, director of marketing and strategy, told me:

> 'In terms of key success factors, there is an old Chinese proverb,
> "The fish rots from the head". Unless you've got an MD who absolutely
> embraces the purpose and is continually driving the right behaviours and
> urging the organization's success, it won't happen. He is then supported
> by an exec that collectively buys into the programme. It's the executive
> team who take ownership for all the strategy. We've debated it hard, and
> then we've brought it to life through our external brand promise and our
> internal brand purpose, and I think that's very important.'

Insight

Having agreed the purpose, the next step was to get insight from customers that would allow the organization to define what it really meant from the customer perspective and how to deliver it operationally. Like many hotels, Premier Inn collects huge amounts of data from guest feedback surveys and they made this available to Smith+co. We took this data and analysed nearly half a million records of frequent customers to determine the value drivers for the brand and the current experience that customers were receiving. The value drivers are those attributes of the offer that encourage repeat and referral behaviour of customers and, as such, are very important to determine if you are to design an experience that differentiates. In the case of Premier Inn we discovered that value for money, room and bed comfort, and warmth of service were all important to the target customers. We also correlated top box satisfaction scores with intention to recommend and from this created our 'ECG' curves showing the actual and the desired experience for customers. Mark Fells, director of digital, explains how this data is used to create insight and inform new product development:

> 'Because we have so many guests who stay with us, we send them
> questionnaires and a huge number respond – over 100,000 every month –
> who rate our products and services as part of their stay and therefore we
> get a very sensitive barometer about every element of the experience.
> For example, we offer a choice of pillows now in response to what our
> customers thought about their pillows. I think the challenge is how do you
> go a stage further and how do you start to build customers into almost
> an ecosystem? We're starting to think about how should we involve some

of our fabulously loyal customers in customer panels, whether they be virtual or real, where we would ask a group of customers to come and review our hotels before they open and tell us what they think works and doesn't. Should they be involved in the building process and actually choosing the site?'

This is powerful but the real opportunity is to get upstream in the capture of customer data so that the experience can be enhanced real-time rather than post-stay. Personalization needs to be tempered with appropriate privacy but offers the means to customize the experience and deliver the purpose much more intentionally:

'If we knew more about our guests upfront, if we could ask their permission to give us more information, we could probably start to serve them different choices that would probably meet their motivations more clearly and start to deliver our purpose earlier in process.'

Mark's point about making different choices in the experience to align more intentionally with the brand purpose is a very important one. As we said in Chapter 10, the customer experience is rather like an ECG line and, just like with a real ECG, a flat line is bad! Customers who experience high points in the customer journey that are aligned with the purpose and promise are much more likely to remember their experience with affection. We will get to this point a little later but first we have to define the promise.

Define

With the volume of data that we had to analyse and the high level of insight this provided, we were in a terrific position to work with a cross-functional team in the Customer Experience Workshop to focus on how the brand would 'stand up' by defining the brand promise and designing the new experience. However, what is vital in this process is to anchor the definition very clearly in the purpose and strategy of the organization. Far too many organizations have brand purposes, strategies, visions, missions and values that are mis-aligned and serve to confuse rather than illuminate. Often the starting point for our work is to take these disparate messages and find a common thread running through them. Fortunately our task was made easier because Simon Jones shares a very similar view and his team's work on the Premier Inn brand strategy provided a clear definition of the personality, values and tone of voice for the brand. All we had to do was to use this as a foundation on which to define the promise:

'Purpose and strategy are clearly related, and therefore it's not the case that we landed on a purpose and then retro-fitted our strategy around it. Nor did we come up with a strategy and then say, "Right, let's think about a decent strapline that will bring this to life for the organization." I think that's where organizations fail in these kinds of exercises. What we have actually done is to be quite reflective about what it is that makes Premier Inn special and different, versus other budget hotel companies, in particular. And in doing so, we've hopefully landed on a series of strategic programmes that are adding value to the people we employ, the guests we attract, and our shareholders, and are really reflective of what we think our purpose is at its heart.

'Therefore, we have a coherent whole, with our purpose expressing our strategy and a strategy that delivers our purpose. The two have been developed in parallel, as opposed to separate and distinct exercises. I've seen lots of examples where businesses have said, "Right, that's our strategy but people are not going to find it very compelling so let's try to give it a sexy sounding name to try and bring it to life." Instead we have tried to run the business honestly, with a set of principles that we feel passionate about and we believe our people feel passionate about, and then we express those in the mantra that is our purpose.'

This is an important point because as we started this work there were a number of changes made at the executive level, including the appointment of Simon Jones as Director of Marketing and Strategy. As a result, the marketing team were working on the brand positioning in parallel to John and Amanda's leadership of the 'Bigger, Bolder, Better' project with the Operations and HR teams. Our role in Smith+co was to help ensure that the various pieces joined up. This is a classic example of 'triad power', where Marketing, HR and Operations must operate as one around a common agenda. Every organization is different. Some have a very well-defined brand platform in place and we can use this as a firm foundation for the customer experience. Others have a loosely defined brand position or perhaps, as with Premier Inn, this is being reviewed, and in this case the purpose and brand promise can help to inform the brand work as well as the operational and HR components. Key to this, however, is that all of the elements are aligned. They came together in the form of a brand pyramid in Premier Inn.

The value of having a purpose and strategy that are closely aligned is that you can communicate this simply and clearly to customers in a way that is much more emotional and engaging than the usual tactical advertising used by so many brands. 'A great night's sleep' is so much more compelling than 'We offer weekend discounts'.

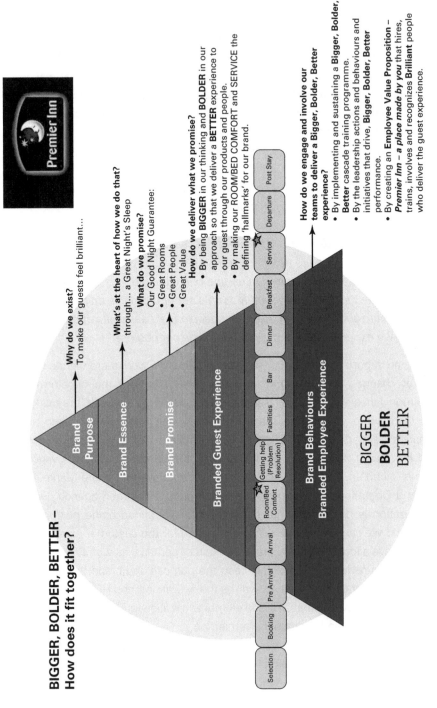

Figure 12.3 Premier Inn campaign: Bigger, Bolder, Better

This was shown very clearly a short while later when Russell Braterman was appointed as Premier Inn's new Brand Marketing Director. After being briefed on the brand purpose, he said, 'That's the TV ad! I just need to turn it into something for an outside audience.' He did.

In January 2014, Premier Inn announced the launch of a £15 million media campaign, its largest ever. The campaign featured the British comedian Lenny Henry. Russell Braterman said:

'The focus of the creative is on Lenny and his enjoyment of sleeping well. The advert sees Lenny in his Premier Inn bed, on a whistlestop tour of the UK. Whether you're a business traveller needing to get a great night's sleep before a big meeting, or if you want to catch a good night of "zzz's" before attending a friend's wedding, there is a Premier Inn just around the corner.'

Image 12.4 The Hypnos bed

The impact of a campaign like this is even greater when you can put a proof point behind it. When your purpose is very clear this can be communicated in the form of a brand promise or guarantee. In the case of Premier Inn it is the 'Good Night Guarantee'. If you don't have a great night's sleep they will refund your money. Few brands are bold enough or brave enough to stand behind their purpose by making a promise to customers about it. The reason is that they do not have the confidence to deliver the promise consistently. To do so requires careful design to ensure that the promise is delivered consistently across every touchpoint.

The Premier Inn promise became 'Great Value, Great Rooms, Great People' backed up by the 'Good Night Guarantee'. So the 'stand up' piece was very clear. Now was the time to decide how to 'stand out'. This gave a very clear steer to designing the experience.

Design

Having spent the first day of our customer experience workshop defining how Premier Inn should 'stand up' we were ready to move on to 'stand out'. We spent the second day of the workshop with our cross-functional team to take the draft promise and then design the experience to deliver it. We looked at the 'ECG' curves and then selected the touchpoints that could become hallmarks for the brand. You can't afford to differentiate at every touchpoint and it would be less memorable if you did, so a key decision is which touch-points to over-index or invest in that will have the greatest impact. John Forrest explains this well:

> 'We have targeted our investment into the things that really matter to the customer. And internally we have a phrase that is, "We only put cost into the system when the consumer values it and is willing to pay for it," because, at the end of the day we are a budget hotel business. There is no point in putting gyms in hotels, for example, because our consumers don't want them. They don't want to pay for them. What they do want is a great bed; they want a clean, comfortable room; they want a decent-quality shower; and a great breakfast to set them up for the day – and that's where we focus our investment.'

This operating model is then supported by the business strategy so that there is total alignment between the purpose, the strategy and the customer experience. Simon Jones goes on to explain this:

> 'We've made choices to support the business model. So, we've chosen, wherever possible, to own and operate our hotels because it gives us greater control of the proposition and it has the happy consequence of ultimately delivering, we think, more sustainable returns over the medium to long term. We've also made choices around how we distribute our inventory. For example, we could go the very easy and seductive route of opening up lots of third-party channels of distribution, which initially would drive incremental revenue, but actually over time would build cost into our system and mean we would lose direct control of our customer.
>
>   'So we've played very carefully with that part of our market. We have one preferred partner, **www.booking.com**. We closely work in

partnership with them and we make sure that how we work with them is complementary to our business rather than competing with our business. We have made active choices, about where we've invested in our central teams and where we've invested in our site teams, because I'm a big advocate that investing averagely across the business doesn't give you returns. We have decided we're going to be famous for service and room comfort. So, we invest in our reception team, and our beds because that's where we think we can maximize the impact for the guest.

'And that means we choose not to differentiate in other areas. I think dinner is quite a good example. We provide a good-quality dinner with a decent choice of dishes, but it's not gourmet food, you know, and the reason we do that is although dinner is important for our guests, it's not the reason why they stay at the hotel.'

Many organizations we work with really struggle to make this kind of strategic choice. They want to serve 'all segments' and be 'better at everything'. The fact is that a great experience is when you are special to someone special. That means having a clear focus on target customers and what they value. The good news is that this choice becomes easier with a purpose, because it serves to guide you, it becomes your compass. John Forrest makes this very point:

'Some of the boldest things that we have done have been because we've got the purpose as our focal point – do we live up to it? For example, we can't have guests feeling brilliant about a bed that's only okay, so we've developed our brilliant Hypnos bed that is way ahead of anything on the market. We rolled out 30,000 beds in 2014, because if we're going to make the guests feel brilliant through a great night's sleep then we have to spend the money to deliver on that promise. The other bold decision is we're going 24/7 on social media, and we're moving to seven days a week on guest relations, because the executive team said "You can't be a business that's about making the guests feel brilliant through a great night's sleep, and then not man your complaints department at the weekend." So that meant committing to over £100,000 on labour to resource it. But it's making a difference every weekend.'

One of the most frequent errors we see organizations make is to buy some sexy new technology and then expect it to deliver a great customer experience. It rarely does. The fact is that the technology should enable the experience, not dictate it. Our view on technology is 'Just because you can, does not mean you should.' The great thing about having a clear purpose, promise and customer experience is that they point towards the technology and processes required to deliver them. This is particularly true in the sexy world of digital, as Mark Fells knows only too well:

'Digital channels have a huge role to play by bringing to life some of the key advantages that the brand has. So, we're trying to find ways to bring to life our rooms, beds and our service to make the brand stickier. Also we are starting to give people more information about the products and services that are available in each particular site by helping them to make an informed choice. So, if the site is particularly good for a sporting venue or if it has just been refurbished or it has our latest new bed that we are rolling out, we are trying to put that across very simply and clearly, very early in the booking process.'

Align

Having defined the promise and designed the experience, the team were now ready to roll this out across the organization and align their 19,000 colleagues with it. But how to do so in a way that was engaging, exciting and experiential? The result was a campaign called 'Bigger, Bolder, Better' and a complete 'Branded Customer Experience' training cascade of the same name.

John Forrest was very clear in his own mind that the purpose was the reason for being, and Amanda Brady was busy crafting an employee proposition to create the culture to support it called 'Premier Inn – a place made by you', but they realized that there was need for a communication campaign that would intentionally align the organization behind both. They believed that this campaign would probably have a life of a few years but that ultimately it would need to be refreshed – but the purpose and employee propositions would not. They would form the DNA of the brand:

'We looked at our business plan and our five-year plan together, and it was all about becoming bigger, but to achieve that we needed to be bolder, and we needed to be better. Bigger, in terms of growth, bolder in terms of our approach to things like marketing and digital, and better in terms of the guest experience; better rooms, better beds, better training. Because we'd put our purpose at the top of the business plan, rather than some statistic or financial goal, the purpose is the "why" and the "Bigger, Bolder, Better" initiative became the "what" and "how". And, of course, the other ingredient is "Premier Inn – a place made by you", our employee value proposition that was created in parallel. We had to work hard to

make sure they were aligned because it would have been a train crash if they had not joined up.'

Many organizations have brand purposes, promises, brand values, employee value propositions, corporate values and so on but they are usually created independently and in isolation by the owning function and thus fail to 'join up'. John Forrest and Amanda Brady jointly sponsored the 'Bigger, Bolder, Better' campaign so that the messaging that went out to the organization was seamless. As soon as the purpose was agreed, Amanda Brady set about defining the employee proposition that would ensure that the way people were recruited, trained and rewarded was consistent with the delivery of the purpose. This would ensure that the culture would enable the brand to 'stand firm' in the long term:

> *'Once we got the purpose, we said, "Right, well, what do we need to do now? What is our vision for our people?" It was very clear that our purpose requires us to hang onto our people because they are the differentiator for our guests. That led to our employee proposition, "Premier Inn – a place made by you". A key factor in developing it was that we utilized the expertise of the teams to develop something that is theirs and for them.*
>
> *'The annual conference was an amazing opportunity to communicate all of this. Initially we let each of the executive teams go off and prepare their speeches, but then when we brought it all together it just didn't flow. So then we talked about how we were going to make this live for people and simplify it. Patrick came up with this idea of being "Bigger, Bolder, Better", so we hung all our messaging around that. All the executive team realigned their scripts to keep homing in on the core message. Every time one of us got up, we either related our presentation to one of the three elements or all of them, and we all used movies as the metaphor, so it was great fun. And then we finished by saying, "Well, that's all great, how are we going to make it happen?" And that was through being really clear about how we were going to cascade it to touch every single team member.*
>
> *'The difference with this cascade training is that everybody felt like they had a part to play. We started from the top and it went all the way down to every team member and I think that worked really well. Second, the line managers are delivering it to their teams and I think their commitment to it is evident, so the team members feel that it must be important because it is their line manager telling them rather than an instructor.*

Image 12.5 The Premier Inn executive team presenting at the 'Bigger, Bolder, Better' event

'This was quite a big task operationally but we were very clear that if we didn't do this, then our competitors might do something better, so to keep ahead of the game we all had to buy into the process. And, actually, as a leader, you have an obligation to make sure that your teams are fully equipped to be able to deliver the promise and also to be made to feel like their contribution really matters. We have just heard that Premier Inn has placed twelfth in the large company category for the Sunday Times 100 Best Companies to Work For *survey from last year to this year. So I think there have been lots of benefits from doing it this way.'*

One of the things that is apparent from these executives is their constancy of purpose and consistency in where the priorities lie. This is partly a result of the process of engagement that Patrick and John led, but also careful attention to alignment. A key part of the 'Bigger, Bolder, Better' campaign was a series of functional workshops that saw each of the executive team lead their teams through the purpose, promise, new experience and how they could support it and their front-line colleagues. Alignment is particularly important when organizations go through structural change or acquisitions. Unless the new people buy into the purpose they can become toxic to the culture. At the time that Premier Inn was launching 'Bigger, Bolder, Better' it was also changing

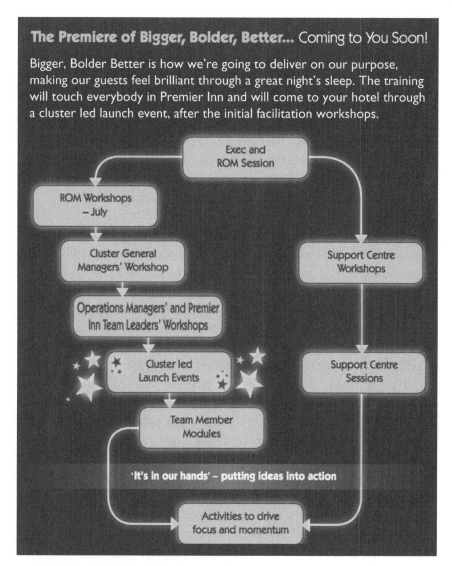

Image 12.6 The 'Bigger, Bolder, Better' cascade

the reporting line of the restaurant business. Patrick quickly realized that the restaurants had to be built into the process:

'I mentioned our restaurant business, where we had people in 350 hotels who weren't quite sure where they belonged. They are Premier Inn now. If you cut them they'll have purple blood. I think this has really helped to pull people together.'

The problem with most annual conferences is that they are just that – annual. The message gets forgotten for the rest of the year. John was determined that this would not happen:

'I decided that my role is to keep our purpose as the single focus and to be relentless in communication. My job is also to celebrate the magic moments, and the heroes, and to shout out when we fail, and fix it. You've got to role model the behaviour. It goes back to what I learnt earlier in my career: what you permit, you promote. If you do something then that makes it all right for everybody else to do the same thing. So I try to set the bar very high and reach for that standard and live the purpose; then I can hold other people to it.

'An important communication tool is my weekly blog. I post good news stories there, so they are available for everybody to read. I'm constantly monitoring what is going on with social media, as well as having a team of people who do it too. I'm encouraging the language and behaviour of our purpose and it's starting to get infectious; people are spotting stories good and bad, and then just pinging them all over the place. So people say, "This is brilliant", "What a great example of making the guests feel brilliant". You've just got to keep using the language. So, for example, "This was a magic moment", or, "You know, I'm not sure this was a magic moment", or, "How's the guest feeling? I doubt they're feeling brilliant?"

'Going back to why we started this initiative, part of it was codifying our culture and now everybody who joins is going through an on-boarding process that takes him or her back through the journey that we've been on, and that is really speeding up people's integration into the business. Because we are all now able to describe, at interview, or induction, what it is that we do, and why we're obsessed about certain things. All of a sudden it's not 15 or 16 different interpretations of what we do; we can articulate it exactly. We're firmly committed to recruiting for attitude, and not for skill. We can train you to do anything, but if you haven't got the attitude that allows you to make people feel brilliant, then we don't want you. Team turnover is at an all-time low and the best in Whitbread. So we're now capable of keeping our people. We've made another bold decision; we're no longer going to be a minimum wage employer, we've taken everybody above minimum wage by introducing our "Team Deal" incentive whereby savings made as a result of improving the customer experience directly benefit our people. We have also introduced variable pay, and pay for progression scheme, which all help to improve the deal for our teams – we've made a commitment to hold on to our people.'

If you are determined to hold on to your people you need to make sure they are the right people in the first place. We often tell our clients 'Hire for DNA, not MBA.' In other words, hire people first and foremost who fit your culture, not those who are the best qualified. Amanda and her team reviewed the recruitment process accordingly and started an initiative called 'Brilliant Beginnings':

> 'Our "Brilliant Beginnings" recruitment process has been designed to make sure we recruit people who've got the right personality and attitude and who will really care about delivering for our customers. That is very important for us, and I don't think it matters whether they are 16 or 65. As long as they are behind what we are trying to achieve, and understand it and the role they can play as an individual, it doesn't matter what educational background they have.
>
> '"Brilliant Beginnings" is also an on-boarding process. When team members join us we allow them to be themselves at work. We don't try to tailor them to the organization. We tell them about our purpose and that what we are about is creating a great customer experience that makes our guests feel brilliant through a great night's sleep. We tell them that anything they can do to support that will help.
>
> They feel like they are part of a family within their unit and within the brand. I think people are very proud to work for Premier Inn. They know that what we say we're going to do we will deliver, not just for the customer, but for them too. I think all those things are connected. I hear them saying every day how much we've changed their lives and how much this is not just a job to them, but it feels like an extended family.'

Alignment becomes even more complex as you think about extending this across functions, cultures and geographies but, arguably, it then becomes even more important, as John Forrest explains:

> 'The next step is to share our purpose with our international business. As they start to grow, we need to provide them with the DNA of Premier Inn and lock them into our purpose to make sure they don't make decisions that are not aligned. So, yes, you can buy a cheaper bed, but you are not allowed to because we're about making our guests feel brilliant, and so if you're going to put a purple sign over the door, then you have to live up to the things we stand for.
>
> '"Bigger, Bolder, Better" is a campaign that allows us to share the purpose with 19,000 employees across the organization, in the centre, and out in hotels. We needed to get everybody to understand what

we're about, and then give them insight and training, and empowerment to make sure they are able to make that purpose come to life. The conference was just the reveal. Then it took us six months to train people to be ready to deliver the material. That was followed by launch events and people were saying, "Oh, this material is brilliant, it's great that we are actually talking about what we should be talking about," and they got really excited about it. I'm also really excited and proud of the fact that our new Marketing Director, Russell Braterman, took one look at our brand purpose video and used it as the basis for our external campaign.'

Measure

One of the key success factors is ensuring that the organization 'stands firm' and the efforts are sustained through measuring and rewarding the right things. If you say that customer experience is important but only measure sales, people will soon default to selling rather than service. Aligning measures and rewards starts at the top of the organization, as Simon Jones points out:

'We are a very collaborative team whose interests are aligned. What I mean by that is we have a common incentive platform that goes all the way down to the site level, so there are no corporate politics where I'm incentivized to do something that may cause one of my colleagues to fail. Actually, if one of my colleagues fails, I fail. We miss our metrics. And what that means is we have a very supportive, very collaborative culture, and that percolates its way throughout the entire organization. I've worked in very complex, global businesses, which have matrix organizations, and in a lot of those organizations the incentives simply aren't aligned. Therefore, you get an internal rat race, which leads to all sorts of adverse behaviours. We just don't have that.'

One of the things we usually devise with our clients is a 'scorecard' that aligns key customer experience metrics with financial, business, operational and people measures. In the case of Premier Inn they already used the parent company Whitbread's WIN Card system. This stands for 'Whitbread In Numbers' and brings together all of the key business measures. We used this as the basis and simply identified which metrics were going to be the most appropriate to evaluate success. These were agreed as customer advocacy in the form of NPS, employee engagement and invocations (being the amount of money refunded as a result of the 'Good Night Guarantee' being triggered):

'Our promise is important, because the very existence of the guarantee gives our team confidence in our product, because they know ultimately they can stand behind that guarantee when the front line is dealing with guest complaints. The second thing is, we have thought about how we hard wire into the system the delivery of our purpose and our brand promise, through things like our scorecard, which we call our WIN Card, our incentives programme, and our forensic approach to how we audit the sites, and then linking the audit and WIN card to staff incentives. So everyone is lined up behind a very transparent set of metrics that have been developed with the consumer in mind, and then we make sure that day-in-day-out we're delivering that purpose and the promise.'

John Forrest makes the important point that a scorecard of this kind ensures that the purpose and promise become the focus of the organization for the year, not just the annual conference. So what are the results?

'Our financial results are great. This year we achieved the highest guest recommend score that we've ever had. Our net promoter score is 59.8, an all-time high. But I think it's really the softer things, about how it makes the team member feel. Does it give them a reason to come to work? Do they get behind our purpose? I measure our success by some of the little things: I get an e-mail from a team member that says "I've just been on Bigger, Bolder, Better Module Two and it's really inspired me. I'm really looking forward to going back to work to put it into practice." I'm out with John in the business the next couple of days and one of the things I want to do is talk to some team members about how they found the programme. Do they really say, the reason I come to work is to "Make our guests feel brilliant, through a great night's sleep"? Even though our team engagement score is nearly 80 per cent, I think this will increase it. I think it will give people a reason to come to work, and that's what I'm looking for.'

Employee engagement did, in fact, increase. The Hay Group independently measured the employee engagement in 2014 and found that employee understanding and support for the brand purpose were 96 per cent – some 22 points higher than the UK norm and 16 points higher than their top performance benchmark. In 2015, Premier Inn won the Marketing Society award for Employee Engagement. See **ow.ly/Q05vk**. We know from our research that there is a relationship between employee engagement, employee retention, customer experience and customer retention. This has proven to be the case. Premier Inn has seen a significant increase in team member engagement, a reduction in team member turnover, a 26 per cent reduction in 'invocations' – those occasions when the 'Good Night Guarantee' is triggered, and a sharp increase in guest recommendation:

> 'Our turnover has decreased, so we are now at the lowest we've been for a number of years. I think what our purpose has made us do, though, is to focus on what is really important and we have identified that our housekeeping teams are very important. I'm not really sure we gave them as much emphasis as we should have in the past. So we've made some bold decisions about not outsourcing housekeeping in the future.
>
> 'We previously looked at it from a commercial perspective, not from a guest or a people perspective. So what the purpose has done for me as an HR director is to help me put people at the top of the agenda in every level. I'm able to have much more influence to help me get the decisions that I want.'

As every HR director will tell you, being able to influence the executive agenda is a key success factor. Another is sustaining success – and that is where innovation becomes important, not just in the product or technological sense, but in every aspect of the business to ensure that the organization 'stands firm'. We think of innovation as being continually reinventing the business to ensure that results continue to improve. As was said in Chapter 11, '*If you want to stay number one, think like number two.*'

Innovate

Amanda Brady says:

> 'The next step is to think about sustainability. How do we take it to the next level but keep the core principles in place (because they're not going to change)? I think we need to keep refreshing and evolving the campaign so that people feel like they are getting something new but keep the core messages the same. For me, that is a challenge. I do think there is a moment in time now about what comes next. We need to keep up the momentum.
>
> 'As I look towards the future I can see that the digital world is expanding and changing how we communicate. How do you keep up to date with that? I think that challenges a lot of the old principles of HR. For example, although HR has a functional responsibility, we play a bigger part in touching and cutting across all of the disciplines within a business and you have to be equipped to be able to do that. The way

we recruit will be very different in the future. The way that we develop people will be very different. We have a social responsibility but we also have an economic and business responsibility – and how we balance those two things together will be quite a challenge. We have a much more competitive landscape ahead of us, and what might have been good when we were in a recession won't keep us equipped for the future.

I think this campaign will help us but I do think we need to keep thinking about how we refresh and evolve it and make sure everything that we do aligns with it so that we are delivering one common message.'

Patrick Dempsey is also concerned with sustainability:

'We've got to make sure that everybody new coming in goes through the same programme, because otherwise, in two or three years' time, 40 per cent or 50 per cent of the organization will be new. We've got to continue to talk about "Bigger, Bolder, Better." So it will continue to be the theme of our conference this year. We need to continue "Premier Inn – a place made by you". That's how we keep the culture alive. That's the big thing for me, about how we sustain it. (See the video at **ow.ly/Q070**.)

'There is also something in my mind about how to engage our team members with our social initiatives. Over the next two to three years we will offer 1,500 apprenticeships, put 7,000 people into learning; we will have around 2,000 people on work experiences over that period of time, and we will have recruited 3,000–4,000 new people into roles, from the NEET (Not in Education, Employment or Training) population. I wonder how we can weave that into "Premier Inn – a place made by you" so that it's not just about the fabric of the building, it's about the teams and the family you interact with. I would love to create 100,000 opportunities for 16–24-year-olds, school placements and apprenticeships, over the course of my lifetime. I think you can have a personal purpose and a work purpose and for me the two are very linked.'

Patrick Dempsey raises another very important point, and that is the issue of purpose at the level of the individual. When organizational purpose and personal purpose intersect you get a very powerful force for change for good. If brands are to be more than money-making machines for shareholders they have to create value for customers and the society within which they exist. And that is the fundamental premise of this book; we believe that organizations must have a purpose that serves society at large and their customers in particular if they are to survive. Customers want to do business with brands that have authenticity – and people want to work with brands that are values-led. But if you get those two things right the profits will follow anyway.

Innovation is also about anticipating the changes in consumer behaviour and the emerging trends in customer experience. We asked the Premier Inn team to share some of their predictions with us about how they saw customer experience evolving:

'As I look at the trends, I think the whole digital online piece is where we see the future. Use of mobile, less voice, the whole digital platform is changing. How people make bookings, how people interact with us, use of third parties, metasearch. I think this is the biggest trend hitting us. We can't see into the future but what we can do is deliver what we do, very well. Some of those things are not in our control, but I think as long as we go back to what we do and why we do it – and we do it really well – we shall succeed.'

(Patrick Dempsey)

'Clearly, we are looking to link the digital experience with some of our other above-the-line communication, so if you're on the website today you will see a lot of the visual cues that you see in the TV campaign and some of our outdoor campaigns referenced on the website. We will also be talking about some of our innovations around things like our new beds in order to bring that to light in the digital platform.

'I do think there is more we can do, both with the website itself, but also the consumer experience. So, you know, there's no reason why, in the fullness of time, we won't think about how we deliver a great night's sleep through having apps. There are sleep apps that monitor the quality of your sleep, for example. You can think about things like pamper packs that help you to relax, we could record bedtime stories...'

(Simon Jones)

'Engaging customers and getting them to interact with both the brand and the experience, but more importantly with each other, will be key moving forward.

'How do you start to think about digital beyond its transactional form and start to bring the experience to life digitally in a way that complements what customers experience physically? How do you even start to merge the two so that the physical and digital become one? How do you move beyond the transactional and start to think about informing customers, entertaining customers, communicating with customers and serving customers, all through digital platforms? I see that as the big challenge for us going forward.'

(Mark Fells)

Advice for other leaders

Finally, we asked the Premier Inn team what advice they would give to executives starting out on a similar journey:

> 'What I have learned is that you have to accept it's going to take time to get the whole team to sign up to the final purpose, you can't rush it – and don't set off until you have, because everybody will challenge and test you on the way. You don't want anybody wobbling because that will just derail the whole process. But, also be ready for the fact that it is very powerful. So when you get it right, it takes over your life. If you're going to go through the pain and stress of defining it, and then writing it down and codifying your guest experience, then you've got to want to live it.'
>
> (John Forrest)

> 'The lesson that I have learnt about being purpose-led is "Don't treat it as a marketing exercise, but treat it as a broader business exercise", and by that, I mean whatever statements you come up with for your purpose or your promise, you've got to really play through. Ensure that you can credibly deliver it and that it is genuinely hard wired into "the way we do things around here". The second thing is that you've got to view it not as an exercise that you do at a point in time, but as a cultural shift.
>
> 'We would say that we are only on the start of a five-year or 10-year programme and, hopefully, we have made a reasonably good start, but we can't sit here and say that we are absolutely acing the delivery of our purpose, day-in-day-out. And until we have done that we won't rest in our quest to making our guests feel brilliant through a great night's sleep.'
>
> (Simon Jones)

> 'To get people connected to a common purpose is absolutely the right thing to do, because you have 19,000 advocates out there rather than an exec team of seven. You feel it in every business that you go in, it feels like we've done something right, and I think that's quite an achievement on behalf of the whole organization. It's tough though, you've got to stand your ground and be bold. You need to convince your colleagues that it's absolutely the right thing to do and the benefits that it will bring won't happen unless you do it properly. But we have also had some fun and what we have come out with is some great material and a great platform to build a better organization, something that we can replicate right across a bigger business. It has been an inspirational road to be on, to go from nothing to something quite powerful, I think it is quite an achievement.'
>
> (Amanda Brady)

Image 12.7 John Forrest, COO, Premier Inn, accepting the 'Best Midscale Hotel Brand' award at the UK's 'Business Travel Awards 2015'

The Premier Inn team have been very generous in sharing what they learned as well as examples of their materials. I asked Amanda, 'Aren't you worried about confidentiality?'

> 'People think they can just pick up all the material that we have developed and just launch it in their own business but my advice is that you can't. You have to go on the journey and if you don't you won't be as well connected and it won't be on purpose for you. Anyway, why would you want to be doing something that somebody else is doing?
>
> 'I would say to anybody thinking about embarking on this journey, I believe you will reap the benefits but you will undoubtedly have some sticky moments but with them comes a great outcome. So don't shy away from that. You should be bold.'

(Amanda Brady)

As we completed writing this chapter we heard the news that Premier Inn had been awarded 'Best Midscale Hotel Brand' at the UK's 'Business Travel Awards 2015'. The judges concluded: 'This company has left no stone left unturned, reviewing, revisiting and continuously improving every element of its offering, from beds, technology, food, staff training and parking – the list is endless.'

The other news that broke as we were completing our book was that Patrick Dempsey was moving on from Premier Inn, so we asked him what advice he would offer other managing directors, having achieved such a brilliant result at Premier Inn, as the final word:

> 'My advice for anybody embarking on this journey is, first of all, create the sponsorship and leadership from the top of the organization. You've got to have somebody like John Forrest who is really going to lead; it has to be very clear that one person has to lead it and take it right throughout the organization. Make sure that it's not just a one-year project; you've got to keep this going for three to five years. This journey of introducing a purpose and a vision is a bit like an advertising campaign; you've just got to keep it going, keep it going, keep it going, until it's completely embedded in the organization.'

So, in this chapter and the previous chapter we have introduced two informative and, we hope, inspiring case studies about brands in different sectors with different challenges, cultures and business models – but with a common approach to implementing their purpose. So how can you apply these lessons to your own organization?

Well, to make it easier for you we have created a toolkit of best practice tips, tools and techniques that you can find online: **www.smithcoconsultancy.com/cem-toolkit**.

We hope that you have been inspired by these stories. We have tried to allow the tone of voice of these brands and the richness of their learning to shine through. However, if you would like to know even more about the *On Purpose* research, the leaders we interviewed and brands we studied, then turn to the next page.

Note

1 Larry Bossidy and Ram Charan (2004) *Confronting Reality: Doing what matters to get things right*, Crown Business, New York.

On purpose – multichannel

The keynote presentation

In this high-energy, engaging multimedia presentation we take you deep into the minds and thinking of the executives within these companies. We identify the key insights underlying these organizations' success – principles that you can take away and apply to your business. You will be inspired to develop new ideas to exceed your customer expectations, and the knowledge to translate these ideas into practical actions that will accelerate your organization's growth.

In designing a keynote presentation to meet the specific needs of your event, we will draw upon those stories and examples from our research that are most likely to resonate with your audience and align with the themes of your conference.

On Purpose – The Masters Programme

Eight practices define the essence of being *On Purpose*. They describe the actions and behaviours of the brands we studied. In this book and in our online toolkit we share some of the techniques that we use to help organizations become purposeful in their direction and in the experience they deliver to customers. We hope that you will apply the learning to your own organization, but if you need greater immersion and intensive coaching speak to us about our one-day or two-day 'On Purpose Masters Programme'. This workshop is designed to take executive teams through the principles, case studies and apply the learning in a highly interactive way to your own organization. The one-day programme uses case studies to illustrate the principles; the two-day programme allows us to apply these principles to your own situation with coaching from the facilitators.

Led by the two authors of *On Purpose*, Shaun Smith and Andy Milligan, the Masters Programme is designed for executives who have probably already embarked on a customer experience initiative but are ready to take it to the next level. We will conduct our On Purpose survey with your delegates and compile a report of our findings. This will be used to guide discussion and to focus on the areas of opportunity for your organization.

Visit our website at **http://www.smithcoconsultancy.com**, or for more information contact **jd@smithcoconsultancy.com**.

The authors

Shaun Smith

Since the mid-1990s Shaun has been a key catalyst in expanding management focus from the tactical issues of customer service to the much wider and strategic issue of customer experience. He has developed some of the latest thinking and practice around this subject, helping organizations worldwide to create compelling customer experiences that achieve brand differentiation and long-term customer loyalty.

He has featured a number of times on the *Ask the Expert* programme on CNBC and is co-author of five critically acclaimed business books. His first book with Andy Milligan, *Uncommon Practice: People who deliver a great brand experience*, examines those companies that create exceptional customer experiences. His second book, *Managing the Customer Experience: Turning customers into advocates*, reveals how leaders can build this kind of competitive advantage for their own organizations. *See, Feel, Think, Do: The power of instinct in business*, also co-authored with Andy Milligan, explores how highly successful business leaders and entrepreneurs use the power of instinct to achieve results, and *Bold: How to be brave in business and win* picked up from their first book and explored brands that were transforming their markets. *Bold* was awarded 'Business e-Book of the Year' in 2012.

Andy and Shaun's latest book, *On Purpose*, develops their thinking to explore why and how the bold brands do what they do.

Shaun is co-founder and partner in the customer experience consultancy Smith+co, which works with leading brands around the world to design, develop and deliver dramatic customer experiences. Shaun is a fellow of the Professional Speakers Association, a member of the Global Speakers Federation and has been awarded the Professional Speaking Award for Excellence. For more information visit: **http://www.smithcoconsultancy.com/speeches-and-workshops/about-our-speakers** or email Shaun for his speaker profile at **ss@smithcoconsultancy.com**.

Andy Milligan

Andy Milligan is a leading international consultant on brand and business culture. He has worked for almost 25 years advising major organizations on strategies for brand building, customer experience and internal culture as well as running seminars and conferences on brand alignment and employee engagement worldwide. Andy has worked on a wide range of projects internationally and across a number of market sectors including airlines, financial services, packaged goods, telecommunications, sports and leisure. He has directed major projects in Japan, South Korea, Singapore, the United States and throughout Europe.

Andy appears regularly in the media to comment on brand issues including appearances on CNN, Sky, CNBC and the BBC. He is an acclaimed author on the subject of branding and has published four bestselling books: *Uncommon Practice: People who deliver a great brand experience* and *See, Feel, Think, Do: The power of instinct in business* with Shaun Smith, *Brand it like Beckham*, which analyses how the Beckham brand has become a global phenomenon, and *Don't Mess With The Logo*, co-written with the designer Jon Edge, which has been described as doing 'for brand management what the Haynes workshop manuals do for cars'. Making it simple, easy to understand and enjoyable!

Andy is a founder and partner in The Caffeine Partnership, a strategic consultancy which helps leaders to deliver brand-led growth. For more information visit **www.thecaffeinepartnership.com**.

Acknowledgements

First of all, a big thank you to Janine Dyer who created the online toolkit and provided invaluable feedback and suggestions on the manuscript.

Thanks to the members and associates of the Smith+co team who wrote the 'guest panels' on their various areas of expertise: Alison Battisby, Vanessa Hamilton, Linda Moir, Claudio Toyama and Tim Wade. You can find their profiles and read more about their perspectives on our website: **http://www.smithcoconsultancy.com/about-us/meet-the-experts**.

Thanks to Tim Sefton who conducted the research with the giffgaff executives and provided invaluable help with this case study.

For their assistance with the On Purpose survey distribution we thank our friends at Mycustomer.com, see: **http://www.mycustomer.com/**; CustomerThink.com, see: **http://www.customerthink.com/**; GCEM.com, see: **http://gccrm.com/eng/content_e.jsp**. If you haven't seen these portals you should. They are an invaluable source of all the latest and best thinking around customer experience.

Our CEM partners, TOTE-M, in the Netherlands for their help conducting the research and customer experience workshops at Liberty Global. See: **http://www.tote-m.com/en/**.

To Claudio Toyama, Smith+co's director of customer and employee insight, for conducting and analysing the quantitative research; and Tanja Kirtley who helped obtain the necessary approvals from the many people we interviewed.

Finally, thanks to Helen Kogan, Jasmin Naim and the team at Kogan Page, our publishers, for their enthusiasm and tremendous support for the book.

Index

Note: *italics* indicate a Figure, Image or Table in the text.

CPSIA information can be obtained at www.ICGtesting.com
Printed in the USA
LVOW01s2324030915

452758LV00006B/7/P